# WHISTLEBLOWING
# AROUND THE WORLD
## Law, Culture & Practice

Edited by Richard Calland & Guy Dehn

In honour of Satyendra Dubey.

Richard Calland dedicates this book to men and women everywhere who speak out against injustice whenever they find it.

Guy Dehn dedicates this book to his parents.

Published by The Open Democracy Advice Centre (ODAC),
Cape Town, South Africa and
Public Concern at Work (PCaW), London, UK,
in partnership with The British Council.

# WHISTLEBLOWING AROUND THE WORLD

## Law, Culture & Practice

Edited by Richard Calland & Guy Dehn

ODAC & PCaW
in partnership with
the British Council:
Southern Africa

2004

Published by ODAC, 6 Spin St, Cape Town 8001 &
PCaW, 16 Baldwins Gardens, London ECIN 7RJ
in partnership with the British Council: Southern Africa

© ODAC/PCaW 2004

ISBN 1-919798-56-0

First published 2004

Editing and production by Idasa Publishing
Design and layout by Magenta Media
Bound and printed by Logoprint, Cape Town

# PREFACE & ACKNOWLEDGEMENTS

This is a book about whistleblowing and whistleblowers. Because the way in which whistleblowers are seen and heard is changing, we felt it was time to offer a unique North, South, East, West comparative review of the state of whistleblowing around the world. In doing so, this book looks at American, Australasian, British, Japanese and South African approaches. It does not attempt to jostle with the growing body of academic work on the subject, but instead focuses on what legislative protection and civil society support is available to public interest whistleblowers, how these work and where they fail in practice.

As such, we hope the book will be a practical guide for NGOs, public and private bodies, and policy-makers alike. That is why we include copies of materials for training, advocacy and reform campaigning, as well as the actual laws, in the CD-Rom that accompanies the book. Many thanks are due to Lorraine Stober of ODAC for gathering together the various documents.

We head two organisations whose mission it is to promote practical and effective solutions to help embed the concept of a safe alternative to silence as a means to free, accountable and well-governed organisations and societies. In this work, we are privileged to encounter and work with whistleblowers – men and women of distinction and courage. We are pleased to carry the voices of four whistleblowers in this book, including an account from Enron whistleblower, Sherron Watkins. But behind these celebrated cases, we pay tribute to the increasing numbers of people who are now questioning suspect conduct and challenging abuse, and who are doing so in a successful but low-profile way.

We hope the book will promote best practice, and thereby contribute to the international debate about the role of whistleblowing. Mirroring perhaps the sense of isolation that many whistleblowers experience, activism around the world on this subject has been somewhat disjointed until now. But now we see a critical mass of expertise and activism emerging. By "joining the dots" between these local endeavours, the global anti-corruption agenda can be served – a further example of the "Think Global and Act Local" notion.

We wish to express our gratitude to the British Council for the depth and commitment of its partnership in this project and its support for both our organisations. The Council's support has enabled a real bridge to be built between Public Concern at Work and the Open Democracy Advice Centre –

between the UK and South Africa. It is a great example of a North-South collaboration, and we wish to pay tribute in particular to the vision of Jean September, head of governance for the British Council: Southern Africa, without whom this book would not have been possible.

We are lucky to have persuaded not just a group of whistleblowers to share their experience with us, but also some of the leading experts from around the world. We are particularly pleased to have such an authoritative contribution from Tom Devine, who has provided dedicated support for whistleblowers for much of his professional life.

In addition, we must thank the following people: Helena Kennedy, chair of the British Council, for her encouragement and support for the road-show of workshops and seminars that we intend to accompany the launch of the book; Laura Neuman of the Carter Center for agreeing, under great pressure of other commitments, to work with Sherron Watkins on her chapter; Moira Levy and her colleagues in Idasa Publishing for the excellent copy editing and co-ordination of production of this book; and Mandy Darling of Magenta Media for her creativity on the design front. Finally, we wish to thank our colleagues for their hard work on this book. Contributions from a number of the relevant staff members appear in this volume. Organisations are nothing without the people that work within them and we are both fortunate to lead teams of exceptional individuals.

Guy Dehn and Richard Calland,
London and Cape Town, 29 February 2004

# CONTENTS

# CONTRIBUTORS' BIOGRAPHIES

## Richard Calland

Richard Calland is Executive Director of the Open Democracy Advice Centre in Cape Town and Programme Manager of the Right to Know programme at the Institute for Democracy in South Africa (Idasa). He is co-author (with Alison Tilley) of *The Right to Know, The Right to Live: Access to Information and Socio-Economic Justice* (ODAC: 2002). Calland was a leading member of the ten-organisation Open Democracy Campaign Group that conducted extensive research and lobbied intensively in relation to the South African whistleblower protection law, the Protected Disclosures Act, 2000. Calland is a member of the International Task Team on Transparency of the Institute for Public Dialogue at Columbia University, and consults extensively around the world on transparency policy, access to information law and anti-corruption strategies.

## Guy Dehn

Guy Dehn is the Director of Public Concern at Work, the whistleblowing charity. He leads on the policy and legal work and was closely involved in settling the scope and detail of the Public Interest Disclosure Act, 1998. He also advises organisations and governments in the UK and abroad on how to promote an open and accountable culture. Before founding Public Concern at Work in 1993, Dehn was legal officer to the National Consumer Council for six years and subsequently served as an elected member of the Council of Consumers' Association. He is also a practising barrister and chair of the Allen Lane Foundation.

## Charles Lewis

Charles Lewis is the founder and Executive Director of the Center for Public Integrity, a non-profit, non-partisan watchdog organisation in Washington, US that conducts investigative reporting and research on public policy issues. Lewis has written or co-written several of the Center's books and studies, including *The Buying of the President 2004* (2004). Lewis formed the International Consortium of Investigative Journalists and Global Access, a Center project to monitor and report on corruption and government accountability throughout the world. From 1977 to 1988, Lewis did investigative reporting at ABC News and at CBS News. He serves on the board of the Fund for Investigative Journalism and is a member of the Society of Professional Journalists, Investigative Reporters and Editors, and the Committee to Protect Journalists.

## Harry Templeton

Harry Templeton is the Scottish Director of Public Concern at Work and has a particular role in its public education work across the UK. Previously he was a printer and union official at Mirror Group Newspapers.

## Victoria Johnson

Victoria Johnson practised law in Cape Town for seven years, primarily in the field of civil litigation. She joined the city council as a senior legal advisor for four years and then resigned to look after her newly born son. She now works part time as a legal consultant at a Cape Town firm.

## Robin Van den Hende

Robin Van den Hende is the caseworker at Public Concern at Work. He is the initial contact on the helpline, and helps with the charity's policy and public education work.

## Sherron Watkins

Sherron Watkins, former Vice-President of the Enron Corporation, was named one of *Time* magazine's 2002 Persons of the Year. Now an independent speaker and consultant, she is co-author of *Power Failure, the Inside Story of the Collapse of Enron* (2003). Prior to joining Enron in 1993, Watkins worked for three years as the portfolio manager of MG Trade Finance Corporation and for eight years in the auditing group of Arthur Andersen.

## Tom Devine

Tom Devine, Legal Director of the Government Accountability Project, has worked as a whistleblower advocate for more than two decades. Author of the *Whistleblower's Survival Guide*, Devine has served as counsel on every major whistleblower law passed in the US at federal level since the 1980s. He is the author of the whistleblower provisions of the Organization of American States' model anti-corruption law. Devine regularly speaks to international audiences about whistleblower protection, occupational free speech and national security.

## Anna Myers

Anna Myers is Deputy Director of Public Concern at Work and manages the charity's confidential helpline. She is also a lead trainer of senior managers on how to handle whistleblowing concerns. Myers, who qualified in Canada, is a solicitor in England and Wales.

## Kirsten Trott

Kisten Trott qualified as a solicitor in Australia. Now based in the UK, she works as an International Policy Executive for the Law Society of England and Wales. Previously she worked as legal advisor at Public Concern at Work.

## Mukelani Dimba

Mukelani Dimba is a Training Consultant at the Open Democracy Advice Centre in Cape Town. He has an academic background in management and labour law and is part of the Training and Consultancy Services Unit, which advises the public and private sectors on how to use the access to information legislation in South Africa.

## Lorraine Stober

Lorraine Stober is the whistleblowing helpline advisor at the Open Democracy Advice Centre. She has an economics degree and a labour law diploma from the University of Stellenbosch. Before joining the Open Democracy Advice Centre in 2002 she practised labour dispute resolution.

## Bill Thomson

Bill Thomson trains and advises individuals and organisations on the Protected Disclosures and the Promotion of Access to Information Acts for the Open Democracy Advice Centre. A labour arbitrator and mediator with Tokiso Dispute Settlement, and an environmental mediator with the South African Department of Environmental Affairs and Tourism, Thomson was also previously a Director at the conflict resolution organisation, the Independent Mediation Service of South Africa (IMSSA).

## Yukiko Miki

Yukiko Miki is the Executive Director of the Information Clearinghouse Japan. This is an independent not-for-profit organisation, based in Tokyo, which focuses on freedom of information and government accountability. It assists individuals, trains organisations and lobbies for and on legislation.

## Koji Morioka

Koji Morioka is professor of political economy at Kansai University; head of Kabunushi (Shareholders) Ombudsman, a non-profit organisation of lawyers, accountants, academics and shareholders, and co-leader of Public Interest Speak-up Advisers (PISA) in Japan.

## Evelyn Oakley

Evelyn Oakley is the company secretary of Public Concern at Work, having helped set up the charity in 1992.

## Alison Tilley

Alison Tilley is Project Director of the Open Democracy Advice Centre. Before that she practised law in the private sector and then joined the Black Sash civil rights organisation as its first civil society legislation monitor. Later she was appointed National Advocacy Manager of the Black Sash. She is also a trustee of the Women's Legal Centre.

## Brian Martin

Brian Martin is International Director and past president of Whistleblowers Australia. He is also associate professor in Science, Technology and Society at the University of Wollongong. He is the author of books and articles on dissent, non-violent action, democracy, scientific controversies and other topics.

# CIVIL SOCIETY ORGANISATIONS

**Open Democracy Advice Centre (ODAC)**
Cape Town Democracy Centre
6 Spin Street
Cape Town
8001
South Africa
Tel: 2721 4675673
Fax: 2721 4612814
e-mail: odac@opendemocracy.org.za
website: www.opendemocracy.org.za

**Public Concern at Work (PCaW)**
Suite 306
16 Baldwins Gardens
London
EC1N 7RJ
United Kingdom
Tel: (0044) 20 7404 6609
Fax: (0044) 20 7404 6576
e-mail: whistle@pcaw.co.uk
website: www.whistleblowing.org.uk

**Government Accountability Project (GAP)**
1612 K St. NW # 400
Washington D.C.
20006
United States of America
Tel: (001) 202 408 0034
Fax: (001) 202 408 9855
website:www.whistleblower.org

## Whistleblowers Australia

P.O. Box U12.9
Wollongong University
NSW
2500
Australia
website: www.whistleblowers.org.au

## Information Clearinghouse Japan

108 Kiunkaku Building 3 Azumi-cho
Shinjuku-ku,
Tokyo
160-0005
Japan
Tel: 81 3 5269 1846
Fax: 81 3 5269 0944
e-mail: yukiko.miki@nifty.com
website: www.foi-asia.org

## Public Interest Speak-up Advisors (PISA)

e-mail: pisa@rf7.so-net.ne.jp
website: http://www006.upp.so-net.ne.jp/pisa/ (no information in English)

## British Council

Steve Shaw
Governance Team
British Council
Bridgewater House
58 Whitworth Street
Manchester
M1 6BB UK
Tel: 00 44 1616 957 7102
e-mail: stephen.shaw@britishcouncil.org

Jean September
Director of Governance
Associated Magazine House
3rd Floor
21 St. John's Street
Cape Town
Tel: 2721 4606660
Fax: 2721 4606691
e-mail: jean.september@britishcouncil.org.za

# FOREWORD

# WHISTLEBLOWING AROUND THE WORLD

*Helena Kennedy*

Sometimes something happens somewhere in the world and you remember exactly where you were and what you were doing when you heard about it. Everyone recalls vividly where they were when they heard about the World Trade Center attacks on September 11, 2001. Those old enough recall where they were when they heard that John F. Kennedy had been assassinated. And most people probably remember where they were when they heard or watched as the space shuttle, Challenger, exploded, 13 seconds after it took off into the clear blue skies of south-eastern America. Six professional astronauts perished at that moment. As did a seventh member of the crew, a woman teacher who had won a national competition to accompany the mission. Her husband and children watched in horror, as did millions around the world. It could and should have been prevented. Roger Boisjoly was a senior scientist working on the shuttle. He had been warning NASA of a design fault. He was so concerned about the safety of the spacecraft that even the night before he was urging that the launch be postponed. Tragically, his message, like that of so many whistleblowers, was ignored.

But as the editors of this book note in their Introduction, both culturally and legally, things are changing. Whistleblowing is coming of age. There is a growing recognition around the world that people who encounter corruption and wrongdoing must be given as safe an environment as possible to be able to tell someone in authority what they know. In both the UK and South Africa rail disasters, at Paddington and Muldersvlei respectively, concerns about safety had been raised by responsible employees but ignored by irresponsible employers. In the banking sector, in the Maxwell and BCCI scandals, there were people who knew what was going on and wanted to blow the whistle but did know to whom to turn and did not trust that they themselves would not suffer reprisals for doing so.

Secrecy is no longer acceptable; too many lives and livelihoods have been lost or destroyed because a whistle could not be blown. But too often the voice of the honest worker or citizen has been drowned out by abusive, unaccountable bosses. Invariably, staying silent *was* the only option. Creating a safe alternative to silence represents a difficult challenge, legally and culturally; separating the message from the messenger is still obstructed by vested interests, deeply ingrained sociological habits and attitudes, and by the limitations of the law.

However, there is an emerging new experience around the world, which deserves a wider audience so that practitioners, civil society activists and policy-makers can learn from it. This new experience derives from the state-of-the-art approach taken by the UK in its Public Interest Disclosure Act 1998, with a fresh conceptualisation that was adapted by South Africa in its Protected Disclosures Act 2000. Now Japan and other countries are considering a similar course, prompting an important change in relations between employees and management. Whistleblowing laws and policies thereby become a further instrument for transformation in the workplace: this has a ripple effect on the culture outside and the practices of organisational accountability and individual responsibility. The UK-SA-Japan approach to whistleblowing differs from that of the US, which includes the use of rewards and incentives to trigger reports to the state and has been adopted in Korea and elsewhere.

Supported by the British Council, a substantial partnership between two NGOs, one from the North – Public Concern at Work in London – and the other, the Open Democracy Advice Centre in South Africa, has grown over the past three years. The two organisations have led their fields in the promotion of the rights of whistleblowers and in their cutting edge projects providing free, confidential legal advice for whistleblowers and training for employers. Their respective founders advise national and international bodies on whistleblowing and governance and are well placed to develop, lead and edit this comparative review of whistleblowing around the world, which is aimed at producing a practical toolkit for NGOs and other bodies in different regions to address this issue in the context of their own cultures. There is now a growing interest in whistleblowing around the world and the new thinking should be shared. I am proud of the contribution that the British Council has made and will continue to make to this specific endeavour and I trust that this book will attract the attention it deserves.

Baroness Helena Kennedy

Chairperson of the British Council and an internationally renowned human rights lawyer and activist.

# PART 1:

# SETTING THE SCENE

# INTRODUCTION

## WHISTLEBLOWING AROUND THE WORLD: THE STATE OF THE ART

### THE ROLE OF THE INDIVIDUAL, ORGANISATIONS, THE STATE, THE MEDIA, THE LAW AND CIVIL SOCIETY

*By Richard Calland and Guy Dehn*

---

**Whistleblowing** - [a] Bringing an activity to a sharp conclusion as if by the blast of a whistle (*Oxford English Dictionary*); [b] Raising a concern about wrongdoing within an organisation or through an independent structure associated with it (*UK Committee on Standards in Public Life*); [c] Giving information (usually to the authorities) about illegal or underhand practices (*Chambers Dictionary*); [d] Exposing to the press a wrongdoing or cover-up in a business or government office (*US, Brewers Dictionary*); [e] (*origins*) Police officer summoning public help to apprehend a criminal; referee stopping play after a foul in football.

## Why whistleblowing matters

Whistleblowing matters to all organisations and all people. This is because every business and public body faces the risk that something it does will go seriously wrong. The risk may be that some food you are about to buy is badly contaminated, that the train your family will travel on is unsafe, that the surgeon who will operate on your child is incompetent, that a hazardous substance is being dumped near your home or that your savings or taxes are being stolen. Whenever such a risk arises from the activities of an organisation, the first people to know about it will usually be those who work in or with the organisation. Yet while employees are the people best placed to raise the concern and so enable the risk to be removed or reduced, they are also the people who have the most to lose if they do.

Unless organisations foster a culture that declares and demonstrates that it is safe and accepted to raise a genuine concern about wrongdoing, employees will assume that they face victimisation, losing their job or damaging their career. The consequence is that most employees will stay silent where there is a threat — even a grave one — to the interests of others, be they consumers, passengers, patients, communities, taxpayers or shareholders. This silence can mean that those in charge of organisations place their trust in the systems that they oversee rather than in the people who operate them. This denies them a fail-safe opportunity to deal with a serious problem before it causes real damage.

So whether you are a consumer, an employee who may believe something is going badly wrong or a manager or an employer who wants to run a proper organisation, whistleblowing matters. It helps us to understand how we can deal with such threats and wrongdoing and how we can counter the breakdown in communication that subverts accountability in the workplace. That this breakdown can undermine the public interest is clear when we remember that the most successful way the police deter, detect and clear up crimes is through information communicated to them by the public. Yet in workplaces across the world, law, culture and practice give a strong message that employees should turn a blind eye to wrongdoing and should not raise their concerns internally or externally.

The consequence of this culture is that it discourages normal, decent people from questioning wrongdoing that they come across in their jobs. It encourages employees to be guided exclusively by their own short-term interests and undermines any sense of mutual interest between the workforce, the organisation and those it serves. While its effect is most damaging and direct in relation to workplace wrongdoing, it also influences the way employees behave when — whether travelling home or shopping at the weekend — they come across crime in their community. Conditioned to turn a blind eye in the workplace, this culture can only encourage them to walk away from their community.

These are the "big picture" reasons why whistleblowing matters. But to understand how you, your organisation or group can address this issue, we must first consider the position of the individual employee who realises that there is some wrongdoing or threat to the public interest.

In practical terms, if an employee is concerned about some wrongdoing or risk in the workplace that threatens others, he or she has four options. These are

- To stay silent;
- To blow the whistle internally;

- To blow the whistle outside; or

- To leak the information anonymously.

## Silence and society

Silence is the option of least risk for the individual employee who comes across wrongdoing in the workplace. It is the default option for many reasons. The employee will realise that his or her suspicions could be mistaken or that there may be an innocent explanation for the conduct. Where colleagues are also aware of the suspect conduct but are staying silent, the employee will wonder why he or she alone should speak out. Where the wrongdoing seems clear to the employee, he or she will assume that those in more senior positions have also seen it and are implicated in some way and so will see little reason to pursue the matter internally. In societies where unions are scarce or their independence has been compromised, the employee will be left without help or guidance on who to approach and how. In organisations where labour relations are adversarial and whistleblowing is unwelcome, the employee will be expected to prove the wrongdoing, even though it clearly would be far better if those in charge investigated the matter. Finally, unless employees believe there is a good chance that something will be done to address the wrongdoing, there will be no reason why they should consider risking their own position.

Even if the employee is not deterred by any or all of these reasons, he or she will rightly need to consider their private interests and those of their family before raising the matter. Without any reassurance to the contrary, the employee will fear workplace reprisal – be it harassment, isolation or dismissal. Thus, without guidance and reassurance on what to do, it is inevitable that most employees stay silent. The reasons that people are now re-evaluating whistleblowing are because the costs of this silence have become too high. It means that:

- Consumers, shareholders and communities are left at risk with neither the information nor the opportunity to protect their own interests;

- Unscrupulous managers or employees are given a reason to believe that "anything goes";

- Those in charge are denied the chance to look into concerns about wrongdoing and to avert real problems; and

- Debates and reforms tend to focus on ways to improve the system, rather than on the conduct of the people who have to make it work.

# Whistleblowing and the employer

Recognising the damaging effects of this culture, the UK Committee on Standards in Public Life recommended steps that organisations could take to reassure and enable staff to raise concerns constructively. One of the reasons that the Committee was set up was loss of public confidence caused by incidents of wrongdoing which had not come to light before real damage was done (caused or facilitated by silence), and by rumours of misconduct or sleaze that were difficult to effectively refute or substantiate (often caused by anonymous stories that circulated around). While its recommendations on whistleblowing were directed at public bodies, the message applies to organisations in all sectors.

> *Placing staff in a position where they feel driven to approach the media to ventilate concerns is unsatisfactory both for the staff member and the organisation. We observed in our First Report that it was far better for systems to be put in place which encouraged staff to raise worries within the organisation, yet allowed recourse to the parent department where necessary. An effective internal system for the raising of concerns should include:*
>
> - *A clear statement that wrongdoing is taken seriously in the organisation and an indication of the sorts of matters regarded as wrongdoing;*
> - *Respect for the confidentiality of staff raising concerns if they wish, and an opportunity to raise concerns outside the line management structure;*
> - *Access to independent advice;*
> - *Penalties for making false and malicious allegations;*
> - *An indication of the proper way in which concerns may be raised outside the organisation if necessary.*[1]

At the heart of this approach is the recognition that without safe means for concerns to be raised and addressed, the only options employees have are silence or feeding a rumour mill that can only undermine public confidence. While these options appear as alternatives, they are in fact linked because though the organisation is kept in the dark the employee's silence is rarely absolute. In many cases the employee will mention the concern about the wrongdoing to immediate family or close friends (who are unable to do anything but sympathise with the employee's plight) and through them the unchecked allegation can gain its own demoralising momentum.

---

[1] UK Committee on Standards in Public Life, *Second Report*, May 1996, p 22 and *Third Report*, July 1997, p.49.

In formulating its recommendations, the Committee took account of good practice in the private sector where in genuinely competitive markets there has been a growing recognition that the early reporting of suspected wrongdoing was in the organisation's self-interest and a key aspect of effective self-regulation. The reason for this is that, as every shopkeeper and small business person knows, if an organisation suffers wrongdoing or damages its consumers they will likely take their custom elsewhere.

In terms of shifting cultures, an analogy can be drawn with the approach taken by large corporations to feedback from consumers. Businesses in sectors that became more competitive over the past 20 years realised the need to try and build lasting relationships with their customers. Aware of surveys that one dissatisfied customer would tell ten or more people of their unhappy experience, market leaders started to solicit feedback from customers rather than wait for complaints. They found that even if they did not satisfy the particular complaint, the mere fact they had considered it would substantially improve the customer's attitude to the company. This was in contrast to the approach adopted by monopolistic organisations, which treated and treat consumers – once the purchase had been completed – as troublesome, if not untrustworthy, complainants.

The approach to information from the workforce has been equally negative. The assumption is that employees will only raise personal grievances because they do not recognise or identify with the wellbeing of the organisation. This assumption has informed a raft of laws and practices on workplace relationships and so, in turn, has inevitably influenced the way employees are conditioned to behave in the workplace. This is not just misguided but self-defeating as information from the workforce is vital as it enables the organisation to put a potential problem right before it causes any real damage to it, its reputation or its stakeholders.

The self-interest of organisations in promoting whistleblowing is now being recognised and increasingly employers are beginning to provide safe whistleblowing routes for staff. While many of these are in response to recent legislation, the most effective are those in which the organisation's leaders realise the importance of providing an alternative to (but not a substitute for) line management. Without it they give their managers a monopolistic control over the information which goes to those in charge. As with any monopoly, one weak link – be it a corrupt, lazy, sick or incompetent manager – will break the communication chain and stop those in charge getting information which could be critical to the success or failure of the organisation.

There are two other ancillary benefits for organisations. First, the new approach to whistleblowing reminds everyone in an organisation that they owe a loyalty to the organisation and not just to their manager. Secondly, providing a safe alternative to silence is one of the most effective ways to deter and discourage people from abusing their position and authority.

## Whistleblowing outside

Obviously not all employers will act responsibly, and in such cases an outside disclosure is the only effective way of averting a problem before real damage is done. So outside disclosures must be protected in any effective whistleblowing arrangements. Understood and applied properly, such arrangements allow the authorities to distinguish those organisations that can rightly be given the chance to address such problems themselves from those that cannot. In this way whistleblowing cultures will make regulation more efficient.

Such outside disclosures raise ethical and legal issues of confidentiality and secrecy. They also influence the balance of relationships between business, the state and the media. An outside disclosure will more often than not involve some regulatory intervention and, at worst, unjustified adverse publicity. At the very least this will cause inconvenience and disruption to an organisation that would have dealt with the matter properly had it been told of the concern directly. In such cases where the employer would have addressed the matter responsibly, the value of an external disclosure is questionable because regulators and the media, when they receive such information, will mostly put the facts straight back to those in charge of the organisation. It is clear from this that a workplace where outside disclosures are seen and used as the first port of call is evidence at the least of poor management and weak leadership.

Until recently, in most legal systems there has been no protection for an employee who makes an outside disclosure – even if it is made in good faith and is justified and reasonable. Accordingly, such disclosures have often been made anonymously, raising the difficult issues we address in the next section. Unless your country or organisation wants to encourage anonymous disclosures, you have every reason why both in law and practice you should explain when outside disclosures, openly made, are permitted and protected.

Where a whistleblowing culture exists staff will not fear raising a concern internally and so protecting outside disclosures is something that should cause no fear to any well-run organisation. Indeed it will see how such a provision works to its advantage. Firstly, without there being an external body to which staff may safely and openly go, some employees will lack the confidence to believe that any internal scheme is a genuine attempt to hear and address such concerns. Secondly, asserting the role of such an outside body (be it a regulator, parliament, shareholders or the wider public) makes real the principle of accountability by reminding everyone in the organisation who is accountable for what and to whom. This can engender a sense of self-discipline across the organisation as people know they can readily be expected to account for their conduct. Finally, the clear message that employees have a safe external route is a powerful incentive for managers to promote and deliver the organisation's own whistleblowing scheme.

## Anonymous disclosures

Without safe routes for whistleblowing concerns to be raised openly and addressed properly, anonymous disclosures are the likely alternative to silence. Here it is important to distinguish anonymous from confidential disclosures. An anonymous disclosure is one sent in a brown envelope or a message left on an answer machine, with little or no possibility of identifying or contacting the whistleblower or verifying the information. By contrast, a confidential disclosure is where the recipient knows the identity of the person but agrees not to disclose it if and when the information is used.

As to the message, anonymity raises real problems as it makes the concern more difficult to investigate, the facts more difficult to corroborate and excludes the possibility of clarifying any ambiguous information or asking for more.

As to the messenger, an anonymous disclosure focuses more attention on and speculation about his or her identity than open whistleblowing. The result is that anonymity is no guarantee that the source of the information will not be deduced. Where the allegations are serious, those implicated will try to identify the source and as the net draws in and innocent colleagues are suspected, the pressure on the source to own up becomes intense. In the context of disclosures from the workplace, the identity of an anonymous source is identified far more often than not. When this happens, the fact that the employee acted anonymously will be claimed as a sign of bad faith, shame or dishonesty, and will be used to undermine any suggestion that he or she was acting in the public interest.

As anonymity makes it harder to address the message and can also harm the messenger, it has little to commend it from either point of view. Looked at in a wider sense, anonymity also has little virtue. Firstly, whether anonymous disclosures are made internally or externally, they are tainted by the fact that anonymity will always be the cloak preferred by a malicious person. Secondly, anonymous information can give the organisation that receives it unaccountable and unlimited power over what to do with it. As it is anonymous, it is entirely left to the discretion of the body whether to use, ignore or conceal the information. This is because its decision is not open to question by the anonymous informant and because nobody else knows it has the information. Anonymity therefore fuels mistrust and makes the powerful unaccountable.

## So what is whistleblowing?

As this book shows, whistleblowing is now used to describe the options available to an employee to raise concerns about workplace wrongdoing. It refers to the disclosure of wrongdoing that threatens others, rather than a personal grievance. Whistleblowing covers the spectrum of such communication, from raising the concern with managers, with those in charge of the organisation, with regulators or with the public (be it through the media or otherwise). And the purpose of whistleblowing is not the pursuit of some private vendetta but so that the risk can be assessed and, where appropriate, reduced or removed.

Whistleblowers stand up to be counted and raise their concerns openly. Thus they are the opposite of the anonymous informer that authoritarian systems nurture. And they are different from the confidential or "off-the-record" sources that journalists will also depend on to inform their stories. This is what we mean by whistleblowing and whistleblowers in this book.

Whistleblowing is a positive activity and people do not have to be victimised to be whistleblowers. Many people all over the world raise concerns about dangers and wrongdoing in the workplace and the issues are dealt with properly and their lives and careers progress unaffected. They too are whistleblowers, though they remain – no doubt to their personal satisfaction – largely unknown. Public perception, however, is informed by those whistleblowing cases that do enter the public domain and so we turn now to the four whistleblowers in this book and consider the issues that their cases raise.

## The four whistleblowers

The most famous of the whistleblowers featured in this book is Sherron Watkins. She gives an exclusive account of her whistleblowing experience at Enron. She was one of three whistleblowers named *Time* person of the year in 2002/3, an honour normally reserved for world statesmen. As *Time* said in its citation, Watkins and her two fellow whistleblowers – Cynthia Cooper who had worked at WorldCom and FBI agent Colleen Rowley – "were people who did right just by doing their jobs rightly – which means ferociously, with eyes open and with the bravery the rest of us always hope we have and may never know if we do".

Watkins raised her concerns about the financial problems at Enron with its chairman some months before its collapse. Her internal whistleblowing helped to call a halt to the massive wrongdoing at Enron and to ensure that a cover-up was not an option. Importantly, in terms of public perceptions, Watkins survived in her job. As she writes, "I recognise that my story is one with a happy ending. I was not vilified, I was not without other means of earning an income, and I was able to remain in Houston and did not have to uproot my family. Congressional reports and external auditors confirmed my allegations. I was named a *Time* Person of the Year."

Harry Templeton, however, had a much harder time. He recounts his efforts to stop a media magnate from plundering the employees' £400 million pension fund. Templeton's whistleblowing took place in the UK in the late 1980s and few then were willing to give a whistleblower a fair hearing. Templeton was sacked and vilified for his efforts. It was only after Maxwell had drowned in suspicious circumstances and his theft of the whole pension fund was discovered that people realised that Templeton had been right all along. Although Templeton's career in the print industry had been terminated, his personal story shows that even when hounded, whistleblowers do not need to become victims.

Moving to our case study from South Africa, an in-house lawyer, Victoria Johnson, took issue with the political leadership of the city of Cape Town over its arrogant approach to the public it had been elected to serve. While she is right to say that the underlying issue – the renaming of two city streets – was an ostensibly minor one, her principled stand and eventual vindication has helped to establish new standards of accountable governance in the Western Cape. As to her own career, it too has survived, though Johnson has had to endure criticism, painful soul-searching and anxiety.

Dr Jiang Yanyong's role in exposing the Chinese authorities' impulse to conceal the incidence of SARS shows that the need for whistleblowers exists the world over. In a global economy this may seem obvious, but this incident makes it clear that even if one country is trying to create a whistleblowing-friendly culture, the well-being of its people can still depend on a lone individual in another part of the world. As Robin Van den Hende's account shows, the fact that Dr Yanyong has been publicly recognised for his role at home is further evidence of a changing culture.

So, how typical are these four whistleblowers? None of them expected their whistleblowing to be easy or risk-free. All of them had strong personal ethics and examined their own consciences against this. Each has retained self-respect, though Johnson's is qualified by her remark that her betrayal of her boss has tinged her role with a degree of shame and discomfort. Each of them blew the whistle openly (and on this it is notable that Watkins' initial anonymous reports had come to nothing). All of the four (and Dr Yanyong with a remarkable insistence) were ready to accept responsibility for their actions – so demonstrating that they practised what they preached. In each case, they were not denouncers or accusers but witnesses who let the facts speak for themselves, and this too is an essential element of true whistleblowing.

## Whistleblowing and the media

Whistleblowing is a key way to deliver accountability (by which we mean that people are expected to explain their conduct). Where someone in a position of power has been informed about likely wrongdoing, he or she will know that if they ignore the risk and the concern proves well-founded and serious damage will be done, the reasonableness of their own conduct will be scrutinised. In the end, whatever concerns there may be about the independence, priorities or interests of the media in any country, the media is an essential means by which conduct is capable of being scrutinised and those in positions of power are called to account for their actions.

This is not to say that the media should be the first port of call for all whistleblowers because the mere existence of a free media (whether at home or abroad) has a latent, deterrent effect on misconduct. This is clear from the popular maxim people use when faced with a difficult decision: "Would I be happy to see my action reported in the media?" This valuable and sensible test leads to one of two results. The first is that you only act in a way for which you are ready to account. The second is you decide you do not have to act in such a way as you will use your influence to try and ensure that you will not have to account for your actions. As whistleblowing is the most effective, if not the only, check on this second course of conduct, the symbiotic relationship between whistleblowing and the role of the media is clear.

Sherron Watkins' case demonstrates this vividly as her internal whistleblowing proved to be the equivalent to a smoking gun. She chose to raise her concern internally, as she wanted to give the company a chance to try to salvage the situation and as she believed Ken Lay – Enron's chairman –

was a decent man. But once she had clearly sounded the alarm to those in charge of the company, they realised that they would be expected to account for their response to her warnings. And so the options of saying that they had no idea things were so bad, of covering up or of scapegoating some middle-ranking executives should the company collapse were no longer viable. And when her memos were discovered the media was quick to explain that their existence meant those responsible now had less chance of getting away with it.

So even though Watkins did not blow the whistle to the media, its presence influenced the way Enron responded to her internal whistleblowing. In addition, her internal whistleblowing was all the more well judged if, as some have reported, the power and influence of Enron was so great that there was a strong reluctance in the US media to question the company's success. This influence and the legal pressures the company could have brought to bear meant it was unlikely whistleblowing directly to the press would have achieved anything. This is not wild speculation as the story about Jeffrey Wigand's whistleblowing on the tobacco industry – dramatised in the Hollywood movie "The Insider" – shows. In this case one of the leading US investigative programmes on TV – CBS's "60 Minutes" – decided not to broadcast the whistleblower's story for legal and/or commercial reasons that were irrelevant and unacceptable to the lead journalist, Lowell Bergman. The only way Bergman was able to get the programme aired was by using all his skills as an investigative reporter to blow the whistle on CBS to the *Wall Street Journal* and the *New York Times*.

Templeton's case raises similar issues. He worked for a media magnate whose power was such that no UK media or journalist (other than the satirical magazine, *Private Eye*) would report Maxwell's misconduct, nor his misuse of the pension fund – even when it was the reason that Templeton and his colleagues had gone on strike. Equally the political and financial influence of Maxwell was so great that few, if any, elsewhere were willing to hear what Templeton was saying, preferring instead to accept Maxwell's view that Templeton was just a wild man from the north. With no media outlet prepared to run the story and with no regulatory oversight of pensions in the UK in the late 1980s, Templeton had no option but to fight the abuse himself.

However, neither Templeton's case nor "The Insider" is a good guide to the general role of the media in whistleblowing as they both involved whistleblowing about the media. This is clear from the other case studies. While Johnson blew the whistle internally on the misconduct of some of the political leadership in the Western Cape, it was not long before the media picked up the story (a likelihood that seems to be particularly great for those who work in or around political life). The attention the media then brought ensured that the issue would not go away even if Johnson chose to or felt pressured not to pursue her concerns in the face of strong opposition. In this way the media proved vital allies in her whistleblowing, even though they were not the first port of call. Their attention helped to separate the message from the messenger and their interest in and witnessing of the events can only have discouraged any serious attempts to victimise her.

The support Johnson received from the media takes us back, briefly, to Watkins' case as she too benefited from its coverage. When her own position was at its lowest ebb, the media discovered her memos in the congressional documents and she says that its attention gave her a "sense of safety and sanity", even though she felt uncomfortable at being at the centre of a media circus. In the light of this, as Watkins suffered no real reprisal, it is no surprise that whistleblowers who are victimised often talk of the vital support and strength the media has given them. This is due not only to the fact that the media act as a witness themselves but that they highlight – and may help redress – the inequality in bargaining power between the parties if the dispute moves towards legal action.

Dr Yanyong was a classic media whistleblower, who went straight to the press. His public disclosure about the threat of SARS was undoubtedly justified by the gravity and imminence of the risk to human health, and by the cover-up of the facts. However, Yanyong's initial approach to Chinese and Hong Kong media was not picked up or covered until his letter found its way swiftly to the international media which ran the story (thus also enabling the Chinese press to cover it more easily). Without qualifying or distancing himself from his media disclosure in any way, Yanyong also pursued his concerns openly with the Chinese authorities insisting that he should be held accountable for his actions. As with Johnson's case, the fact that there was media interest ensured that the authorities were obliged to deal with the message and would have thought twice before taking any action against the whistleblower.

While one should not generalise from these four cases, they do show that the relationship between whistleblowing and the media is a vital one and one which – beyond the simple point about accountability – is of necessity complex, rich and unique. Even if Watkins had blown the whistle to the authorities – as the post-Enron legislation in the US now encourages and protects – the mere fact that the media was there to scrutinise the way the authorities dealt with her warnings would have helped ensure that they did their job diligently, whatever power and influence Enron may have had.

This symbiotic relationship between the media and whistleblowing is discussed in the interview with Chuck Lewis, a leading public interest journalist in the US, which follows this introduction. While emphasising that reporting "benefits magnificently from and is enriched by the views of insiders", he recognises the distinction between the whistleblower (or "source-plus" as he calls it) who speaks openly and on the record, and the confidential source whose views inform or inspire a journalist's story. His description of the pressures that journalists are under and his explanation of why parts of the media dislike dealing with whistleblowers helps explain from a journalist's perspective why this relationship can be so fraught.

Lewis's description of these pressures throws light on the practical reality of being a journalist, which was compared by a former US Supreme Court judge to that of a "fragile bark on a stormy sea". This shows more consideration to the work of journalists than that demonstrated by Lord Hutton in his report into the death of scientist Dr David Kelly. Kelly had been the source for the BBC's questioning of the authority of a British government claim that Iraq's military threat justified pre-emptive action. In the light of Lewis's view (which we share) that the media is more inextricably bound to a whistleblower – as its own credibility will be undermined if that of the whistleblower is – than it will be to an unnamed source, one can wonder how events would have unravelled had David Kelly blown the whistle openly.

Lewis recognises that many people do not want to go anywhere near the media – either as a source or as a whistleblower – and in his interview speculates that the occurrence of a true media whistleblower (such as Dr Yanyong) is about one in a million. He observes that for every one of these, journalists have to deal with a good number of whistleblowers who are "obsessed by their own personal situation". The problems and distractions these cause impact not only on journalists but also on other bodies they deal with across the community (as Brian Martin of the Australian whistleblowing group remarks whistleblowers, too, can be awkward people). In some cases the cause of this obsession is the result of the whistleblowing, but in others it has much to do with the way some individuals respond to the plight, pride and priorities of the human condition and to the fact that modern western society has become so personalised that we are all encouraged to see the messenger rather than the message.

Moving beyond western societies, Lewis remarks on the dangers that investigative journalists, their sources and whistleblowers can face in developing democracies and transitional economies. Where these are real issues their impact goes go far beyond whistleblowing, but as Jiang Yanyong's case shows the international media may be able to provide some essential and effective scrutiny.

While recognising whistleblowing laws as vitally important in any democracy, Lewis rightly cautions against arrangements that draw the whistleblower into an exhausting internal scheme. Not only do such arrangements risk obscuring rather than asserting accountability, they can confuse the message with the messenger. So to what extent can whistleblowing legislation help?

## Whistleblowing and the law

In constructing whistleblowing or any other legislation, one has to be clear what one is trying to achieve both for the big and small picture, and one needs to make a call on how the law – which will always be something of a blunt instrument – can avoid doing harm, while being as effective as possible in securing the desired result. To this end, one should consult with key interests and understand and try to meet their legitimate concerns. In the context of whistleblowing, one should also take account of other factors in the country which dictate or influence people's conduct when faced with questioning or addressing wrongdoing.

In planning any whistleblowing legislation, we believe one can helpfully look at the experience in other countries and Part 3 of this book contains a review and critique of some of the main legislative schemes. But even if the approach of any country to any particular issue seems sound, one should not assume that its answer will necessarily fit your own country. This is because the role of the law differs so greatly between countries, not only in the protection it offers, the balances it strikes and how accessible it is, but also in the culture it reflects.

The oldest whistleblowing legislation is the False Claims Act, introduced during the American civil war as the only effective way to deter and detect companies which were selling defective guns and munitions to the warring sides. It provided that the whistleblower is entitled to a cut of any financial savings that the government secures or recovers as a result of the disclosure. Tom Devine – a leading US public interest attorney – shows that similar US whistleblower laws that enable "people who do good to do well" have brought colossal savings to public finances. While there are moral hazards in such an approach, it is one of the few legislative schemes that is not triggered by the victimisation of the whistleblower.

Aside from such reward-based legislation, the US also has a plethora of different and conflicting provisions that now apply to its whistleblowers, as Devine demonstrates in his contribution to this volume. Despite his profound frustration at the way the laws that apply to government employees have been subverted by the courts, it is clear from the striking examples he offers that Devine and other campaigners have helped US whistleblowers to secure some major victories in the public interest.

While US whistleblower protection has historically focused on government-related activities, it seems that some of the national security reforms post-9/11 may perversely undermine much of this basic whistleblower protection. If this proves to be the case, US corporate sector whistleblowers who have, post-Enron, been given protection will now be in a stronger position than their public sector counterparts. While it will be interesting to see how this new corporate sector legislation will work in a country where there is no general labour law protecting employees, the simple approach it takes to disclosures contrasts with that in the UK legislation.

The disclosure regime for US corporate whistleblowers gives them equal protection – and so offers no guidance – whether they raise the matter with their employer, the authorities or Congress. The UK legislation, however, has a tiered disclosure regime. It starts by providing virtually automatic protection for internal whistleblowing; then, whether or not the whistle is blown internally first, disclosures to the authorities are readily (though not quite so easily) protected. Wider public disclosures, however, have to be justified and reasonable if the whistleblower is to be protected and the UK's legislation is rare if not unique in that it has protected a number of media disclosures.

As Anna Myers explains in her assessment of the UK's Public Interest Disclosure Act, while its aims are to protect whistleblowers, it was constructed not to launch a thousand lawsuits but to signal a change in culture where organisations and society would be more likely to address the message rather than shoot the messenger. The disasters and scandals she lists that set the background to the legislation explain why such an approach was felt necessary in the UK. A downside of this approach is that it may encourage some employees to persist in trying to work the internal system when an external disclosure would be more effective for the public interest and less exhausting for the employee.

The UK's disclosure regime promotes the idea that, unless the employer assures staff that they can safely blow the whistle internally, they are unlikely to warn the employer of any problems. So to avoid the disruption or bad publicity of an external disclosure or the disaster that may follow silence, it's in the employer's interest to make it safe for staff to raise concerns and to deal with them properly. Equally, should the employer victimise the whistleblower, not only will that draw attention to its own wrongdoing but it will also have to compensate the whistleblower for all his or her losses.

Myers suggests that one main benefit of the UK law has been its declaratory effect, as it has helped shift perceptions about whistleblowing and about ways to deter and tackle wrongdoing. In this respect the approach of the Public Interest Disclosure Act can be seen as a British response to the point Devine makes that, at best, the potential of a whistleblower law is to be effective as a last resort. Its approach also chimes with the observation that organisational leadership can be more significant than legal rights in this area as the UK law seems to have had some success in encouraging organisations to reconsider the value of whistleblowing and prompting many leaders to embrace it.

While it will take a generation or more before one can assess whether such an attempt to shift cultural values has had any real effect, the Public Interest Disclosure Act seems to be working reasonably well so far. Myers cites tentative evidence from the public sector that it has impacted on the incidence of wrongdoing and demonstrates that the law has been used successfully by internal and external whistleblowers from both the public and private sectors.

Kirsten Trott's careful analysis of the numerous whistleblowing laws in Australia and New Zealand is of necessity more abstract as there is so little evidence about how they are working in practice. The main reason for this is that the enforcement of the legislation there is a matter primarily for the authorities themselves. While in the UK and the US the whistleblower can initiate a claim of victimisation, the laws in Australia are predominantly enforced by criminal or administrative actions brought by the authorities. With legislative schemes that criminalise both the managers who victimise whistleblowers and the whistleblowers who stray beyond the precise statutory protection, it is perhaps no surprise that there have been no prosecutions.

As Trott notes, research needs to be undertaken into the various schemes to see how far they have encouraged Australasian public sector employees to blow the whistle, whether they have discouraged reprisals and whether they have deterred wrongdoing.

While the Australasian legislation focuses on the public sector (following the emphasis of the approach in the US pre-Enron), it is proposed – by contrast – that the draft law in Japan will apply only to the private sector. As Yukiko Miki and Koji Morioka show in their respective chapters, the cultural and social pressures for corporate loyalty in Japan present a real challenge to any whistleblowing scheme. These are so great that, notwithstanding the very strong labour protections Japan provides, hardly any employee has blown the whistle in the past however grave the dangers. It appears that the Japanese law may look for guidance to the UK whistleblowing legislation. With such a strong tradition of corporate loyalty in Japan, the adoption of a legislative scheme based on the mutual interest between employer, employee and the public interest is both modest and radical at the same time. For this (albeit, to many Westerners, incongruous) reason, Japan may prove well suited to reap the benefits of this approach. However, if the new law were to protect only disclosures about one of several hundred specific criminal offences it is difficult to see how this will embed or build on any mutual interest.

Whatever may happen in Japan and the UK, the potential application of this mutual interest approach to whistleblowing in transitional economies takes one to the experience in South Africa. Its Protected Disclosures Act, in force for over two years, is closely modelled on the UK legislation and it is clear from the chapter by Mukelani Dimba, Lorraine Stober and Bill Thomson that the challenges this approach faces are intense. How can legal protections against reprisals be sustainable where life is cheap and the labour supply plentiful in the context of a 40% unemployment rate? In a country where the recent past has been clouded by the role of *impipis* or state informers, how soon can we fashion a benign approach to whistleblowers? Recognising the wider benefits that a common interest can make meaningful in a transitional economy, South Africa is now considering whether to widen the legislative scheme beyond the workplace.

Of the four case studies, it is only Victoria Johnson who could at the relevant time have been protected by her country's whistleblowing legislation. Though she did not have to bring a claim, it is clear from her account that its existence helped guide her actions and strengthen her resolve. Had the US legislation for corporate whistleblowers existed in the 1990s, it is at least possible that Watkins or one of her colleagues would have blown the whistle earlier, either internally or to the authorities. Had they done so only to be victimised, their resulting legal claim would have attracted scrutiny not only of the reprisal but also of the alleged wrongdoing and so much damage and distress would have been avoided. The same result may have happened in Templeton's case had the legislation been in force, though what is clear is that he would have been fully compensated for his losses even if it did not stop Maxwell. So, as the case studies show, when one considers the effect any legislation may have one has to view it in the context of the other factors and levers that exist and can be brought to bear on the issue, interests and players.

For this reason, even where any given whistleblowing legislation appears to be strong and clear, employees still need to take real care. As Sherron Watkins remarks, "a lot of whistleblowers choose not to seek legal assistance because they have done nothing wrong. I think that a lawyer is really necessary and not someone that the company pays." This is not just because the lawyer can advise on legal rights and obligations, but because he or she can offer tactical advice and can help ensure that the whistleblower keeps sight of the wood for the trees.

## Whistleblowing and civil society

Recognising this, civil society groups in Australia, Japan, South Africa, the UK and the US have separately seen the need to offer legal advice to employees on whether and how they can blow the whistle and to offer varying levels of support thereafter. Talking through such conflicts of loyalty with an independent person helps the individual reach an informed decision provided that (as the Government Accountability Project [GAP], the US not-for-profit organisation urges) the first rule for any whistleblowing organisation – to cause no harm to one's client – is adhered to.

As significantly, the existence of a civil society group addressing this issue in any given country can help to tilt the balance so that organisations are less swift to discourage, ignore or suppress whistleblowing. In this way, they can strengthen the hand of prospective whistleblowers even where they have not approached the group for advice. As the experience in South Africa, the UK and the US shows, a civil society group addressing whistleblowing can also help influence attitudes to organisational accountability and leadership, quite aside from its client work.

Turning to wider cultural issues, civil society is best placed to promote the case that people be encouraged to question rather than simply denounce and to explain why the right to question another's conduct is no greater nor less than the right of others to question one's own. By informing debates about the roles of whistleblowing, accountability and the public interest, civil society groups can provide the context within which honest, decent people can see whistleblowing as a public good and something worth considering. As more people begin to see whistleblowing in this light, those who are tempted to abuse positions of power will think twice as they can no longer rely on the system's pressures on staff to stay silent.

As Part 4 of this book shows, the civil society responses, rightly, reflect the culture, legal tradition and sociology of each country. In Australia there is, essentially, a mutual support group for whistleblowers. In Japan, civil society provides expert advice to employees on whether and how to blow the whistle. This is similar to the approach in the UK and South Africa, though the whistleblowing groups there also train employers, unions and regulators on leadership, openness and accountability. In the US, the group is more whistleblower than whistleblowing and campaigns and litigates on individual cases.

The experience from the US, UK and South Africa is that civil society groups can also exercise real influence over the scope and content of whistleblowing legislation and drawing on that experience these groups are now able to offer support and guidance on initiatives elsewhere.

This book, then, is for activists, employees, leaders, legislators, managers, policy-makers, practitioners and professionals across the public and private sectors. Its review of the state of whistleblowing around the world – North, South, East and West – shows that a critical mass is beginning to accumulate internationally. We hope this book will encourage and help you to join up the dots, linking law and policy with culture and practice, so that you can help chart the right course for your own organisation and society. Only if the good intentions of any law are matched by a change in culture can a safe alternative to silence be created. Only then can the principle of accountability work in practice and protect the public interest.

# THE JOURNALIST AND THE WHISTLEBLOWER: A SYMBIOTIC RELATIONSHIP

*Chuck Lewis in conversation with Richard Calland*

Richard Calland: What is the nature of the relationship between the journalist and the whistleblower?

Chuck Lewis: The whistleblower, by definition, at least in the US context, tends to resort to this fairly dramatic and courageous, and arguably edgy, situation because they have already tried to work from inside. They have talked to their superior or they have decided that their superior is part of the problem. Usually a whistleblower is at their wits end and the internal dissent and discourse has run its course and, in fact, is not a practical means of expression. So the whistleblower then has no choice but to go public and to go to the media.

I think in all reporting the journalist benefits magnificently from, and is enriched by, the view of insiders. It is all part and parcel of someone feeling that something is wrong and wanting to express it. It is much simpler to mention it to your boss or to write an internal memo. To go through what a whistleblower goes through, not only for the next months or years, but possibly altering the rest of their life, you can be sure that they have thought about it and even attempted to act internally.

I am very suspicious of internal safeguards, because sometimes you can set up internal systems that sound wonderful, but the whistleblower is still shunned. If they have gone public or are suspected of talking to outsiders, or just don't want to play along because they clearly don't like what is going on and have made it clear internally, no one speaks to them in lunchrooms. They are excluded from meetings. You can have all the internal safeguards you want, but it is going to be a miserable daily existence. So, while you should try to protect them internally, in the end the whistleblower frequently needs more than that.

RC: Would you see the press as a place of safety for the whistleblower?

CL: It is a place of safety. It is the one place outside the powerful – almost terrifyingly so – instruments of government. It is the one place you can shine a light on government or you can talk about government so that the public will learn about what you have heard or found out or know. There really is only one place, and that is the media. That sets up a whole set of issues that are complicated because a lot of the media is seriously flawed. A lot of news organisations do not have a serious commitment to investigative journalism and a lot of news organisations and/or re-porters are not equipped to deal with whistleblowers. There are some-times situations where there are so many whistleblowers, scores of them, that in a given situation the news organisation is ill-equipped to absorb all the information. That is assuming that they even want to go there.

The other problem with whistleblowers is that a lot of journalists roll their eyes; sometimes whistleblowers, a good number of them, are ob-sessed with their own personal situation and their own individual cir-cumstances. Their usefulness to journalists is somewhat circumscribed by the parochial nature of the information they provide. The person gets so obsessed – maybe justifiably on some level – that they can be-come somewhat paranoid, given the pressures brought on them, to the point that they may become unstable. Many journalists don't really want to deal with whistleblowers. It takes a certain kind of journalist and a certain kind of news outlet to be ready and receptive.

RC: So, given those reasons, the media may prove to be not much of a safe haven, but rather an equally precarious place. Would it not depend very much on the state of the media and the particular media organisation to whom the whistleblower turns?

CL: Exactly. There are so many subjective things that could happen in each individual case with each whistleblower, which is why the media is one place where there could be a happy ending where the public interest is served. But for each of those cases there are probably many, many failed connections, where the whistleblower doesn't call the right person or calls them on deadline. So there also needs to be legal protections for whistleblowers, whether they are of an internal or external nature. Each country needs to have a regime in place to protect whistleblowers be-cause what they are doing is so vitally important to any democracy. The media could be, and in fact is, an extraordinarily important part of this equation, but it is certainly not the only outlet.

RC: I think I am right in saying that you worked for *60 Minutes* and knew both Lowell Bergman and Mike Wallace, both made famous by the Hol-lywood film, *The Insider?*

CL: I was a producer for CBS News's *60 Minutes* and worked with senior correspondent Mike Wallace for five years in the mid-1980s. He was a friend and colleague of Lowell Bergman, with whom I also worked at ABC News years earlier. Indeed, it was Bergman who suggested to Wallace and the other powers that be at CBS that they hire me back in 1984.

RC: To what extent do you think the *60 Minutes* story, which led to the making of the movie, *The Insider*, is a classic example of what can happen and what can go wrong?

CL: I think it is a pretty classic case. What is usual is that most journalists get frustrated, their shoulders slump a little lower and they walk a little slower, and they go on to the next story slightly beaten down by the experience of having a story spiked for bad, un-journalistic reasons. It is very unusual that a journalist ends up becoming a celebrity and having a movie made about them. That is the part that is unrealistic. I am sure several people at the higher reaches of CBS would have other comments to make about the movie, but I do think it is fairly classic.

In journalism, inside and outside the US, there are powerful corporate or sometimes political interests that play their part. They sometimes get into the news sausage-making process and interfere with it and try to manipulate it in an ugly way. Individual journalists, line producers, associate television producers, or (even) a specific individual print reporter inside a newspaper, are what former supreme court Justice Douglas referred to as a "fragile bark on a stormy sea".

You are in a news organisation but you are not always sure how deeply committed that organisation is to quality journalism. So, in some ways, the plight of the individual journalist is not unlike the plight of the whistleblower inside his or her government or corporate setting. In fact, the journalist becomes a whistleblower of sorts. Lowell Bergman in the case of *The Insider* was a whistleblower. He blew the whistle in an astonishing set of circumstances, actually hooking up with Hollywood. The whole thing was first played out in the media itself – the media didn't just casually discover the story. The first place Bergman went to was his colleagues in the media who wrote about it, particularly the *Wall Street Journal*. There was a public furore over it and CBS was then in an embarrassing situation, which was almost unprecedented for the network. Events then took on a life of their own, but Bergman's whistleblowing started the whole process and the finishing touches were the movie. That is not the usual process for any whistleblower or writer.

RC: But up until that point, the classic nature of it suggests a sort of symbiotic relationship between the journalist and the whistleblower and in a sense the load, which is a very heavy burden, becomes somewhat shared when that relationship forms. Is that a fair way to describe it?

CL: That is absolutely fair. Jeffrey Wigand and Bergman I believe first met in Louisville, Kentucky in a hotel lobby and Bergman began to spend hours and hours trying to understand the circumstances and the information itself and trying to coach and nudge Wigand into cooperating with him and trying to navigate legality problems such as the confidentiality agreement which was of course a huge issue. So, there does emerge a symbiosis and a kind of informal pact. And it is classic, but it doesn't always end up on a show that goes to 40 million people as in a case like this. The classic arrangement between source or whistleblower and reporter is one of the most fundamental parts of journalism.

Usually you don't know who the source is. Frequently he or she will furnish documents or leak information to the journalist and it is not necessary, especially in print journalism, for that person to go public. Part of the problem is that the medium of television requires someone to say this and it can't be Mike Wallace doing a voice-over, saying that they know there is a person out there. You can only do that for one or two sentences, but then it won't carry weight, because of production values in television and the way television works. So in most of the classic cases the whistleblower source usually helps a journalist tell a story, whereas a journalist protects a normal source and will even go to prison to protect and keep that source from ever being revealed or identified. It is a little unusual for our source to publicly fall on his or her sword.

RC: So for the average journalist there presumably is not a huge distinction between a whistleblower and a normal source. Is that true and what are the dangers of that, in that we know that whistleblowers are not just a source?

CL: I would call them a "source plus". A source is someone who is willing to speak, sometimes in a very complicated, even dangerous situation. A person deciding to speak, or to leak any document, can be doing something not only courageous and gutsy, but professionally stupid. I am glad they do it, but it is incredibly risky. The act of being a source and making a phone call when the reporter's phone records might be retrieved, might be retrieved by the government, or just trying to meet someone in a park or in the corner of a smoky bar when you could be photographed or followed by government agents or private security, is extremely precarious. The journalist is deeply grateful for that level of interest and commitment to whatever the subject is.

A whistleblower is someone who does all of those things, but is also capable of going public, and is frequently willing to go public, to talk about what they saw or did. For the public the news media is then endorsing this person and saying to the public, with a neon sign, that this person is courageous, authentic, they know what they are talking about. Many sources also do, but this person is willing to go public and in that sense, they are in it together. If there is a backlash, the criticism will not only be of the whistleblower. It will be of the news organisation that chose to trumpet and showcase his or her information; they are bound inextricably together once the story appears. The stakes can be incredibly high.

RC: Why was there no media exposure of the whistleblowers in the Enron and Worldcom cases before the two companies collapsed?

CL: Sherron Watkins from Enron wrote an internal memo saying she's not so sure of some of these things, a sort of internal cautionary flashing light. When the Enron thing started to topple, people discovered the memo and she was deemed a hero, but prior to the revelations she chose actually not to go public, as a classic whistleblower would. I don't want to sound tough, but let's be honest. In the case of Enron and Worldcom people were getting rich from the subterfuge. These are companies that were cooking their books, lying to shareholders, to the stock exchange and to the public, and most of the people at the corporate level and even at the mid-levels were all getting rich. They were building up their retirement pensions, creating nest eggs for their families. They all had a vested financial interest in everything they said either being true or at least working. This company will stay afloat, and not only stay afloat, but flourish. Even if things weren't quite the way they were supposed to be, they would rationalise that other companies do it too and that is the way things are and they get used to the idea that what they are doing is not a felony. They will adapt to it because it is frankly extraordinarily lucrative and convenient to them and their families.

We cannot underestimate the risk. Not only can you lose your job and be sued civilly for possibly violating a confidentiality agreement or be sued by your own company or government in the cases of corporate whistleblowers, you are also going to be broke. You are going to be without any visible means of support. You are going to be unemployable. It is not just what you are doing to your company, it is also what you are saying to all your friends and colleagues and fellow employees – "I'm not going to keep making all this money, because I don't like the way we are making it". You are also deeming yourself a royal pain in the ass to any other prospective company who will hire you. Who wants someone that is going to rock the boat and bring out the bugles if there is the slightest problem? Can you trust that person? Will they be loyal? You are betwixt and between: you don't want to do anything illegal, but you also don't want to make yourself unemployable for the next five, 10, 20 years, where it is on your record that you brought the house of cards down with your courageous "whistleblowing".

We tend to think that whistleblowers are everywhere and it is common for there to be whistleblowers. But actually they are extremely rare, particularly ones who are credible and know what they are talking about and who don't have skeletons in their closet and have the psychological make-up to withstand the heat and all the pressure and don't mind taking a hit financially. You are talking about a one in a million type of person. It is exceedingly rare to find a whistleblower who can withstand the heat and the scrutiny that is going to occur. So more often than not people keep quiet and more often than not they don't go public. Maybe they send an internal memo in a brown paper envelope to a journalist and then instead of being a whistleblower they become an anonymous source. They find other ways to fight their personal demons in the middle of the night. They want to look themselves in the mirror and justify that they have a family, mouths to feed, they don't like what is going on so they will try to help shine a light and so they do something that is slightly less courageous, less public, less dramatic, but also constructive to society and to the broad social and political fabric.

RC: Do you think there is a case for specifically training investigative journalists on whistleblowing?

CL: I don't know if it takes special training as much as a special temperament. Most journalists are under incredible pressure, which I don't think the public fully appreciates. Most journalists have to turn out a certain number of words per day or they are fired. There are serious, major problems with the commercial media and even in the publicly supported media in most countries around the world, where investigative reporting is not doing well. A lot of important stories are not being told in specific countries and especially in the cross-borders where it is more costly, more dangerous, more difficult, logistically more cumbersome. Any good journalist who's been around for a few years and has dealt with sources, can often deal with whistleblowers. The problem with a lot of journalists is, like everyone in life, they get a bit old and crusty and start thinking they know everything. They start becoming a little less open-minded. What often happens is a whistleblower doesn't know how to approach a journalist properly. Sometimes whistleblowers will do things that are irritating, like call during a breaking story or on a deadline. It is a common sense thing. Journalist will have 10 phone messages and they don't get to call number seven back for one or two weeks and the whistleblower takes it so personally, they get mad and don't want to talk to the journalist any longer.

RC: What about developing or emerging democracies where the press may be weaker, less experienced and possibly less free?

CL: This already delicate dynamic between reporter and whistleblower or source is more dicey when the news media organisations are weak or controlled by the government. How secure will a whistleblower feel if the supposedly "free" press is merely an arm of the state? In some countries, the news media is owned by organised crime thugs – how much unfettered investigative reporting about corruption will be published under those circumstances, and how safe is any whistleblower or source who talks to any hired journalist working in that milieu? And what about the fates of reporters and whistleblowers under the knife of threatened libel action in which the media organisation is financially fragile and unable or unwilling to stand behind publishing the truth? Is exposing the truth worth risking your life or your family's livelihood? Investigative journalism in new, embryonic democracies is a precarious adventure.

# PART 2:

## CASE STUDIES – NORTH, SOUTH, EAST & WEST

# BLOWING THE WHISTLE ON A
# NEWSPAPER MAGNATE

*By Harry Templeton*

In 1984 when Robert Maxwell took over Mirror Group Newspapers from Reed International, I wasn't too pleased – to put it mildly. I'd never actually met him, but I knew of him and his murky reputation. He was already a major employer of printers and journalists in Scotland through his involvement with the Radio Times and several other publications, but every report I received from people whose opinions I respected was adverse. He was regarded as a bully, an opportunist, a liar, a cheat, a criminal, a self-publicist, a low-life masquerading as a reformed entrepreneur and mystery surrounded the source of his wealth. The dogs in the street were barking that he was definitely not a man to be trusted. So ask yourself – would you have been wary? The consequences of this man's intrusion into my working life turned out to be far more serious than I could have imagined for me and my family.

I was 37 years old, married to my wife, Faye, and had five children. We were (and remain) a working class family with a mortgage, a car, a reasonable standard of living – able to afford holidays abroad occasionally. We are just ordinary folk. I had been working for the past 14 years in Glasgow for the Mirror Group titles – *The Daily Record* and *The Sunday Mail* – as a printer operating the presses. I had become the "Imperial Father" or Senior Shop Steward of the trade union within that office. My union involvement was part-time, and I was a working member of my crew. It was a 24-hour a day, seven day a week business, and we operated shift patterns and rotas to meet production requirements with most actual printing being done overnight.

We had embraced new technology, printed in full colour and dominated the Scottish daily newspaper market. Ours was the most profitable part of the Mirror Group. We had secured a wage and conditions package other tradesmen would die for. The future looked bright and traditionally this was seen as a "job for life" – if such a thing existed.

I was aware that Reed International wanted out of newspaper publishing for their own strategic reasons but we weren't too concerned because they originally announced that they intended to sell to the widest spread of public ownership. They suggested that the papers could ultimately be owned by their readers, rather than by any individual or group. They had appointed an ex-building managing director to oversee that laudable, if somewhat radical, process. Shamefully, to my mind, they reneged on the deal and accepted Maxwell's offer instead. Despite his protestations of director responsibility and duty to shareholders, I couldn't resist telling the chairman of Reed International what I thought of him and his apparent scant regard for the fate of those who'd made the company millions over the years.

I was introduced to Maxwell within days of his unwelcome takeover. I found him to be a larger-than-life character who appeared to believe his own publicity. He expected other people to jump to his every command and comply with his every whim. He had an almost uncanny ability to detect weakness in other people, and to exploit that to maximum advantage for his benefit. He could size up and categorise people very quickly and I found this to be one of his most potent tools in his constant quest for power. I found out very early on that power and influence were what motivated Maxwell and not money, as most people assumed. The availability of money was just a means to achieve his ultimate goals.

He lived up to his reputation at that initial meeting and tried to bully our delegation, even at that early stage. I am the second youngest of a family of 12, born and brought up on a Glasgow housing estate, and I'm sure he realised at that meeting that I don't bully easily!

He reminded us "who pays your wages" (even though he'd only taken over ownership two days earlier and hadn't actually paid us anything yet)! He said that he alone could decide whether existing deals on wages and conditions would continue and if we didn't like it we could leave. He announced that he intended implementing a survival plan for what he described as "this ailing company" though in Scotland we were not surprised because he had had survival plans for every company he'd every bought previously. My concern was that it was his survival, rather than my own and that of the 1 300 people I represented, that was his priority.

Initially, during the early months following his acquisition of the group, he concentrated his efforts on gaining complete control and maximising the profitability of the group titles based in London. He decimated the workforce and imposed Draconian conditions on them as part of "their" survival plan. He had convinced them by a virtuoso performance at a mass meeting that they worked for a sleeping giant company, which only required his Midas touch to awaken and regain its position as industry leader – guaranteeing them long-term employment security. This, when many then faced redundancy or early retirement at minimum legal rates only made more attractive by enhanced payments financed from our pension funds.

Our major concern in Scotland was this apparent misuse of pension fund monies. Our colleagues in the south eventually shared our misgivings, and set up an internal group they called the pension conference. I was part of the Scottish delegation who attended the tactics meetings. We agreed on the nature of the problem, but not on the strategy for dealing with it. The majority decision was that the pension conference would seek urgent meetings with Maxwell to make him aware of our concerns. They believed that they could then appeal to his sense of fair play and seek assurances that pension fund monies would only be used to provide retirement income reflecting service entitlement. Reluctantly, the rest of us followed the majority. Maxwell denied every request, saying that when he bought the company he bought control of the pension funds and insisting that pensions were non-negotiable, and no concern of unions or elected union representatives. Our people became painfully aware that the tactics they had adopted to deal with former employers would fail palpably when dealing with this very different animal.

Still concerned and faced with this attitude we in Scotland looked at other options. The pension scheme was considered at the time to be a model one to which others aspired. The ultimate benefits were related to both salary and length of service and were close to the maximum levels allowed for such schemes under Tax Authority rules. Administration and control of the scheme was shared by a Board of Trustees representing in equal measure both the employer and the workers. There were 14 members in total – seven employer-appointed representatives and seven worker representatives. On the face of it, it was a safe, secure structure envied by other workers in different situations.

Service on such boards was not an attractive option under normal circumstances, as much of the work was seen as mundane and complicated, and how many workers either knew or cared how the scheme operated so long as their pension was acceptable when they themselves retired?

However, these were obviously not normal circumstances and the Scottish-based workers decided to replace our existing trustee with myself. This required us to call for an election after our man announced his resignation. Maxwell became aware of our intentions and tried everything in his power to thwart my joining the Board of Trustees. He insisted on adherence to rules about election to the Board that nobody knew existed and which had not been followed on other occasions when change had occurred. Each worker had to write individual letters to him giving their name, National Insurance number and Scheme Membership number. They then had to confirm their vote for me as the only candidate and then sign and date their voting paper. Many were disqualified for "rule violation" or deemed "spoilt papers".

However, after my overwhelming election victory even he had to accept my appointment, but he refused me entry to my first Board meeting until the part of the agenda labelled "any other business". This device effectively kept me out of yet another meeting but convinced me entirely that service on that Board and access to its work was imperative.

These Trustee Board meetings had been held infrequently while Reed International owned the group; sometimes only three or four times a year. They made policy decisions for scheme administration and control. Since the scheme was a long established one their function was mainly to ensure that everything was functioning as it should. Most decisions on policy had been taken years before. The Board I had been elected onto under Maxwell was vastly different and required frequent meetings to consider all of the policy changes proposed. We often met six or seven times monthly. We often met at very short notice to consider some perceived "crises" that we needed to urgently address. These invariably turned out to be rule or policy changes which required Board assent to allow him to do whatever he planned doing anyway.

It was obvious to me from my first meeting that opposition to his schemes would be very difficult on the Board. The apparent equality of representation belied the reality of its operation. Firstly, although both sides were numerically equal, Maxwell, as the employer, retained the permanent chairmanship of the Board and, in that capacity, he had a second and casting vote in the event of tied votes. The six employer representatives who accompanied him always voted in support of him and seldom spoke, unless chosen to introduce a topic he wanted discussed anyway. They obviously would never dissent from his line, presumably under threat of instant dismissal.

The other trade union representatives (I was the one representing Scotland) were a mixture of the naive and the opportunistic. Quite a number had, since Maxwell's takeover, been promoted to better paid jobs within the group. Others believed that he must be trustworthy because he was a successful business tycoon who employed thousands of people and who they assumed must possess higher moral standards than their own.

Maxwell always stressed his conveniently held view that the Board's function was not to negotiate or argue about pensions. Our function was to run the scheme for the benefit of the pensioners. As such we should look at options available in different circumstances and agree how best to proceed without the need to record any dissenting votes. This oft-repeated mantra didn't square with his decision that he should react to a favourable actuarial report by suspending indefinitely employer contributions to the fund after having only paid nine months worth. Control of a fund worth more than he had paid for the whole company, and into which he'd only ever pay £9 million, was good business and explained his "darling of the city" public perception at that time.

To me he was attempting to cover his tracks by stating that any changes proposed were Board decisions rather than Robert Maxwell ones and that as the chair of the Board he was bound to carry out its policy in the pensioners' best interests.

A number of related events were happening to me personally during this period. I started to get unsolicited, casual, verbal offers for promotion in the plant. Usually at some social gathering or after a meeting I'd be approached privately by some manager who would remark how he'd been impressed by the way I conducted myself and my business and that I obviously wasn't afraid of accepting responsibility. I'd be asked to indicate whether a job on the opposite side of the fence would ever be of interest. Mischievously, I used to ask what they were thinking of on my behalf. I'd remind them that I was a "big fish" where I was, on the union side. Supervisory jobs were initially mooted; when the "fish" didn't bite, these became pressroom manager posts and ultimately a Production Director appointment. To my amusement, the status of the offer-makers increased in line with the standing of the offer made. It still wasn't tempting to know that I could move from pressroom to boardroom in one swoop. My next move would have been out of the door – but they never projected that far ahead.

Also around that same time I started receiving unsigned letters about pension law and practice on London School of Economics headed notepaper. To this day I don't know who my mystery correspondent was. However, he or she obviously knew about my dilemma and was keen to offer advice on various subjects. I was sent papers about trustee board responsibility and power. These often had sections highlighted to stress their importance.

I also found an increasing number of acquaintances (never friends) starting graphic conversations that culminated in warnings that Maxwell was not a man to be crossed and was capable of anything - and they always stressed *anything*.

And even the minutes of trustees meetings were being "doctored" to such an extent that when I read them I wondered whether I'd been there or not. Items were added or removed from the record. I was often denied an agenda prior to arrival, though others present seemed to have been fully briefed about the topics for discussion that day.

Any doubts I had entertained about the importance of the role I'd been elected to perform on behalf of myself and those I represented were swept away as events continued to unfold.

I'd been advised that others agreed that his intention was to use the "adherence to Board decisions" line as a cover. My unknown advisor from the London School of Economics indicated that I would frustrate this by insisting whenever necessary that votes be taken and dissent recorded in the minutes. I began voicing my dissent whenever I deemed it appropriate and always insisted that votes be taken. Maxwell was apparently more acceptable to the other trustees than me and I regularly lost these 13 to 1, or 12 to 2 on a good day.

Quite often I would instinctively force votes for reasons not immediately obvious to myself. I did this because I noticed certain behavioural patterns Maxwell had. For example he'd often look at me as if to say, "I may be fooling some of this lot, but you know what I'm really about". Most times I neither had enough information nor intelligence to figure out what he was doing; but this self-conscious look gave him away and I'd often find out later what it was all about. I think he had a sneaking regard for me, possibly because all attempts to get me "on side" had failed. Unfortunately, I was having little success in my efforts to stop him plundering our pension fund and was at best seen as an overgrown terrier biting annoyingly at his ankles.

My efforts to recruit assistance to supplement my own activity by attracting more powerful figures to give their support fell on deaf ears. My national union General Secretary never replied to a letter I'd sent via my local Glasgow-based full-time official. Political figures made it clear that they didn't want to be involved. I could write volumes speculating on their motives but suffice to say I stood reluctantly in splendid isolation.

I was surprised generally by the lack of understanding most people had of pensions and how they worked. Another hurdle I faced was the fact that pensions were then largely controlled by ancient, wholly inappropriate, Trust Law under which change is difficult and contentious issues are resolved slowly by reference to previous case history and convention. This was highlighted when I tried going to the law to contest a particularly damaging decision of the Trustee Board. I was told that I could not personally bring a case but would have to find a pensioner likely to be disadvantaged by the implementation of the decision. That pensioner could then start legal action against me and the other trustees. The progress of the action through the courts would take years and be very expensive with absolutely no guarantee of ultimate success. Effectively, this avenue was closed to me as well, because finding a pensioner rich and healthy enough to withstand the pressure over years was not a realistic option.

Finding support for justice and fair dealing was proving very hard, while Maxwell continued to push through all the changes required to plunder the scheme assets. Going public with our case was not an option, either – Maxwell had exposed the myth of Britain having a free press. Always willing and financially able to sue any publication or media group for saying or writing anything adverse, he was a master at controlling their output. Even media rivals would not promote our story because the establishment controlled the multi-billion pound pension industry and both they and successive governments were considering doing to others what Maxwell was doing to Mirror Group employees. Asset stripping firms and their pension schemes had become acceptable practice, encouraged by cash hungry individuals and groups of shareholders.

So I embarked on an internal campaign of enlightenment. Although Maxwell insisted that the business transacted at Trustee Board meetings was subject to absolute confidentiality, like the meetings of any Board of Management running a business, I chose to ignore that conventional restriction. I reported back fully to those I was elected to represent. I took the view that pensions were another name for wages in retirement and that, as such, matters that affected pensions were every bit as important as annual wage and condition negotiations. Adverse changes were equally unacceptable in both cases.

They agreed, and we fought back using the only weapon ultimately available to workers: when Maxwell threatened damaging change we threatened the production of the Scottish titles. We had the power, because no one is interested in yesterday's news, lost revenue cannot be recouped following industrial action and advertising income is jeopardised. You may think this extreme but, in my experience, it is always the last resort and was in this case. We saw no other way to stop the wrongdoing being foisted upon us by this ruthless character who focused exclusively on getting his way without regard to others.

On a number of occasions we took action and stopped the presses. It was often subsequently portrayed publicly that we had taken "wild cat" action for some other purpose, but he knew and we knew what it was all about, and we managed to force a rethink on some issues. I was gradually becoming something more than a nuisance to Maxwell. Others saw us having some success in opposition and were keen to emulate our action.

I continued my efforts to at least delay changes going through on the Board of Trustees. You might find it interesting to know how Maxwell managed to get some of the more controversial decisions through the Board of Trustees. He was a clever speaker and fantastic at manipulating others. As an example, I'll talk you through his getting agreement that investment of funds be done in-house.

He raised a point at a meeting where he expressed concern that the scheme was paying too much to investment consultants and fund managers. He began by pointing out from the previous year's accounts that we had paid three companies more than £3 million to invest the bulk of the £460 million in the fund at that time. He then said that this money could be better utilised to increase pensions in payment. He told us that he had selflessly researched the situation and found out that we could afford to employ our own internal fund manager and that, although the best ones didn't come cheap, he reckoned we could press one into service by offering an employment contract costing £300,000 per annum. This was a huge salary at the time, but much less than these investment companies were charging us.

He asked whether there was any opposition to his proposal for change. As usual, I was the solitary opponent. The naive accepted what he said at face value; the more sinister characters, whom I suspected he'd bought, had just been given a plausible excuse to support him. Cynic that I was learning to be, I assumed that he wanted the green light to buy himself a £300,000 p.a. "yes man" who would be prepared to rubber stamp Maxwell's investment decisions as if they were his own. I knew that pension increases would take a long time coming through as a result of this apparent cost-cutting exercise.

This was an oft-repeated tactic, where he proposed something that, if it had been proposed by someone more trustworthy, would have sounded both reasonable and plausible – but from him was scheming manipulation with ulterior motive. I used to say he gave willing associates a hook to hang their coats on lest they be unable to dream up justification for supporting him at a later date. He had a warped genius for such things.

I made people aware that Maxwell had decided that the company would pay for periodic actuarial valuations of the scheme. He claimed that this was to save the scheme substantial amounts of money and release even more to pay increased pensions, but it had another attraction for someone like him. It meant that although we as trustees were shown the resultant reports, we were denied information about the assumptions the actuaries had based their calculations upon. These were very important, as changing one or more of them would alter the outcome dramatically. When I asked to be given access to this information I was told it was "commercially sensitive" and therefore invaluable to competitors in the newspaper industry. This denial meant we had access to the answer without knowing what the sum had been. We were told the scheme had a huge surplus and that this meant that he could suspend indefinitely the company's contributions because the actuaries had reported that there was more than enough in there to meet present and future benefit commitments to pensioners. I had no way of knowing whether that was true or not.

When the surplus was announced we, in Scotland, proposed alternative uses for the "extra" money available from past contributions growing in value in an expanding equity market. We suggested improvements in scheme benefits, and that pensions be index linked in future. Maxwell's much trumpeted concern for the poor pensioners didn't extend to agreeing to improve their lot. He quickly rejected any such proposals.

Incidents like this and other events I was involved in were forcing Maxwell's activities regarding the pension scheme into the open and under the spotlight. He didn't like that one bit and would have preferred people to be blinded to these nefarious acts and sidetracked into concentrating on his image-making PR activity. Our daily newspaper title became known in Scotland as the *Daily Maxwell* and was getting a reputation akin to that of a comic rather than a tabloid. It was jokingly suggested that we might change to a broadsheet to allow full body photographs of "Captain Bob" to accompany his serialised adventures masquerading as an authorised biography.

But even he could not hope to fool all of the people all of the time and more were becoming alarmed about what was being done to their pension scheme.

Then suddenly I was dismissed in February 1988. I was charged with gross industrial misconduct, accused of threatening a fellow worker that if he refused to take part in our industrial action and go on strike that I'd do him some physical harm. This was alleged to have happened close to the folder mechanism on a running printing press. The noise level there is 104 decibels and it is impossible to hear someone shouting into your ear. Even more surprisingly, a witness came forward claiming to have overheard the threat being uttered from his location in the reel storage level 15 ft below and separated by a metal floor. I was forced to clear my locker and escorted from the building. Those involved apparently signed affidavits confirming the accuracy of their evidence.

I was informed that Maxwell would conduct a kangaroo court hearing in London two days later where he would consider the evidence, take stock of any statement I had to make and consider any appeal for clemency. I went along, accompanied by my local, full-time union official. Little or no mention was made of my "offence". I was never shown the evidence against me and only found out about the second individual involved (the "witness") when Maxwell named him. The discussion was more about my trade union and pension Trustee Board activity. I was informed that I was being dismissed and that my chairman supported his local manager's decision that "bullying could not be tolerated".

I was told that Maxwell was aware that I could bring the workforce in Scotland out on strike to support any claim I had of unfair dismissal. He threatened that if I did so he would use new Tory government industrial laws to sue me personally for any losses sustained by the company as a result. He told me that one night's lost production cost somewhere between £150,000 and £200,000 at that time. I wished him luck and said that it's hard getting blood from a stone. All my money was in debt and should he trace any my wife hadn't any plans for, then perhaps we could split that.

Realising that that particular threat hadn't worked, he delivered what was to be the telling blow to my Achilles Heel. He reminded me that he either owned outright, or had a share in, 90% of the companies in the Glasgow area who employed printers. He said that if I brought the men out on strike he would sack all of them and ensure that they would never work again in the local area. He insisted he could live with that prospect and asked whether I could. He knew I couldn't and when I turned to my full-time union official expecting his intervention to support me and tell Maxwell that that option wouldn't be tolerated by the union, he was too busy admiring the shine on his shoes for eye contact. His silence was deafening.

I knew immediately the significance of this man's response. I was the only one present who was hearing the threat just uttered for the first time. I was being sold down the river and treated as the sacrificial lamb. Maxwell expressed "regret" that it had ended this way and sanctioned a £20,000 payment to ease hardship on my family. He then asked whether there was any more he could do for me. Curious, I asked what he thought that might be – ironically he offered investment advice for the sum available. I suggested as an alternative that he consider adding another zero to the cheque. He declined.

I was escorted to the ACAS offices in London to find out whether I'd been dismissed "fairly". The lady who interviewed me privately immediately detected that gross industrial misconduct was not the real reason for my sacking and told me that I wasn't the first. She said that officially I had no right to any compensation and advised that I take the money offered and run; it was probably more than I'd have received taking and winning an unfair dismissal case.

On my return to Glasgow I met my former colleagues and told them what had happened. They wanted to strike immediately in my support and demand my reinstatement. I had to insist that they didn't jeopardise their own and their families' futures.

I'd been beaten in an unequal struggle and regretted my inability to muster the support of more powerful allies. My greatest concern was that my family was going to suffer for my beliefs. However, I knew I was right and had no regrets about what I'd done – I only wished that I'd been more successful.

I was unemployed for the first time since leaving school. I was also to discover that I'd been "black-listed" as a troublemaker. It is claimed such lists don't exist but I believe my name was there in gold letters. Printing in Scotland is a small industry and a closed community. I'd apply for jobs I was overqualified for and wouldn't even get an interview. When I went along to interviews arranged by my union I often felt sorry for the person who was interviewing me – they would react as if they had been instructed to interview Che Guevara and expected me to arrive armed with a rifle at least. I was seen as the offender in this situation.

I'd done nothing wrong except try to thwart a tyrannical, megalomaniac bully from using the pension funds of thousands of innocent people for his own ends and to expand his empire. I'd tried to ensure that money set aside for their retirement income was available to them alone. Yet society looked upon me as a villain.

A family man, and the only wage earner, I couldn't afford to wallow in self pity, and I quickly set about creating a new career for myself away from the printing industry that had rejected me. My knowledge of pensions came in useful in this regard. I became a financial advisor and having struggled for several years have now found success in my new occupation. My family unit remains as strong and loving as ever. We kept the house and managed to minimise the effects of my initial reduced earnings capacity on family life generally. I'm a lucky man.

I tend not to dwell on the past or what might have been. I'm not a worrier and look at circumstances as I find them, consider my options, and then act accordingly.

I obviously followed events at Mirror Group. Maxwell was allowed to continue on his chosen evil path until his accidental death by drowning. Subsequently, and in my view significantly, the full extent of his wrongdoing – the theft of some £400 million from the pension fund – only then became public knowledge. To this day I believe that were he still around he would still be keeping a lid on the situation. Unfortunately, pensioners suffered, and some died prematurely worrying about their ability to manage financially when pension payments they relied upon were either suspended or stopped completely.

Inevitably, official inquiries into how such a thing could happen followed. I was also then portrayed as a visionary and vindicated for my foresight and early opposition. It all seemed pointless and an exercise in closing the stable door. Millions of pounds were squandered in the pursuit of an explanation and to allocate blame; only one parliamentary committee called me as a witness and like all of the other judicial fiascos it resulted for me in an inconclusive whitewash allowing the pensions industry to continue almost unabated and largely self-regulated. Radical change, apparently too extreme for political acceptability, is required to make pensions secure, but the opposition is rich, powerful and well dug in.

Why do I remain a supporter of whistleblowing, such that I am now the Scottish Director of Public Concern at Work? I believe that our more educated and informed modern society will one day change its perception of whistleblowers and will realise that someone who raises a genuine concern about wrongdoing isn't a sneak or a grass. Whistleblowers generally see something happening that is wrong and that represents a risk of some kind to themselves or to other people, and they want something done to prevent the wrongdoing resulting in disaster. Health and safety problems, fraud and corruption, environmental damage all pose threats to society, and in many cases could have their damaging effects minimised if warnings were heeded early on.

To "shoot the messenger", or to stand back and allow others to do so, will eventually, I'm sure, be recognised as a short-sighted policy resulting in greater and more expensive problems. You shouldn't need to be brave, foolhardy, naive or lacking ambition to sound the alarm. You shouldn't have to worry about adverse reaction or potential personal detriment. You are being responsible, and keeping quiet shouldn't even be considered as an option. Lives, jobs and vast sums of money could be saved annually by people just like you and me being encouraged to bear witness with impunity.

My life goes on – it was only a job I lost after all – and I retained all the important things: the love of my family, my self respect, my personal values and my integrity.

I'd do it all again if required but I'd hope to be more successful second time around.

# PUBLIC DECEPTION IN CAPE TOWN:
## STORY OF AN INSIDER WITNESS

*By Victoria Johnson*

My experience of being a "whistleblower" involved what may at first seem a rather banal issue – a proposal by the Cape Town mayor to rename two streets. But, quite amazingly, this proposal ended up turning into an embarrassing and damaging scandal, leading to the mayor's resignation amidst allegations of fraud and maladministration. It also sparked a bitter political battle within the official opposition party in South Africa, causing it to ultimately split.

At the time, in early 2001, I was a senior legal advisor for the City of Cape Town. It was an interesting time to be working in local government; a protracted and complex restructuring of local government, spanning many years, had just culminated in the creation of entirely new local structures countrywide. The City of Cape Town was one of a handful of large "unicities" established as part of this process. It was formed by the merger of seven municipalities, giving it an annual budget of just over R9 billion and a staff of about 27 000. The legal framework for local government had been over-hauled and contained many innovations including, for the first time, the ability of individual councillors to wield significant executive powers.

The person elected to the new and powerful position of mayor was Peter Marais, a well-known and charismatic Democratic Alliance (DA) politician. The DA, the largest opposition party in South Africa, was created when erstwhile foes the Democratic Party (DP) and the New National Party (NNP) decided to pool their resources and enter into a strategic alliance. Together they had managed to narrowly defeat the ANC for control of the city in a fiercely contested local election. Because of legal technicalities, at the time the new party could only be validly formed at local level. At the provincial and national level the DP and NNP, although in a contractual alliance, continued to exist separately.

Because the structures and powers of the city, both administrative and political, were essentially being created from scratch there was an enormous amount of strategic and legal work to be done to get everything into place. A "corporate centre" was created to concentrate on finalising these tasks and certain officials were seconded to this centre. The entire top management structure of the administration had yet to be agreed and people still had to be appointed to the new positions, a process that would take a long time. Importantly, these top management positions would be subject to political approval by the Council's Executive Committee. This fluidity, or call it insecurity, in the top management of the city would later play a role in my decision on how to report the fraud and maladministration I came across.

My boss at the time, Ben Kieser, was seconded to act as head of the legal department, a powerful position given the nature and sheer volume of legal work involved. I was seconded to work with him, as was an office assistant, Ms Davids. I had worked in Mr Kieser's office for about three years prior to this and we had developed a very open and robust working relationship. He was ambitious and strongly politically connected, primarily on the NNP side of the DA, and was intolerant of those standing in his way. He was very good at what he did, and it did not take him long to work himself into the mayor's inner circle, a position of trust few other officials enjoyed.

Only a few months into our secondment Mr Kieser told me that the mayor had decided to propose changing the names of two prominent streets in Cape Town – Adderley Street and Wale Street. The idea was to rename them Nelson Mandela and F. W. De Klerk Avenues respectively. In this way the mayor would "make his mark" in his new position. Mr Kieser told me to draft the report to Council making the proposal and to handle the necessary public participation process.

The proposal was announced and adverts placed in the press calling for public comment. All comments had to be directed to my office. The response was rapid and fierce – and entirely negative. The issue became headline news in the local papers and the letters pages were packed with objections. Most people had no objection to honouring De Klerk and Mandela – it was the choice of the two historic streets that was objected to. Many people suggested renaming other streets in Cape Town, streets whose names had strong apartheid connotations and were long overdue for a change.

I naively thought that with this overwhelming negative response the mayor would abandon his proposal and choose some other way of honouring Mandela and De Klerk. I could not have been more wrong.

The mayor's personal spokesman, Mr Smit, was closely involved in the planning for the street renaming ceremony and was in my office every other day checking on the status of the comments. One day, when I was telling him about the flood of objections, he told me "not to worry" as 300 letters of support would be arriving (this said with a grin and a wink). In later conversations "300" changed to "500", I assumed to deal with the continuing influx of objections. Mr Smit did not say where these letters were coming from, but for me the implication was clear – they would not be genuine letters of support. Mr Smit later admitted making these statements but said he was actually referring to other letters that were apparently being organised by churches and not to the batch of almost 500 suspect documents he ultimately did deliver to me. I was shocked and angered by what he had told me, but instinctively felt it unwise to express those feelings. I was not sure what would happen, or what I would ultimately do, but as an immediate precaution I set up a system of hand numbering the objections as they came in so that "fake" positive submissions could not be easily fed in and back-dated. I told our office assistant, Ms Davids, (who I trusted implicitly) what Mr Smit had said, as I needed her help in doing the numbering and also to look out for any potentially fake letters. And then I waited to see what, if anything, would happen.

It was not long before I was told by Mr Kieser to keep all information regarding the comments secret. No one was to see them or even know how many objections there were. A few days later the documents were removed from my office and hidden in the mayor's office for a few days because, I was told, the deputy mayor, Belinda Walker, was looking for them. I was told that on no account was I to give the deputy mayor or Member of Provincial Legislature Robin Carlisle access to these documents, and that if I was asked I should say that they were with the mayor. As both the deputy mayor and Mr Carlisle were staunch DP members, I began to suspect that the street renaming proposal had become the subject of a fight between the NNP and DP components of the DA.

Tensions between the two partners in the DA had been the subject of periodic speculation in the press long before the street renaming proposal. Although these tensions were denied by the DA at the time, they were quite apparent to anyone working closely with the politicians. In fact, at times, the level of mutual distrust almost reached the realms of the paranoid and was quite fascinating to watch.

At this time, Mr Kieser confided in me that getting the proposal through had become the mayor's biggest political battle and that he would literally "stand or fall" on whether he was successful. When it was pointed out that this made a farce of the public participation process his response was "fuck the public".

On the last day of the official commenting period, a Monday, the front page headline of the Cape Town morning daily, the *Cape Times*, quoted the mayor as saying there was an "overwhelming" positive response to his proposal. This was when the seriousness of my situation really sunk in. At the time there were about 550 objections, including many from respected institutions and organisations, and only seven letters of support (some of which were questionable).

That afternoon Mr Smit came into my office and handed me a batch of almost 500 "letters" and petitions supporting the mayor's proposal. His statement when handing them to me was, "*this* is how you win elections". As soon as he left my office I looked at the documents and was speechless. A cursory glance made me sure that they were forgeries. I was struck at the lack of subtlety, the stupidity.

The mayor was quoted a few days later as saying the letters of support outweighed the objections by 2.5 to 1 (ironically, even if you counted the forgeries as valid, they *still* would not have outweighed the objections). This again made front page news, and I pointed out to Mr Kieser that what the mayor had publicly said was patently wrong. His response was to suggest that I count each individual name on the many "petitions" supporting the proposal as separate "yes" votes and to count each petition objecting to the proposal as only one objection, regardless of how many names appeared on it. This was to enable the letters of support to "build up a lead". Needless to say, I did not follow this instruction. Mr Kieser later admitted making the suggestion but said he did so merely out of interest's sake to see what the result would be.

I knew that I was sitting on a time bomb and had to take some action, but I simply did not know what to do. I really wanted to remain anonymous and saw an approach to the media as a real and desirable option. At that stage I had no desire to implicate any particular individuals, but just wanted to bring the fraud to light so that it could be investigated. I was wary of trusting the city's internal authorities as I either did not know them or could not guess their loyalties in what was at the time a politically explosive issue. The only senior manager in a permanent position was in fact the head of the whole organisation, the city manager. But he had not yet taken up the position, was a total stranger to me, and was then based in Johannesburg. I knew that reporting the matter to one of the acting managers would mean asking them to take on the mayor (and the very powerful head of legal services) at great risk to their own career. I was in no doubt that if the allegations were not followed up avidly enough, or were covered up, I would be the one left to suffer. As I was the chief breadwinner in my family at the time, with a young baby, I did not want to unnecessarily prejudice my future.

I decided to appoint an attorney primarily so that I could discuss my options in an entirely confidential and safe setting. I was naturally aware of the new "whistleblower" legislation, which had very recently come into force in South Africa; the Protected Disclosures Act, 2000. After studying this Act I realised that it may be problematic relying on its protection in the case of an approach to the media as it was clear the Act preferred a disclosure to be made to the employer. Although the Act allowed disclosure to the media, it did so only if one or more of a list of applicable conditions existed and it was these conditions which were of some concern to me. For example, an approach to the media would be protected if I believed I would suffer what the Act calls "occupational detriment" by reporting the matter to my employer. Although I felt certain that I would suffer occupational detriment, I wondered how I would go about proving it if I were challenged. I felt that any attempt to show that I would probably be treated unfairly would necessarily involve my making further, probably defamatory, accusations against powerful people in the city, something I was loath to do.

Another potential condition allowing a report to the media was if I believed the evidence of the impropriety would be destroyed or concealed if I reported it internally. Again, I felt that although there was some chance of this happening I was not comfortable having to justify my actions with that "suspicion" as my defence. Again, how would I go about showing that that suspicion was reasonable? All in all, the Act left me feeling very exposed when it came to reporting to the media and my attorney recommended that I report the matter to the acting city manager, Dr Fisher, which I then did.

I had just gone on two weeks leave and so arranged to meet Dr Fisher at his home. I told him that there were "problems" in the street renaming process but that I was too scared to give any details, or to implicate any particular individuals. I urged him to try and access the submissions as soon as possible but warned him it may be difficult to get to them as even the deputy mayor was being denied access. He agreed to keep the fact that I had approached him entirely confidential and we agreed that I would send him an "anonymous" note asking him to investigate potential wrongdoing in the public participation process. He would then use this note as justification for asking for the documents. My idea was that I would then be "forced" to co-operate and give relevant information to whoever would be investigating the matter. It was important to me not to be seen as having willingly betrayed my superiors.

About a week later a report appeared in the weekly *Mail and Guardian* newspaper alleging fraud in the street renaming process. This newspaper has a reputation of being a fearless "corruption-busting" publication and general thorn in the side of the powers that be.

Mr Kieser called me in from my leave to attend an urgent meeting on what to do about the press article. I dreaded this meeting as I was extremely anxious to ensure that Mr Kieser did not suspect me of any disloyalty.

I arrived at work to find Mr Smit, Mr Kieser and the mayor's strategic advisor in my office with the newspaper report. Although I was greeted in a friendly manner, I immediately sensed that I was being studied as a possible suspect in the leak. Mr Kieser told me, in a threatening tone, that they would find the person who "did this" (pointing to the article) and he would person-ally make sure that person went down even if it meant he went down with him or her. He said that the most important thing to do was to find out who leaked the article and then to ensure that there was no link between the fraudu-lent documents and the mayor as the mayor's job was on the line. The fact that there were hundreds of forgeries in the submissions hardly warranted a mention.

That evening I emailed Dr Fisher and told him about the meeting and that all they seemed interested in was finding the source of the leak and not in investigating the false documents. I specifically told him in this email that I would not be prepared to give my information to any investigation controlled by either the legal office or the mayor's office. Although he did not yet know the details of the information I had (i.e. which specific people were involved), the implications of my request must have been clear to him.

Despite this, when I got back from leave I found that a one-man "com-mission" had been appointed in the form of a senior advocate to investigate the "integrity" of the public participation process and, specifically, to find out who leaked information to the press. The commission was toothless in that it could not subpoena anyone or demand any documents.

Initially I had expected this commission to contact me before almost anyone else as I was the one with the most hands-on knowledge of the public participation process. But the weeks passed and I was not contacted. (By the time I was ultimately contacted, events had reached a point where it was almost pointless for me to meet the advocate.) I felt in a state of limbo, not sure what more I should or could do.

Some time before, a multi-party sub-committee had been established to assist Council with the street renaming process. After the newspaper article alleging fraud was published, this committee was tasked with looking through the submissions and evaluating them. As part of this process they were in-structed to "disregard" suspect (i.e. fraudulent) submissions. I was concerned about this and, after an argument with the legal consultant retained to assist the committee, took it upon myself to simply photocopy all the submissions and hand deliver them to the office of the senior advocate. As it turned out, the sub-committee for reasons known only to themselves (and for which they were later criticised), did not employ a handwriting expert in their evaluation of the submissions and so missed a large portion of the fraudulent documents.

Meanwhile, the push to get the proposal through continued. Although I was ostensibly in charge of the public participation process, I found out purely by chance that the commenting period had in fact been extended to enable "the churches" to submit comments. This extension was not advertised, and "the churches" turned out to be the church of the mayor's private "spiritual advisor", Pastor Noble. He ended up delivering a supermarket packet filled with just over 100 standard form letters supporting the proposal. A later audit of these showed that some congregants had decided to put their names to the proposal more than once.

Mr Kieser also instructed me to manipulate the "categorisation" of the objections to portray that a large portion of objections were not to the idea itself, but merely to the "wasted costs" of changing the street names – an issue I was told would be easiest for the mayor to neutralise in argument. They had worked out the cost of the exercise to be about only R15 000 (i.e. essentially just the cost of changing the signs).

At this point I started feeling powerless; this "cover-up", and the spin being put on the fake documents (there were even suggestions that the forgeries had been "planted" by the ANC to discredit the mayor), were so relentless and effective that I knew I would have to take more active steps to reveal the truth. The "investigation" of the fraudulent documents was being controlled and guided by the very people I would implicate and I could not understand why the acting city manager was not taking more active control. I started to feel increasingly isolated and stressed. The strain and guilt of keeping up the pretence of still being "loyal" to those I would later implicate was becoming almost unbearable.

I decided the safest way to report the matter was by way of a very detailed affidavit (to avoid "spin" being put on what I said) given simultaneously to a spread of senior managers as well as the deputy mayor. In this way I felt safe from any smaller alliances being created against me, but it necessitated a clear betrayal of Mr Kieser and of Mr Smit's trust in me. In the run-up to finalising my affidavit I kept wavering about whether I could go ahead with it. It was without doubt the most difficult decision I have ever had to make.

I used the Protected Disclosures Act when handing the affidavit over by asking the recipients for written confirmation that I would suffer no detriment (as described in all its forms in the Act) as a consequence of handing the affidavit over. Although I knew I was already protected by the Act, it was important to me to have this written confirmation as a "double" safeguard.

When I handed the affidavit to the deputy mayor she asked if I would allow her to show the contents, in the utmost confidence, to the leader of the DA, Tony Leon. This was because of the potentially serious damage the DA may suffer as a result of the contents. After discussing this with my attorney I agreed to her confidentially showing Mr Leon the contents. However, the next morning, a senior office bearer of the DA, called me "as a courtesy" to inform me that the DA would be publishing my affidavit at a press conference within the next few hours. He was very friendly and expressed great support for me (as did another senior DA advisor, in a call a short while later) but, underlying that, I was not sure whether I was being asked for my permission or whether the press conference was a *fait accompli*. I realised that if I did not expressly say "no" to the publication of my affidavit, my silence could be taken as assent and, although I did not object to the general substance of my accusations being in the public domain, I felt intensely uncomfortable about actually publishing the very detailed incidents I had described. I felt I was in a position where it was impossible to say no and, because of the acute stress I felt on hearing of the impending press conference, I found it difficult to think clearly. I called my attorney who thankfully found an out for me by raising the issue of defamation – I could validly say to the DA that I was unable to agree to the publication of my affidavit as I would then personally be at risk of a defamation claim. This is what I did, and the press conference went ahead without my consent.

As soon as my employer heard of the press conference I was immediately put on "special leave" as it was clear the workplace would be intolerable for me, and Mr Kieser and Mr Smit were suspended. I found the media attention almost unbearable and left town for a few days to try to escape.

The street renaming proposal was formally withdrawn and within days former High Court Judge, Willem Heath was appointed to hold a formal investigation into the matter. I was warned there would be a public hearing and I would be required to give evidence. A senior counsel was appointed at the city's expense to personally represent the mayor while the city appointed its own senior counsel to protect its rights. I was initially told, even after the hearings had been running for a while, that the city would not cover any legal costs for me, despite the fact that I would be the prime target of attack. I appointed counsel at my own risk and was pleased that the city ultimately reversed its decision and paid for my legal representation.

It is difficult to describe the anxiety I felt before having to give evidence – I had not seen Mr Kieser, Mr Smit or the mayor since handing in my affidavit and the thought of publicly facing them and accusing them seemed almost unreal. Advocate Heath's office had assured me the hearings would not be televised but on the morning I was to give evidence I found out this was not the case, which added considerably to my stress. In retrospect I would have demanded some say in how I was to give evidence, but at the time I was caught up in a process that I felt I had no control over.

I was first to give evidence and the strategy of the mayor, Mr Kieser and Mr Smit was clear from the start. They subjected me to a vicious attack on both a professional and personal level. This went on for almost two days and was accompanied throughout by the mayor, Mr Smit and Mr Kieser staring at me as aggressively as they could, rolling their eyes and giggling. It was so bad that my counsel said he wanted to complain to Advocate Heath and ask them to be moved. I asked him not to as, strangely enough, I found that watching them trying so hard to put me off actually made it slightly easier to get through the cross-examination.

One of the main "defences" by those I had accused was that my affidavit ignored the "paper trail", and that this paper trail showed that the public participation process was managed in a responsible and above board manner. Ironically, the very reports used as their defence ended up being a source of further criticism for misrepresentations contained in them.

Before the start of the public hearings I had been privately warned by a disgusted NNP politician of a plan to accuse me of merely being a DP puppet. This seemed a predictable ploy to undermine my motives given the fight that had already been going on between the NNP and DP on this issue. Shortly after I received the warning I was contacted by certain journalists saying that they had "heard" that I was actually a DP member, a personal friend of the deputy mayor's, that the DP had drafted my affidavit, and so on. These rumours were so obviously false and so easily refutable that they never went any further although, years later, some of the rumours still stick.

At the hearings I had the distinct impression that I was merely a pawn in someone else's fight; a fight between the DP and NNP components of the DA. The hearings seemed to me to be really about the battle to get rid of Peter Marais. It seemed unstructured and not detailed enough, this was in part because it was so rushed and there had been almost no time to prepare. In his final report Advocate Heath was highly critical of the mayor, Mr Kieser and Mr Smit. He did not find them culpable of fraud, but recommended disciplinary action against all three on the grounds of maladministration. As far as the forgeries were concerned, his findings confirmed evidence of fraud and he recommended that the matter be reported to the South African Police Services for further investigation.

There followed an embarrassing game of "musical chairs" in Western Cape politics, which can perhaps be summed up as follows. Marais was cleared of any wrongdoing by a closed Council committee of his peers; he was expelled from the DA (and so from being mayor); he launched a court case following which he was reinstated; he resigned as mayor; the NNP split from the DA and entered into an alliance with the ANC; the power shifted at provincial level and the premier of the Western Cape (Gerald Morkel) lost the premiership; Marais became premier; Morkel became mayor; Marais lost the premiership after allegations of sexual impropriety; Morkel lost the mayorship after a further political shift when floor crossing legislation was implemented; Marais faced charges of corruption and left the NNP to form his own party.

When I got back to work it was a great struggle to settle down. In the background subtle, and not so subtle, threats were made. For example, in a private discussion regarding the street renaming issue I was reminded by a certain councillor that in this country "a woman is raped every nine seconds". I was also told a number of times of apparent plans to sue me for "millions". But this had to be balanced against the overwhelming support I was shown by members of the public (total strangers who called me at work) and employees of the city who bombarded me with emails and other messages of support.

It was only in the subsequent closed disciplinary hearings of Mr Smit and Mr Kieser that I truly felt the full detailed facts of the whole saga were being put forward in a logical and clear way. A top legal firm had been appointed to act for the city and had painstakingly prepared their case. I was their chief witness and underwent three days of cross-examination by Mr Kieser who represented himself and Mr Smit in the hearings. But Mr Kieser subsequently resigned and Mr Smit's contract lapsed before the hearing could be completed, and so he also left the city's employ.

As a mark of Mr Kieser's political connections, after his resignation he was almost immediately appointed as a "strategic advisor" for the then new mayor, Morkel. The fact that the city signed the contract appointing him to this position was without doubt the deepest betrayal I experienced in the whole saga. This was especially as I would inevitably have to, and did, work with him in his new position. Fortunately his appointment only lasted a few months after which he was due to be appointed to a position in what was then Mr Marais' premier's office but this did not come about as Mr Marais subsequently lost the premiership.

One of the aspects of being a whistlebower which came as a surprise to me, and which I suppose must be a common feature in these types of matters, was the fact that there never seemed an "end" to the matter. I suppose I had hoped for some final objective "finding" after which a line would be drawn and it would be over. The reality was that it lingered on quite actively for more than a year, and, as much as I tried to put it behind me, something would happen which would necessitate a reaction from me. For example, a battle went on for many months by those loyal to the Marais/NNP faction to try to charge the deputy mayor with a disciplinary offence for giving my affidavit to Tony Leon. I invariably got drawn into the battle as it suited their fight against the deputy mayor to discredit me whenever possible.

The after effects still go on. Two years after the event I was given a message that the NNP caucus had apparently been discussing me and "had not forgotten" what I did. The message was given to a close colleague, allegedly by an NNP politician, and I can only assume it was meant to get to me. I have no idea whether the caucus ever did make this statement, but the fact that someone wanted me to think they did was disquieting. And, almost three years later, after I had resigned from the city I was asked to join a consortium tendering for work from provincial government. The lead tenderers were contacted by more than one ANC politician who queried my inclusion, given that I was actually a "senior strategic advisor" to the DA.

A number of people have asked whether I would do what I did again. I have no hesitation in saying I would, but my first choice would still be to try and expose and stop the fraud without having to make detailed allegations against individuals. But in my case, even after the fraud was exposed in the newspaper report, the people implicated did not back off. They attempted to cover up what had happened and to bully the proposal through with even greater vigour, so I felt I had no choice.

I feel a deep sense of ambiguity over what I did – whatever one may say about doing the right thing, it does not change the fact that I broke a fundamental social rule by betraying someone I worked closely with and who trusted me. No matter which way I think about it, or try to rationalise it, that fact will never go away and so my memory of the time is always tinged with an underlying sense of discomfort and shame.

# JIANG YANYONG AND SARS

*By Robin Van Den Hende*

Jiang Yanyong is a Chinese whistleblower. He saved lives by revealing the cover-up of the spread of a fatal virus. His actions resulted in corrective action and an unprecedented display of accountability by the Chinese government. However, the most extraordinary thing is that Jiang has received official praise and has not suffered the victimisation of previous Chinese whistleblowers.

In November 2002, cases of atypical pneumonia began to occur in Guangdong province in southern China. It was characterised by a high fever, a dry cough and shortness of breath or breathing difficulties.[1] It was only on 11 February 2003 that the Chinese government officially reported the outbreak to the World Health Organisation (WHO).[2] By this time the virus had potentially been spread widely by the millions of people who had travelled from Guangdong for the New Year celebrations.[3] On 21 February, an infected medical doctor from Guangdong checked into a hotel in Hong Kong.

---

[1] Department of Health, *Severe Acute Respiratory Syndrome; Frequently Asked Questions,* 16 May 2003, www.doh.gov.uk/sars/faqs.htm

[2] World Health Organisation, *Severe Acute Respiratory Syndrome (SARS): Status of the Outbreak and Lessons for the Immediate Future,* 20 May 2003, pg. 1.

[3] Gittings, John, "After Months of Cover-Up, China Says SARS Crisis is 10 Times Worse than Admitted," *The Guardian,* 21 April 2003.

Over the next few days, guests and visitors to that hotel spread the illness around the world along international air travel routes.[4]

The illness they carried was named Severe Acute Respiratory Syndrome (SARS) and was later discovered to be a new form of corona virus.[5] With no vaccine and no treatment, SARS forced health authorities to resort to isolation and quarantine. Proving fatal in about 15% of cases,[6] the spread of SARS around the world was accompanied by mass anxiety and the fear that this was a repeat of the 1917 influenza pandemic. On 15 March, WHO issued rare, emergency travel recommendations to alert health authorities and the public to what was perceived as a worldwide threat to health.[7]

One of the people in China watching these developments unfold was a 71-year-old, Communist Party member called Jiang Yanyong. He had joined the People's Liberation Army (PLA) in 1954, before moving to the PLA's General Hospital No. 301 in Beijing in 1957. In 1968, at the height of the Cultural Revolution, Jiang was branded a counter-revolutionary and was banished to feed horses at a military-run ranch. Despite this, he returned to Hospital No. 301 and rose to become director of surgery. In 1989 he treated those injured during the army crackdown on pro-democracy demonstrators in Tiananmen Square. On the tenth anniversary of the massacre he accused the authorities of lying when they claimed no protesters had been killed. By 2003, Jiang was semi-retired. He spent his days reading books, surfing the Internet and occasionally doing surgery. Every Monday he did the rounds of Hospital No. 301.[8] However, the SARS crisis interrupted his quiet life.

At the beginning of March, the annual sessions of China's legislative assemblies were meeting in Beijing and the Chinese authorities wanted to avoid any embarrassing "instability" during such important events. If SARS arrived in China's capital city it would be embarrassing, suggesting that the Communist leadership and state health system were failing to control the spread of the virus.

At this time, a colleague told Jiang that an old man being treated at Hospital No. 301 was suspected of having SARS. His colleague said that the patient was transferred to Hospital No. 302, an infectious disease hospital,

---

[4] World Health Organisation, *Severe Acute Respiratory Syndrome (SARS): Status of the Outbreak and Lessons for the Immediate Future*, 20 May 2003, pg. 1.

[5] Department of Health, *Severe Acute Respiratory Syndrome; Frequently Asked Questions*, 16 May 2003, www.doh.gov.uk/ sars/faqs.htm

[6] World Health Organisation, *Severe Acute Respiratory Syndrome (SARS): Status of the Outbreak and Lessons for the Immediate Future*, 20 May 2003, pg. 2-3.

[7] Ibid. and pg. 4.

[8] "SARS Whistleblower Breathing Sign of Relief," *The People's Daily*, 21 May 2003; Kang Lim, Benjamin, "SARS Cover-Up Whistleblower Doctor Gagged," *The Manila Times*, 24 May 2003.

for treatment. However, Hospital No. 302 had no experience of SARS and as a result ten members of the medical staff became infected. The old man died two days after being admitted. When his wife became ill, she was also admitted to Hospital No. 302 and shared her husband's fate. It was only at this point that Ministry of Health officials informed hospital leaders that Beijing had cases of SARS. The hospital officials were forbidden to publicise what they had learned about the arrival of SARS in Beijing.[9] We will never know whether such publicity might have lead to increased precautions and so saved lives.

Soon after this, a patient was admitted to Hospital No. 301 with liver and gallbladder diseases. This patient developed SARS symptoms and was moved to Hospital No. 309, but later died. However, two doctors and three nurses at Hospital No. 301 became infected, forcing the closure of several wards.[10]

A diagnosis of SARS in a former classmate and colleague at the end of March prompted Jiang to talk to Hospital No. 309 (which by that stage had become the PLA's SARS Control and Prevention Centre) about SARS. Jiang was told that there had already been 40 patients at Hospital No. 309 who were suspected of having SARS or had been diagnosed with it. Of these, six had died. The next day, Jiang was told that this had increased to 60 patients and seven deaths. He also found out that there were 40 SARS patients at Hospital No. 302.[11]

On 3 April, China's Minister of Health, Zhang Wenkang, announced to the world's press that the Chinese government was diligently dealing with SARS and that the spread of the virus was under control. Zhang stated that Beijing had reported 12 SARS cases, of which three had died. Jiang watched this press conference live on television and could not believe what he was hearing.[12]

The next day, Jiang talked to two retired, senior officers from the PLA Logistics Department and discovered that they shared his suspicion of the Minister of Health's figures. After Hospital No. 301 reported 46 SARS cases, Jiang asked the medical managing department of the hospital to immediately report new developments to higher authorities.[13] When Jiang telephoned colleagues at Hospital No. 309 he found them furious at Zhang's statements and

---

[9] Jakes, Susan, "Beijing's SARS Attack," *Time Asia*, 8 April 2003; "A Chinese Doctor's Extraordinary April in 2003," *The People's Daily*, 13 June 2003.

[10] "A Chinese Doctor's Extraordinary April in 2003," *The People's Daily*, 13 June 2003.

[11] Ibid.

[12] Ibid; Jakes, Susan, "Beijing's SARS Attack," *Time Asia*, 8 April 2003.

[13] "A Chinese Doctor's Extraordinary April in 2003," *The People's Daily*, 13 June 2003.

repeated their assertion that they had dealt with 60 SARS cases, including seven deaths. They told him that, as Hospital No. 309 was full to capacity, the PLA Logistics Department had asked Hospital No. 302 to take more patients. Hospital No. 302 itself was dealing with five severely ill SARS cases.[14]

Jiang set out his concerns about the reporting of SARS cases in an email and sent it to state broadcaster CCTV-4 and the pro-Beijing Phoenix TV in Hong Kong.[15] In this email Jiang identified himself, gave contact details and stated that: "As a doctor who cares about people's lives and health, I have a responsibility to aid international and local efforts to prevent the spread of SARS."[16]

Jiang later told *Time Asia* magazine that he wrote the email because "a failure to disclose accurate statistics about the illness will only lead to more deaths".[17] In his email, Jiang stated that Health Minister Zhang's statement to the press was "virtually unbelievable".[18] Jiang quoted the figures for SARS cases that he had been given and ended the email with the statement: "The above information is true and I am accountable for it."[19]

Neither CCTV-4 nor Phoenix TV responded to the email, although it was leaked to foreign media.[20] On 8 April, reporters from the *Wall Street Journal* and *Time* magazine contacted Jiang for an interview. *Time* was the first to publicise Jiang's case and he quickly became the focus of the world's media. The *Time* article was translated into Chinese and spread through the Internet. Jiang's actions alerted China and the rest of the world to the full extent of the epidemic.

Probably by coincidence, the next day a WHO team presented its interim report to the Health Ministry on the Guangdong outbreak. This stated:

> *If SARS is not brought under control in China there will be no chance of controlling the global threat of SARS … Effective disease surveillance and reporting are key strategies in any attempt to control the spread of a serious new communicable disease such as SARS.[21]*

---

[14] Ibid; Jakes, Susan, "Beijing's SARS Attack," *Time Asia*, 8 April 2003.

[15] "SARS Whistleblower Praised," *The Daily Telegraph* (Australia), 28 May 2003.

[16] "A Chinese Doctor's Extraordinary April in 2003," *The People's Daily*, 13 June 2003.

[17] Jakes, Susan, "Beijing's SARS Attack," *Time Asia*, 8 April 2003.

[18] "A Chinese Doctor's Extraordinary April in 2003," *The People's Daily*, 13 June 2003.

[19] Ibid.

[20] "SARS Whistleblower Praised," *The Daily Telegraph* (Australia), 28 May 2003.

[21] World Health Organisation, *Severe Acute Respiratory Syndrome (SARS): Status of the Outbreak and Lessons for the Immediate Future*, 20 May 2003, pg. 8.

The WHO took action. On 10 April it publicly criticised Beijing's SARS reporting system and dispatched a team to investigate. This was followed on 11 April by the designation of Beijing as an infected area.[22]

Meanwhile, Jiang met with the management of Hospital No. 301. He asked them to pass to the higher authorities his suggestion that Zhang admit his mistake and resign, as well as his suggestions for handling the SARS crisis.[23] Jiang stated:

> *If the statistics I reported prove to be wrong, I will immediately announce to the WHO and I will be willing to be punished. If the statistics released by the Ministry of Health are wrong, then please correct them.[24]*

On 12 April, Jiang gave a letter to the management of Hospital No. 301 repeating his assertions and asking them to forward his suggestions to the Ministry of Health. In this letter he wrote:

> *Please send people from the Ministry of Health to verify and check the figures and materials with me … Anyone who makes mistakes should be bold in acknowledging his or her mistakes. No sophistry or falsification is allowed in issuing public information in relation to public health and people's lives.[25]*

It is unclear why Jiang went to his superiors after going to the media. In Europe and the US, workers tend to instinctively blow the whistle to their employers first and only later consider an external disclosure if the issue is not resolved. Jiang may have felt that the media coverage was necessary because of the grave and imminent risks to public health but that this did not relieve him of his personal responsibility for his disclosure. It may also be the case that the media coverage provided him with the protection he needed to confront the PLA hierarchy. Considering his earlier experiences with the Chinese state, Jiang must have been aware of the risks he was running in publicly contradicting the official line and asking that Zhang be held accountable. To then invite his superiors to hold him to account for his actions demonstrates his own strong sense of accountability.

At a press conference on 16 April, the WHO announced that its investigation had found that PLA hospitals in Beijing were not supplying full statistics

---

[22] "A Chinese Doctor's Extraordinary April in 2003," *The People's Daily*, 13 June 2003.

[23] Ibid.

[24] Ibid.

[25] Ibid.

to the Health Ministry. The WHO suggested a figure of between 100 and 200 SARS cases in Beijing. This was far closer to the numbers suggested by Jiang than the 37 cases reported by the government.[26]

On 20 April, the Vice-Minister of Health, Gao Qiang, announced revised figures for SARS in Beijing. He reported 339 diagnosed cases and 402 suspected cases.[27] Gao stated that the figures were only arrived at after the ruling state council sent a special team to investigate and admitted that the Health Ministry had failed to cope with the emergency. The May Day holiday, which involves millions of people travelling across China to their traditional homes, potentially spreading SARS, was cancelled.[28] The government's actions were an unprecedented reversal[29] and admission of fallibility. On the same day, Zhang and Beijing Mayor Meng Xuenong were dismissed. The government also declared that dissemblers would be punished.[30]

In late June, the WHO announced that Hong Kong and Beijing had broken the human-to-human transmission chain, it being 20 days since the last probable SARS case. By early July, the transmission chain had been broken in all the infected areas around the world. The WHO described this as "a striking achievement".[31] Mainland China had reported over 5 200 cases of SARS and over 280 deaths from the virus[32] while initial estimates put the financial cost to the Far East at $30 billion.[33]

The 2003 SARS epidemic was a crisis and a tragedy. In its interim report on the Guangdong outbreak, the WHO commented:

> *Cases during the earliest phase of the SARS outbreak there [in China] were not openly reported, thus allowing a severe disease to become silently established in ways that made further international spread almost inevitable.*[34]

However, the epidemic could have been much worse. We will never be able to quantify how much worse, or how many lives might have been lost, if

---

[26] "China Plays Catch-Up," *Sydney Morning Herald*, 19 April 2003.

[27] "A Chinese Doctor's Extraordinary April in 2003," *The People's Daily*, 13 June 2003.

[28] Gittings, John, "After Months of Cover-Up, China Says SARS Crisis is 10 Times Worse than Admitted," *The Guardian*, 21 April 2003.

[29] "SARS Whistleblower Praised," *The Daily Telegraph* (Australia), 28 May 2003.

[30] Armitage, Catherine, "Will Beijing Heed the Call of Doctor's Whistle?" *The Australian*, 28 April 2003.

[31] World Health Organisation, "*SARS: Breaking the Chains of Transmission*," 5 July 2003.

[32] On 17 May 2003, mainland China had reported 5 209 cases of SARS and 282 deaths. World Health Organisation, *Severe Acute Respiratory Syndrome (SARS): Status of the Outbreak and Lessons for the Immediate Future*, 20 May 2003, pg. 10.

[33] Ibid. pg. 2.

[34] World Health Organisation, *Severe Acute Respiratory Syndrome (SARS): Status of the Outbreak and Lessons for the Immediate Future*, 20 May 2003, pg. 8.

Jiang had not revealed the cover-up of SARS cases in military hospitals in Beijing. Jiang's actions were extraordinary. Even if he might have felt that his age and status lessened the chance of retaliation, he is still a brave man.

This is apparent from the continuing, if sporadic, attempts by the Chinese authorities to limit the release of information. It has been reported that the Ministry of Central Publicity issued a directive to a hospital in Shanxi province, scene of a major SARS outbreak, called "the three no's". This directive apparently stated that there should be no talking to the media, no talking to the public about treating SARS and no talking to the WHO.[35] However, in another incident, two doctors in a military hospital exposed how dozens of SARS patients had been hidden during a visit by WHO representatives. The patients were apparently either moved to a nearby hotel or driven around in ambulances.[36] The generally positive official treatment of Jiang might account for the willingness of these two doctors to come forward.

Chinese state media has praised Jiang as the "honest doctor who lead the way in revealing the truth about the outbreak" and stated that he would be awarded a prize for "services to society".[37] CNN quoted sources as saying that an interview with Jiang in the semi-official China News Service would not have been possible without the approval of those at the very top, meaning the Politburo Standing Committee member in charge of propaganda or even President Hu Jintao. It explained the article as an attempt by the new president to establish his authority by demonstrating liberal credentials.[38]

Jiang has confirmed to foreign media that he is living normally and has not been victimised for raising his concerns.[39] However, Jiang has told foreign media that he is not allowed to speak to them without permission from Hospital No. 301 and reporters' requests for interviews have so far been refused.[40] Jiang has stated that he has not been warned off, but that "as a military member we have our discipline".[41] However one report has suggested that Jiang has also had trouble getting a visa to visit his daughter in the US.[42]

---

[35] Armitage, Catherine, "Will Beijing Heed the Call of Doctor's Whistle?" *The Australian*, 28 April 2003.

[36] Ibid.

[37] "SARS Whistleblower Praised," *The Daily Telegraph* (Australia), 28 May 2003.

[38] Wo-Lap Lam, Willy, "Hu Uses SARS to Tighten Grip," CNN, 20 May 2003.

[39] Ibid; Dickie, Mure and Williams, Frances, "Doctor Who Blew Whistle on China SARS Wins Praise," *The Financial Times*, 22 May 2003; Armitage, Catherine, "Will Beijing Heed the Call of Doctor's Whistle?" *The Australian*, 28 April 2003.

[40] "SARS Whistleblower Praised," *The Daily Telegraph* (Australia), 28 May 2003.

[41] Armitage, Catherine, "Will Beijing Heed the Call of Doctor's Whistle?" *The Australian*, 28 April 2003.

[42] Pomfret, John, "China Closes Beijing Newspaper in Media Crackdown," *The Washington Post*. 20 June 2003.

Jiang's treatment seems to compare well with some earlier Chinese whistleblowers who were viewed as a major threat to order and society, with some being charged with counter-revolution.[43] A recent example is the harassment of Dr Gao Yaojie, a retired obstetrician who revealed to foreign and domestic media an AIDS epidemic among villagers infected by an unsanitary blood-buying industry. Gao has stated that she has been scolded by officials, been the subject of surveillance and has been denied a passport to travel to the US to accept an award for her work.[44] We will not know for some time whether or not Jiang's whistleblowing and the tolerant response of the Chinese authorities is a sign of things to come as China plays a fuller role in the international community.

The significance of Jiang's actions won him the *Time* Asian Person of the Year award for 2003/4. In its citation, *Time* pointed out that what gave Jiang's whistleblowing such power, and what made it attract such attention was that apart from the seriousness of the subject matter, he had made his disclosure openly. As *Time* commented this was in stark contrast to "the anonymous challenges of official truths that has been commonplace in China".

---

[43] Human Rights Watch and Geneva Institute on Psychiatry, *Dangerous Minds; Political Psychiatry in China Today and its Origins in the Mao Era*, 2002, pg. 2-3.

[44] "SARS Whistleblower Praised," *The Daily Telegraph* (Australia), 28 May 2003; Fudong, Han, "Jiang Yanyong Deserves a Prize," *China Economic Times*, 14 May 2003.

# THE EMPEROR'S NEW CLOTHES:
# MY ENRON STORY

*By Sherron Watkins*

"I am incredibly nervous that we will implode in a wave of accounting scandals." It seems aeons ago that I wrote those words in an anonymous memo to Kenneth Lay, chairman and chief executive officer of the Enron Corporation. But it was only August 2001, just a little over two years ago. Within three and a half months of that memo, Enron, a place where I had worked for over eight years, had collapsed under scandal and bankruptcy, and many of my former colleagues face scores of criminal and civil counts for financial wrong-doing.

The best analogy I have found to describe how an "Enron" could happen, how a lethal combination of intimidation and insecurity resulted in a "group think" phenomenon that led to disaster, is to liken it to the Hans Christian Andersen fairytale of the emperor's new clothes. It is perhaps one of the first whistleblower stories. In the old tale the emperor is not focused on running his kingdom, but prefers to focus on his dandy appearance instead. His lack of attention, and his desire to always look his best relative to others, enables two swindlers to enter his inner circle. The swindlers promise to deliver a cloth so fine, so incredible, so beautiful, that the emperor will amaze all that see him. The cloth is expensive, however, and it will cost the kingdom dearly, but the emperor is won over and contracts the two swindlers to weave their magical cloth.

The only hitch is that a person is unable to see the cloth if he is either stupid or not fit for office. As the swindlers commence their fictitious weaving, the emperor sends one of his ministers to check on their progress. The swindlers describe the cloth they are making, its myriad colours, its uncanny ability to change in the light, but the minister sees nothing. He knows he is not stupid, but maybe, just maybe, he is not fit for his office. In a bit of a panic he lies and says he can see the beautiful cloth. A few days later, another minister is sent to check on the progress of the cloth. He too can see nothing, but is faced with the added pressure of knowing the earlier minister was able to see the cloth. He too lies and reports back to the emperor that the cloth is progressing nicely and is indeed fantastic. And so it goes until finally, the whole community is convinced of the superiority of the emperor's new clothes. It was not until the big parade that a small child "blew the whistle" and exclaimed that the emperor was in fact wearing nothing. The emperor felt the chill in the air, knew the boy was most likely correct, but what could he do. He was the emperor; he held his head high and continued along the parade route.

Ken Lay, like the emperor, was unable to see the company's problems. He was focused on being a global ambassador of sorts, flying around to developing countries, meeting with heads of state, touting Enron's clean-burning energy solutions abroad, and at home pushing for energy deregulation and open markets. Certainly, he was not focused on running Enron; he had left that to others, particularly Chief Executive Officer (CEO) Jeff Skilling who was intent on meeting the numbers.

Enron hired the best and the brightest, and that was in the finance and accounting departments as well. Certain hedging structures were employed between late 1999 and 2001 that have since been labelled fraudulent by accounting and securities law experts. The first executive to plead guilty to criminal charges admitting that the Raptor hedging structure (as it was known at Enron) was in fact fraudulent, is currently serving a five-year prison sentence. Surprisingly, this fraudulent structure was discussed with several Enron executives as well as Mr Lay and Enron's board of directors, all of whom approved its use. How could this have happened? Basically, in the very same manner as the emperor's new clothes: the hedging transactions were incredibly complex and were shown to executives at Enron in hurried meetings with experts touting the brilliance of the accounting theories behind these clever structures.

Cutting edge accounting was being invented at Enron; surely an executive would not want to ask questions and show his or her lack of intelligence. Intimidated by complex structures and by overbearing accounting and finance experts, many at the company fell victim to a group-think mentality, accepting an accounting structure they didn't understand. My warnings to Lay were like the boy's warning, and Lay, in effect, turned to the executives around him for a second opinion. To a man, they agreed that he must be wearing clothes, they weren't experts, but Arthur Andersen, Enron's outside auditing firm, had said so. If an executive was suspicious of the accounting structures he didn't let Ken Lay know. It would have been like admitting that he'd never seen the cloth in the first place. His job would be in jeopardy for lying earlier.

Even if Ken Lay had paid heed to my warnings, the company was probably doomed by that point. Questionable financial dealings and aggressive and fraudulent accounting had allowed Enron to grow its off balance sheet debt to fatal levels. None of us knew it back in August of 2001, but Enron did not have a mere $13 billion of long term debt (as reported on its balance sheet); the actual number was closer to $40 billion. A total of $26 billion of debt was either off balance sheet or described differently in the liability section of Enron's financial statements. The structures that Enron began to use for debt arrangements became mind numbingly complex. The smartest accountants teamed with the smartest bankers to bend and twist the accounting rules to make Enron's debt deals look like revenue deals. Nearly all of the questionable deals took place from 1997 to 2001, the period when most of Wall Street considered Enron to be one of the most profitable and exciting companies around.

Enron was *the* place to be. Stocks had gone up steadily every year, and the 8 000 employees in the Houston headquarters and 20 000 employees overall were encouraged and rewarded for thinking outside of the box. I was one of the approximately 300 vice-presidents working at Enron when it collapsed. I was hired into Jeff Skilling's division in 1993, actually to work for Andy Fastow, the man who would become Enron's rather infamous Chief Financial Officer (CFO).

Enron had an investment partnership with CalPERS, the California public employees' retirement system. The partnership was called the Joint Energy Development Investment Limited Partnership or JEDI for short. I was hired to manage JEDI. JEDI was an off balance sheet investment vehicle for Enron. At the time, Enron also had a number of other off balance sheet vehicles in use. Most were one-off type vehicles used to finance the construction or acquisition of large international power plants or natural gas pipelines. All of them, in my opinion, were legitimate vehicles with the debt secured solely by the underlying assets in the vehicles and with limited if any recourse back to Enron and its shareholders.

I held the JEDI portfolio management position for just over three years, until the end of 1996. At the start of 1997, I joined Enron's international group focusing primarily on the acquisition of energy-related assets around the globe. I thoroughly enjoyed working in the international group. The work seemed purposeful. Enron was actually trying to bring cheaper, cleaner power to developing countries. It mirrored Enron's earliest corporate goals when the company's vision was "to become the premier natural gas pipeline in North America".

Enron started life as a merger of two large US-regulated pipeline companies in the mid-80s. Houston Natural Gas, a Texas-based regulated pipeline company, hired Ken Lay as its president and chief executive officer in 1984, and one year later merged with InterNorth, another large US pipeline concern. Within months, Ken Lay came out on top of the merger and was named chief executive officer of the renamed company, Enron. With the US deregulation of energy markets, Enron not only delivered energy but also began brokering energy futures. Jeff Skilling was hired in the late 1980s, initially as a consultant and later as the head of what would become Enron's Wholesale Trading and Merchant business. By studying the coming effects of deregulation of both the gas and power markets and then positioning the company to take advantage of the massive market changes underway, Skilling transformed Enron from a stodgy regulated pipeline business to a state-of-the-art energy trading shop which at its heyday handled over 25% of the US's gas and power transactions. The transformation made us all fairly cocky at Enron. The company was considered the top dog in energy trading, competing companies either moved to Enron's hometown of Houston, Texas, or at least moved their trading operations to Houston. Enron essentially made Houston the Wall Street of energy trading.

In the late 1990s, Enron began a fairly aggressive acquisition strategy of energy assets in emerging and, more importantly, deregulating countries. Enron was looking to repeat its North American success elsewhere, and not just in energy. Enron moved aggressively into the international water sector with the acquisition of Wessex Water in 1998. I joined the international group at the start of 1997 and worked on various acquisitions for Enron International until early 2000. In early 2000, I joined Enron's broadband unit, a start-up business line for Enron. While Enron was looking to replicate its US energy trading success in other parts of the world, the company was also looking at adding more products to its by now very successful US energy trading shop. Over time Enron was trading contracts on paper and pulp, steel, the weather and finally broadband.

By 2001, Enron's vision had changed markedly; from the humble goal of becoming a premier natural gas pipeline company, and then the first natural gas major, Enron had set its sights on becoming the world's leading energy company. Finally, at the start of 2001, its vision was changed to the rather self-branding goal of becoming "The World's Leading Company". Maybe that didn't seem outrageous at the time since reported revenues had grown to over $101 billion a year, making Enron the seventh largest company on the Fortune 500 list. Less than one year later, however, Enron was not known as the world's leading company, it was known as the largest bankruptcy in US history owing $67 billion to creditors.

My life has changed a lot in just over two short years. It is amazing to me what a seemingly innocuous job change can do. In the summer of 2001 I switched jobs at Enron for the last time, taking a less taxing back office position with Andy Fastow, so that I could better manage career and home life. At the time my daughter was two years old, and I wanted to be sure I made time for her.

I had had some heady times at Enron – travelling on the company jets to help sell deals, courting clients in Beaver Creek, Colorado for ski weeks or for a day at the Masters Golf Tournament. I had travelled all around the globe chasing deals for the international group – to Chile, Peru, Panama, the Philippines, Korea, South Africa, Guinea in western Africa, with stop-offs in Hong Kong, London and Paris to woo bankers. But trying to constantly climb the corporate ladder also meant a lot of time away from home – be that in travel or just late night hours at the office. I decided to take a back office job at Enron – a job that would mean less advancement potential, lower bonuses, but at least I'd be home by six o'clock to be with my daughter.

Little did I know that my job change would so patently change my life.

The back office role that I took in June 2001 was simply to prioritise the assets that Enron had for sale – nearly 200 of them, worth billions of dollars. I was reviewing book values, estimated market values, estimating the potential gain or loss on sale, trying to determine where Enron could get the biggest bang for its buck as the company tried to sell assets to raise cash that could be used to lower debt. That is when I ran into what I thought was the worst accounting fraud I'd ever seen.

Enron had allowed Andy Fastow to enter into an unprecedented conflict of interest. Andy was CFO of Enron, where his fiduciary duties meant looking out for the best interests of Enron while also becoming the General Partner of an investment partnership, LJM, where he raised over $400 million of limited partner monies and was charged with maximising returns for limited partners. The trouble was that LJM's business was to do business with Enron. In every transaction Andy had to choose – Enron or LJM.

I did not know it at the time, but we have all since learned that LJM served primarily to help Enron meet its financial statement targets for 1999, 2000 and 2001. Nearly all the transactions had no economic substance, no real risk transfer from Enron to LJM. In the summer of 2001, as I was minding my own business, getting used to a new position, I literally stumbled across the Raptors, LJM vehicles that had agreed to pay Enron a locked in value for certain assets. The Raptor structures were used to hedge Enron's equity investments. Some of those assets were tech investments that had once been high-flying stocks but were now depressingly low priced. By the summer of 2001, these Raptor entities owed Enron in excess of $700 million under these hedge deals.

The spreadsheet I was working with showed several hundred million dollars of that $700 million amount as potential Enron losses. I didn't quite get that, and I started to make some inquiries. The general explanation was that the Enron stock that had been used to capitalise the Raptor entities had declined in value such that the Raptors would have a shortfall and would be unable to fully cover the hedge price owed to Enron. When I asked about the outside capital invested in the Raptor structures, I never heard reassuring answers. Basically, I couldn't find any.

Now I hadn't practised accounting in over 10 years, but I knew accounting had not become that creative. Basically Enron was hedging with itself. My first reaction was to find another job, to get out of the company as fast as I could. However, I also knew that I could not leave Enron without a new job in hand. I had my family to think of. My intention was to confront Jeff Skilling, Enron's newly named chief executive officer, on my last day. The trouble was that Jeff Skilling beat me to it and resigned on August 14, citing personal reasons that never quite materialised. It was Skilling's decision to leave Enron that put all of the problems into context for me. Until then, I could almost convince myself that the situation was not as bad as I imagined, that I had some time on my side. Our stock price was still holding relatively steady at around $45 per share. Although it was not increasing at the astonishing rate that it had in the past years, Skilling continued to talk of the good times ahead. The California power crisis had hit Enron particularly hard, as Enron was seen as the major bad actor and the potential for large settlements in litigation against the company was high. The broadband division was failing. But it was not until Skilling resigned for "personal family reasons" that I knew that there was a lot more trouble ahead. Skilling had always been the mastermind, the front man for Enron. He was driven and I would never believe that he would choose his family over the frenetic exhilarating Enron pace, unless of course he knew something that we, the employees, did not. As I said in my memo to Lay, "the market can't accept that Skilling is leaving his dream job" and neither could we.

Two days after he quit (after less than eight months at the helm), he told the *Wall Street Journal* that his personal reason was primarily that he just couldn't sleep at night. The stock price was going down. In 2001 it started at about $80 per share, but by the summer it was trading at about $45. He was depressed about the stock price, didn't know how he was going to get it back up, and just couldn't sleep at night. It was stressing him out too much, he had about $100 million in the bank, so he basically decided to call in rich. That, to me, is pathetic. I thought there should be the equivalent of a corporate court marshal. A navy battleship captain can't just decide in the middle of a squirmish "I'm tired and I'm going back to land". He gets court marshalled; you can't abandon your crew.

To me, Skilling knew that we had hit an iceberg, that we were taking on water and that it was probably lethal and he was choosing to go home. I thought Ken Lay, who was stepping back in – coming out of retirement to return to the chief executive officer spot – had no knowledge that he was stepping onto a sinking ship. I really acted more from a knee-jerk reaction but I had to let him know that the company had probably committed accounting fraud. I initially sent a one-page anonymous letter to Lay.

Following Skilling's sudden departure, Ken Lay again resumed the chief executive officer job (added to his chairman responsibilities). In an attempt to stop the ever-increasing rumour mill, Mr Lay held an all-employees meeting. The room was filled to capacity with people hoping to hear good news, and he didn't let us down. Mr Lay told us that everything was fine, that he was a proponent of "plain vanilla accounting" and that if anyone was troubled or still had concerns, they should come forward. I felt that he was speaking to my memo, and as the meeting had failed to satisfy my disquiet, I identified myself to the head of our human resources division as the author of the memo and requested a meeting with Mr Lay. I believed that he was sincere in wanting to hear from us, and that his comments about the accounting systems showed that he too had some concerns about the aggressiveness of our bookkeeping. I identified myself quickly because I was fearful that if I did not come forward, Lay would appoint the wrong executives to fill Skilling's job; the ones I felt had been part of the fraud all along. I remain convinced that without my intervention, the fraud would have continued for even longer.

After identifying myself as the author of the anonymous memo, I found myself meeting with Ken Lay the very next week. I came armed with more memos I had drafted to help explain the problems facing the company. I used what I thought was rather plain language to explain myself, starting with "has Enron become a risky place to work? For those of us who didn't get rich over the last few years, can we afford to stay?" I added that "Skilling's abrupt departure will raise suspicions of accounting improprieties and valuation issues. Enron has been very aggressive in its accounting – most notably the Raptor transactions." I tried to negate the Andersen sign off with the following comment, "I realise that we have had a lot of smart people looking at this and a lot of accountants including AA&Co. have blessed the accounting treatment. None of that will protect Enron if these transactions are ever disclosed in the bright light of day."

When I met with Ken Lay, I was both optimistic and naive. I not only expected a thorough investigation, but I also expected Enron to establish a crisis management team to address the financial peril Enron would face when the accounting was exposed, which in my opinion was sure to happen. In the long run companies rarely get away with "cooking the books". But no other top executives came forward to back me up and Ken Lay gravitated towards good news and didn't quite accept what I was saying.

Enron and its team of investigative attorneys decided nothing was amiss, but that we should unwind the transactions that I had questioned because the optics weren't good and they were a distraction from core business. That unwind wiped out $1.2 billion from shareholders' equity and started Enron's free fall, which ultimately ended in bankruptcy, roughly six weeks after the press release of the 2001 third quarter results announcing the unwind.

For my part, I was intent on helping the company survive. Although I had applied for other jobs, none had come through and I remained committed to Enron. Thus, I remained at the company, seeking opportunities to help. I kept trying to get upper management's attention, to let them know that their course of action would not work. I went so far as to send a second group of memos to Ken Lay in late October with ideas for averting the massive crisis and rebuilding investor confidence through re-stating the financial statements, but it was too late. With hindsight, it is clear that I was the last person from whom they would accept help.

Everyone tried to convince me that my analysis was wrong, that I was wrong. They would ask how could one of the state's best law firms and one of the country's best accounting firms have missed all of the problems? I began to feel vulnerable and alienated as my colleagues began avoiding me. People acted as though I wanted to tear down the company. However, it was that very fear, the knowledge of the 20 000 employees and many more stockholders that would lose if Enron collapsed suddenly, that had kept me from going either to the Securities Exchange Commission (SEC) or the media in the first place. When it is someone's life that you are saving, such as Jeffrey Wigand who blew the whistle on the tobacco corporations, you know you are doing the right thing by going outside the company, you can feel comfortable with your decision. In my situation, I wanted Enron to do the right thing. Companies that find financial fraud are better off coming clean with their investors. To be exposed from the outside, from the SEC or the financial press, means almost certain doom.

I was highly frustrated by the events that unfolded at Enron during the late fall of 2001. I felt like I was on the Titanic, that we had hit the iceberg, but instead of manning the life boats, the new top guys in charge were all just elbowing their way to see who would be in the captain's wheelhouse.

In the end, for me, it was the publicity that followed the discovery of my memos by Congress (in a box of subpoenaed documents from Enron) that provided me some sense of safety and sanity, confirming that I was correct when everyone else was pulling away. My colleagues, some of whom were my friends, were a bitter disappointment. I felt betrayed, and I was angry. About the only consolation for me were the hundreds of emails, phone calls and letters from both former and current Enron employees who were so grateful that my memos exist. There was just an overwhelming feeling that justice would prevail, that the people responsible would have less chance to get away with it once my memos came to light.

There have been so many books and articles written about why I blew the whistle. Some say that I was doing it for money. Others claim that I wrote the memos to advance my career at Enron. Still others say it was for retaliation against a poor bonus that Andy gave me in 1995. My true motive probably stems from a prophetic event in my childhood. I was raised with a Christian upbringing in a small town where everyone knew everyone else, and where it was ingrained in me that my actions mattered. My mother raised my younger sister and me to know right from wrong, and to choose correctly. One very hot summer day, at my uncle's grocery store, I took a bite out of an ice cream sandwich from the freezer and put it back half-eaten. Of course someone saw me do it, and proceeded to tell my mother. At that moment, I promised myself never to break the rules again. When I meet my Maker in heaven, I will be asked, "what did you do with the wonderful and special skills that you were given?" I will be able to answer, I was honest and I had integrity. That is the reason that I wrote the memo to Ken Lay, and had I not, the company would have tried to hide the problems for longer and would have caused even more people financial harm.

I never consciously chose to be a whistleblower. I never even considered myself as one until later on, until my memos became the "smoking guns". At the time of writing the memos and going to Lay, I was trying to help the company. I was notifying the correct person of the problem and passing the responsibility onto him. I was doing all that I could, and I truly believed that Lay would do the right thing. I trusted him. Throughout the events of the fall of 2001, I was, in a word, "naive".

When I submitted the anonymous memo to Lay, I also gave a signed copy to my friend, Jeff McMahon. He was, at the time, Enron's treasurer and had worked with me in a previous accounting firm. McMahon was the only other Enron employee that I spoke to about my memo before my meeting with Lay. He was encouraging and even provided me with additional ammunition. But later, when everything had crumbled, he asked me what I had expected to happen when I sent the first, and then subsequent, memo? I had been optimistic that Lay would hire an independent investigator and conduct a thorough audit. I firmly believed that there was time to save the company, and that Lay had the will to do so. Again, I was stupidly naive.

I had not consulted with anyone before beginning this course of action. I spoke with my mother and with a friend before meeting with Lay, but I did not feel as though others could understand or help. Although I was nervous, I was never really fearful as I considered Lay a good man and did not think that he would "shoot the messenger". With hindsight, had I taken a breath and found allies, it might have been different.

When it became clear that Lay was not going to launch a true investigation, I started to worry about my own position and with the encouragement of a close friend, I contacted a lawyer. Although he represented companies, and not employees, he did tell me that whistleblower protections were only available if the employee was asked to do something illegal. That was not my case, so I prepared myself for being fired. Nevertheless, I thought that my dismissal would be a private matter. I was unprepared for the media circus that happened months later on January 14, 2002 when the congressional committee investigating the Enron collapse found my memos in a box of documents and made them public.

Toward the end of 2001, my friends had finally convinced me to hire a lawyer. Luckily he decided to take the case. A lot of whistleblowers cannot get a lawyer as they are not taken seriously, or they choose not to seek legal assistance as they did nothing wrong. I think a lawyer is really necessary, and not someone that the company pays. Prior to engaging an attorney, I was still in "helpful mode". I was shocked when he told me not to speak to Enron's lawyers; this seemed radical. But it was my lawyer that helped me through the "surreal period" when there were camera crews everywhere and I was summoned to testify before Congress. The media needed its heroes and villains, and I became the heroine, though this was not how I saw myself.

I am often asked why I did not leave the company sooner? A company as big as Enron is like a country, and although sometimes you do not appreciate its actions, you do not give up citizenship. I was not willing to give up on Enron that easily. Moreover, had I left in 1996 or 1997 when my misgivings began, no one would have believed that I was voluntarily choosing to leave. The issue of whether I should have gone to the SEC or the media is also raised. Again, I went through the internal channels because once Skilling was out of the picture, I trusted that Lay would act and that my memos would help open the necessary dialogue regarding the company's future. Lay had always presented the image of a good and honest man, a community leader known for charity, so I was certain that he would put the shareholders and employees first. Instead the company's senior executives were incredibly arrogant and continued to convince themselves of the value of their fig leaf compliance programme. Once again, form over substance. It was such lunacy.

As with other whistleblowers that I have talked to, I did not want to regret the stand that I did not take. Others from Enron have told me that they wished they had said something. Although I will probably never again receive a traditional job in the private sector, my former colleagues are haunted by different demons: that either they will be considered not smart enough to have figured out the falsities of Enron, or not brave enough to have said something, or they were somehow involved in the complicity. At the end of my tenure at Enron there was a lot of hostility towards me because people were afraid of what I might do next. It got to the point that no one would meet with me without his or her lawyer present. I still live in Houston, and have run into old colleagues. They mainly look away; I think it is because I make them feel like cowards.

Given the same circumstance, I would do it again but would find allies and would come forward sooner. There were early signs: inflated expense reports, nepotism, questionable accounting practices, etc., but I chose to ignore these. I would be more forceful and keep insisting that the company come clean to its shareholders and its employees. When Lay hired the law firm that was implicated in the misdeeds, I should have taken a harder line. One of the take-away lessons for me has been that I want the company in which I work to mirror my own value system. Lay had his sister acting as the company's mandatory travel agent. In a perverse way, this sent the message to people below him that it was acceptable to cut corners. It is important not to brush off ethical lapses, as this can be indicative of even bigger problems. And it is important that we teach this to our children. I see what we are doing to our advantaged youth; we make certain that their futures are never harmed by youthful exuberance. We clean up their mistakes and never force them to take responsibility for their actions. These youth are our future executives, and if we let them get away with cheating now, they will surely do it again later.

In total, over 6 000 people lost their jobs at Enron and many more lost most if not all of their retirement savings. Shareholders of Enron lost over $60 billion of value. Thus far, seven top executives have pleaded guilty and one is serving time in prison. Andy Fastow, who many have accused as being one of the most culpable, has pleaded guilty and is due a ten-year prison term on the basis that he will cooperate with the authorities.

Many damning reports have been issued on Enron, and the company's demise helped bring about a new law, the Sarbanes-Oxley Act. Sarbanes-Oxley mandates annual assessments of controls and accounting procedures, and the new bill clearly takes aim at the rampant abuses that have shaken investors. It represents a broad overhaul of corporate fraud, accounting and securities laws: criminal fraud has been defined to include engaging in any "scheme or artifice" to defraud shareholders and chief executives and chief financial officers of publicly traded companies must certify their financial statements and will face up to 20 years in jail if they "knowingly or wilfully" allow materially misleading information into their financial statements. This will ensure that no future executive can utilise the Ken Lay defence, "that they did not know of the problems". But I worry that the law might get watered down and become another internal control measure that does not work.

Being a whistleblower can easily turn into a lose-lose situation. You can lose your job and be painted as a troublemaker. For others to be encouraged to come forward there must be a better system of confidential or third party reporting, and the law must be strengthened so that the monetary damages received for unlawful termination are sufficient to motivate companies to do the right thing, to avoid terminating the employment of employees that deliver bad news. Although I felt like a lone fish swimming against the tide, I recognise that my story is one with a happy ending. I was not vilified, I was not without other means of earning an income (in my case through lectures and books) and I was able to remain in Houston and did not have to uproot my family. Congressional reports and external auditors confirmed my allegations. I was named *Time* Person of the Year at the end of 2002, along with two other whistleblowers. Though my case may be unique, if faced with the same situation again, I would blow the whistle.

# PART 3:

# LEGAL RESPONSES FROM AROUND THE WORLD

# WHISTLEBLOWING IN THE UNITED STATES: THE GAP BETWEEN VISION AND LESSONS LEARNED

*By Tom Devine*

Freedom of speech to challenge abuses of power is a part of America's identity dating to the Declaration of Independence, and institutionalised as the first amendment in the Bill of Rights to the Constitution. Consistent with that spirit, the US has set the pace creating a vision for whistleblower rights through a sea change in attitudes that sparked a legal revolution. Legislators compare whistleblower protection to "taxpayer protection".[1] Representative Schroeder offered that analogy on the House floor just prior to final passage of the Whistleblower Protection Act (WPA),[2] the best known law of its kind. Representative Derwinski went even farther in 1978 prior to initial creation of the statutory right. "The term 'whistleblower' is like 'motherhood', and we are all for whistleblowing apparently."[3]

In the WPA, protected speech under this principle is defined as lawfully disclosing information that an employee or applicant reasonably believes evidences illegality, gross waste, gross mismanagement, abuses of authority, or a substantial and specific danger to public health or safety. If disclosure is specifically prohibited by statute or Executive Order as classified on national security grounds, an employee is only protected if the disclosure is made to the agency chief or delegee, an agency Inspector General, or the US Office of Special Counsel.[4] While consistent with this principle, legally binding parallel definitions throughout federal and state law create a dizzying number of variations. For purposes of this analysis, a "whistleblower" reflects the following composite definition: "an employee who exercises free speech rights to challenge abuses of power that betray the public trust".

Statutory laws extending freedom of speech to workplace-based dissent are enacted unanimously, because opposition would be political suicide. A

---

[1]   135 <u>Cong</u>. <u>Rec</u>. H751 (daily ed. Mar. 21, 1989) (remarks of Rep. Schroeder). *Markup Meetings on H.R. 11280 of the House Comm. on Post Office and Civil Service*, 95th Cong., 2d Sess. 19 (1978).

[2]   5 USC 1101 <u>et</u> seq. *Markup Meetings on H.R. 11280 of the House Comm. on Post Office and Civil Service*, 95th Cong., 2d Sess. 19 (1978).

[3]   *Markup Meetings on H.R. 11280 of the House Comm. on Post Office and Civil Service*, 95th Cong., 2d Sess. 19 (1978).

[4]   5 USC 2302(b)(8).

broad network of laws also covers state and local government workers. The Civil Rights Act provides rights against first amendment violations.[5] Altogether 42 states and the District of Columbia also have statutes protecting civil servants.[6] Even military service members have whistleblower rights.[7]

Corporate employees have a plethora of rights. Altogether 34 federal statutes have corporate whistleblower rights generally characterised as witness protection.[8] Most frequently they are in environmental reforms like the Superfund law[9] or transportation laws such as for the airlines industry.[10] They extend to employees of financial institutions in response to disasters such as the savings and loan collapse,[11] and to government contractor employees.[12] In 2002 whistleblowers at publicly traded corporations reached the promised land in US law for disclosures evidencing misconduct that threatens shareholder investments – the right to a jury trial in district court under the most sympathetic legal burdens of proof. The new rights were enacted as part of the Sarbanes-Oxley corporate accountability law, in response to the Enron and MCI Worldcom scandals.[13] They are included in criminal law for obstruction of a government investigation.[14]

The laws reflect a corresponding cultural revolution, with whistleblowers lionised in Hollywood movies and on the cover of national magazines. Because they made a difference by challenging abuses of power *Time* magazine honoured three women whistleblowers – Coleen Rowley from the Federal Bureau of Investigation, Sherron Watkins from the Enron Corporation and Cynthia Cooper from MCI Worldcom – as its "Persons of the Year.[15] *Business Week* decreed 2002 the "year of the whistleblower".[16]

At the same time, the US has set the pace in creating opportunities for lessons learned. The growing pains for new rights too often have been fatal for whistleblowers victimised by a legal system that at times has created more victims than it has helped. And despite popular acclaim, within the workplace

---

[5]  42 USC 1983.

[6]  Vaughn, "State Whistleblower Statutes and the Future of Whistleblower Protection," 51 *Admin. L. Rev.* 581 (1999).

[7]  10 USC 1032.

[8]  For a comprehensive analysis of US whistleblower statutes and regulations through 2001, see Kohn, *Concepts and Procedures in Whistleblower Law* 79-98, 141 (Quorum, 2001), ("Kohn").

[9]  42 USC 9610.

[10]  49 USC 42121.

[11]  12 USC 1441a, 1790b, and 1831j.

[12]  31 USC 3730(h).

[13]  18 USC 1514A.

[14]  18 USC 1505.

[15]  *Time* (December 30, 2002).

[16]  "The Whistleblowers: Special Report," *Business Week* (January 13, 2002).

whistleblowing continues to be known as the sound of professional suicide, what celebrated US Pentagon whistleblower Ernie Fitzgerald calls "committing the truth" because you're treated like you committed a crime.

And things may be getting far worse. The most vivid lesson learned could be the fragility of free speech laws when the government responds to national security threats by imposing secrecy. That has been an almost obsessive policy offensive by the current US government since the 9/11 World Trade Center attack One example is hybrid secrecy categories – "Critical Infrastructure Information" (CII) and "Sensitive But Unclassified" (SBU) – for information unable to qualify as legitimately classified. Nonetheless, these new categories have all the secrecy status of classified information without any of the accountability, and are enforced through blanket gag orders with far more heavy-handed penalties than ever have existed for classified leaks. This gag campaign threatens to create a back door Official Secrets Act in the United States by criminalising disclosures that previously were the point of whistleblower laws.[17]

This chapter will survey the range sharp contradictions and lessons learned from the legal and cultural revolutions around whistleblowing in the US.

## Positives

There is little question that the United States' primary positive contribution has been pioneering leadership to create a beachhead for principles in the modern law of employment dissent. The evolution of whistleblower rights is unsurpassed as a vibrant, dynamically evolving growth sector of the US legal system. Enthusiasm has reached a point where lawyers may have the right and duty to blow the whistle on clients in some circumstances, starting to crumble one of the nation's most sacred pillars of secrecy.[18]

This enthusiasm has spread the seeds for whistleblower rights to nearly every nook and cranny of US law. The phenomenon began quietly in 1959, when California's Supreme Court became the first state to create a "public policy exception" to traditional English common law's employment "at will" doctrine that allowed the employment of private employees to be terminated for any reason or no reason under traditional master-servant doctrines.[19] This means corporate whistleblowers can sue in state court to seek punitive damages

---

[17] (Infra, at 17-19).

[18] This statutory breakthrough is at section 307 of the Sarbanes-Oxley law, 15 USC 7201 et seq.

[19] *Petermann v. International Brotherhood of Teamsters*, 174 Cal. App. 2d 184, 344 P. 2d 25 (1959).

from a jury if they are harassed for defending the public. In the ensuing 44 years, 40 states have adopted the public policy exception.[20]

In 1968, the US Supreme Court extended first amendment protection to government workers, from federal civil servants to local public school teachers. The Court established a clear mandate in principle, to be assessed on a case-by-case basis, balancing the government's right to efficient management against the public's right to know. "[A]bsent proof of false statements knowingly or recklessly made … [the] exercise of his right to speak on matters of public importance may not furnish the basis for his dismissal from public employment."[21] Previously the first amendment protected citizens from repression for criticising politicians, but government workers were gagged from freedom to use their professional expertise for dissent on behalf of the public.

Despite this mandate, the case-by-case balancing test for constitutional rights institutionalised uncertainty both for workers and employers. It became clear that a consistent boundary was necessary with objective conditions to satisfy the balancing test. In the Civil Service Reform Act of 1978,[22] Congress created statutory free speech rights for employees to blow the whistle through a legislative mandate favouring disclosure when an employee discloses information that s/he reasonably believes is evidence of illegality, abuse of authority, gross waste, gross mismanagement or a substantial and specific danger to public health or safety.[23] Whistleblower laws have spread like weeds ever since. There are literally hundreds of statutes in the 42 states that have adopted the principle.[24]

The plethora of new laws has sparked flexibility to expand the scope of protected activity. For example, the WPA extended freedom of dissent to those who walk the talk by "refusing to obey an order that would require the individual to violate a law".[25] Traditionally legal rights were limited to protesting an illegal order that still had to be obeyed.[26] Often scandals have led to changes that put teeth in whistleblower rights. For example, in 1998 the District of Columbia responded to corruption scandals by strengthening its whistleblower law with a unique resource for accountability: make attempted reprisal a two-edged sword for bureaucratic bullies. Whistleblowers who are

---

[20] Kohn, supra note 8, at 25-56.

[21] *Pickering v. Board of Education*, 391 US 563 (1968).

[22] Pub.L. No. 95-454, 92 Stat. 1111 (West 2002).

[23] 5 USC 2302(b)(8). See n.4, supra. For an exhaustive, word by word review of this statutory root for US whistleblower law, see Robert G. Vaughn, *Statutory Protection of Whistleblowers in the Federal Executive Branch*, 1982 U. Ill. L. Rev. 615 (1982).

[24] Vaughn, Supra n 6.

[25] 5 USC 2302(b)(9)(D).

[26] Robert G. Vaughn, *Public Employees and the Right to Disobey*, 29 Hastings L. J. 261 (1977).

fired may counterclaim as part of their trial to seek dismissal of those who engaged in the retaliation.[27]

One of the most fundamental breakthroughs for US whistleblowers was a legal revolution in the burdens of proof to win a ruling that their rights have been violated. Provisions in the WPA of 1989 overhauled these basic ground rules as the most effective way to overturn nine years of hostile decisions interpreting the new civil service law.

The most common reason why whistleblowers lost under the 1978 statute was their inability to establish a *prima facie* case. In the absence of any statutory provision, the Board consistently had adopted the test in *Mt. Healthy v. Doyle*[28] for first amendment relief, which over time has meant an employee must prove that protected speech played a "significant," "dominant" or "motivating" factor in the contested personnel decision.[29]

In the definitive legislative history for the law, Congress left no doubt that it "specifically intended to overrule existing case law, which requires a whistleblower to prove his protected conduct was a 'significant,' 'motivating,' 'substantial,' or 'predominant' factor in a personnel action in order to overturn it."[30]

A statutory provision in the WPA[31] replaced the former synonyms with a new test, both to establish a *prima facie* case and as a bottom line for the quantum of evidence necessary to prevail. Now corrective action must be ordered if the employee "has demonstrated that a disclosure described under section 2302(b)(8) was a contributing factor in the personnel action which was taken or is to be taken against such employee, former employee, or applicant." Although there is no specific statutory definition of "contributing factor," Congress left no question about what it means the standard to entail. During floor speeches and consensus legislative histories submitted prior to several unanimous votes, the primary drafters defined the burden as follows – "any factor, which alone or in connection with other factors, tends to affect in any way the outcome."[32] This is the same definition Senator Levin gave for

---

[27] D.C. Code section 1-1-616.15.

[28] 429 US 274 (1977).

[29] 429 US at 287. See also *Warren v. Dept. of Army*, 804 F. 2d 654 (Fed. Cir. 1986); *S. Rep.* No. 100-413, at 13-14 (1988); *H.R. Rep.* No. 100-274, at 27 (1987); 135 Cong. Rec. 4509 (1989) (statement of Sen. Levin); 135 Cong. Rec. 5035 (1989) (item 7, Joint Explanatory Statement).

[30] Id., at 5033.

[31] 5 USC sections 1214(b)(4)(B)(i) and 1221(e)(1). These provisions refer to the two contexts for whistleblower hearings, respectively, when a government agency seeks relief for the whistleblower, or when the employee pursues redress independently.

[32] 135 Cong. Rec. 4509 (1989) (statement of Senator Levin); Id., at 4518 (statement of Senator Grassley); Id., at 4522 (statement of Senator Pryor); Id., at 5033 (Joint Explanatory Statement of S. 20); id. at 4522 (statement of Rep. Schroeder).

a "material factor" in the original version of S. 508.[33] A concurring letter from Attorney General Thornburgh was consistent. "A 'contributing factor' need not be 'substantial'. The whistleblower's burden is to prove that the whistleblowing contributed in some way to the agency's decision to take the personnel action."[34]

The overhaul was only half complete, however. After the worker establishes a *prima facie* case of retaliation, in US law the employer gets a second bite of the apple – the opportunity to prove it nevertheless would have taken the same action anyway for independent reasons, even if no whistleblowing had ever occurred. The government only had to meet that test by a preponderance of evidence, or anything better than a deadlock.[35] The WPA ended this comparative free ride. Now the government must prove its innocent excuse by "clear and convincing evidence,"[36] the toughest relevant civil law standard.

Congress left no doubt that it intended a new course. After summarising the changes in the *prima facie* test and *Mt. Healthy* affirmative defence, Senator Cohen emphasised: "Those are important changes. They mark significant changes in existing law."[37] The consensus legislative history again put the intent in perspective. "By reducing the excessively heavy burden imposed on the employee under current case law, the legislation will send a strong, clear signal to whistleblowers that Congress intends that they be protected from any retaliation related to their whistleblowing and an equally clear message to those who would discourage whistleblowers from coming forward that reprisals of any kind will not be tolerated. *Whistleblowing should never be a factor that contributes in any way to an adverse personnel action.*"[38]

The package of modified standards leaves whistleblowing on a legal pedestal, at least in theory. No other merit system principles, even the new protection for refusing to violate the law in 5 USC 2302(b)(9)(D), enjoy the same modest burdens to prevail.

The US phenomenon has been contagious internationally. Generally the vehicle has been anti-corruption campaigns designed to stabilise free trade markets for globalisation. To illustrate on the anecdotal level, each year the US State Department directs international government and NGO visitors from over 100 nations to the Government Accountability Project for briefings

---

[33] 134 Cong. Rec. 19,981 (1988).

[34] 135 Cong. Rec. 5033 (1989).

[35] *Mt. Healthy*, 429 US at 287.

[36] 5 USC sections 1214(b)(4)(B)(ii) and 1221(e)(2).

[37] 135 Cong. Rec. 4509 (1989).

[38] 135 Cong. Rec. 5033 (1989) (emphasis added).

on how the free flow of information by whistleblowers through safe channels is the lifeblood for credible, viable anti-corruption campaigns. Without testimony from those who bear witness, they are lifeless empty magnets for cynicism, doomed to failure. Similarly, the State Department has sponsored this theme in speaking tours at locations ranging from Mexico and Jamaica to Slovakia.[39]

More institutionally, the US State Department led efforts to include whistleblower protection in the Organization of American States (OAS) Inter-American Convention Against Corruption. Article III, section 8 of the Convention protects "public servants and private citizens who, in good faith, report acts of corruption".[40] At a November 2000 OAS Office of Legal Co-operation conference, a model law prepared by US NGOs was adopted for recommendations to member nations. The model law incorporates virtually all lessons learned that are discussed below. Its cornerstones are:

- No loopholes to freedom of dissent for individuals or organisations who disclose evidence of corruption or abuse of authority;

- State of the art due process rights through the most sympathetic legal burdens of proof and choice of forum to get a fair chance at justice;

- Provisions to impose accountability on those who engage in retaliation;

- Full access for whistleblowers to make a difference going to court or binding arbitration to directly challenge illegality or abuses of power that create, implement or sustain corruption.[41]

One reason for the sustained free speech momentum has been fierce advocacy reflecting the national tradition, when free speech rights have been threatened. Over a ten-day period in the fall of 2000, a spontaneous coalition of newspapers and good government groups convinced President Clinton to veto an Official Secrets Act previously proposed and championed by his own administration.[42] A more recent weathervane was that, after another fierce protest, in October 2002 the Bush Administration accepted whistleblower protection as the only merit system principle to retain independent due

---

[39] See e.g., US Embassy, Kingston, Jamaica: media release (May 19, 2003); Written remarks for Thomas Devine, Anti-Corruption Conference sponsored by US embassy, Bratislava, Slovakia; American Bar Association-Central European Law Initiative; and Transparency International (June 21, 2001), found at www.whistleblower.org. (Anti-Corruption Briefing).

[40] Inter-American Convention Against Corruption, Organization of American States, OEA/Ser. K/XXXIV.1, CICOR/doc. 14/96 rev. 2, Mar. 29, 1996, entered into force Mar. 6, 1997, 35 I.L.M. 724, 728.

[41] The OAS model law can be found at www.oas.org in Spanish or English. It was drafted by the author, in partnership with Professors Robert Vaughn and Keith Henderson at the American University School of Law in Washington, D.C. A complete analysis of its provisions in the context of evolving international whistleblower law was scheduled for November 2003 publication in the George Washington University International Human Rights Journal.

[42] Revised Statement of the President, *Veto of the Intelligence Authorization Act for Fiscal Year 2001*, White House release (Nov. 4, 2000).

process rights in the newly created Department of Homeland Security.[43] Reconciled to independent enforcement of this principle, the Administration has spared whistleblower protection from elimination of independent due process in proposals to otherwise end it for employees at the Department of Defence.[44]

For US whistleblowers, the most significant factor to thaw the chilling effect is not fear of reprisal, but whether they can make a difference when they risk retaliation. Surveys of federal employees by the US Merit Systems Protection Board repeatedly have confirmed that fear of retaliation is only the number two reason why some 500 000 federal employees choose not to act, representing about half who annually witness illegally or other serious misconduct. The primary reason was that they "did not think anything would be done to correct the activity," by margins of 53-19% in 1980, and 61-37% in 1983.[45]

The US experience has passed this test with flying colours. Consider how they made a difference in the following examples:

- Increasing the government's civil recoveries of fraud in government contracts by over ten times, from $27 million in 1985 to an average of $300 million annually the next ten years after reviving the False Claims Act.[46] For the last two years, the figure has skyrocketed to more than one billion dollars annually, or some 40 times what the government could recover for taxpayers without deputising the whistleblowers.[47] That law allows whistleblowers to file lawsuits challenging fraud in government contracts. There is little question that the False Claims Act is the most effective single law in history for individual whistleblowers to have an impact against corruption. The OAS model law contains a similar section, the Citizens Enforcement Act.[48] The False Claims Act also has roots in English law, reviving *qui tam* suits brought by individual citizens "in the name of the King". Currently this type of statute is known as a "private attorney general" law. The Citizens Enforcement Act would

---

[43] 5 USC 9701(b)(3)(C).

[44] Section 102, H.R.1836, Civil Service and National Security Personnel Improvement Act.

[45] Compare Office of Merit Systems Review and Studies, US Merit Systems Protection Board, *Whistleblowing and the Federal Employee* 3 (1981), with Office of Merit Systems Review and Studies, US Merit Systems Protection Board, *Blowing the Whistle in the Federal Government: A Comparative Analysis of 1980 and 1983 Survey Findings*, 6-7 (1983).

[46] 31 USC 3729 et seq.

[47] US Department of Justice press release, "Justice Department Recovers Over $1 Billion in FY 2002: False Claims Act Recoveries Exceed $10 billion since 1986," (January 6, 2003). Based on US Department of Justice data and releases. For a detailed breakdown of recovery trends, see www.taf.org, the website for Taxpayers Against Fraud (TAF), the NGO that monitors implementation of the False Claims Act.

[48] Model Law, supra note 41, Article 28.

expand the private attorney general model so that citizens could file whistleblower suits against corruption generally.

- Overhauling the FBI's crime laboratory, after exposing consistently unreliable results which compromised major prosecutions including the World Trade Center and Oklahoma bombings.

- Sparking a top-down removal of top management at the US Department of Justice (DOJ), after revealing systematic corruption in the DOJ's programme to train police forces of other nations on how to investigate and prosecute government corruption. Examples included leaks of classified documents as political patronage; overpriced "sweetheart" contracts to unqualified political supporters; cost overruns of up to ten times to obtain research already available for an anti-corruption law enforcement training conference; and use of the government's visa power to bring highly suspect Russian women, such as one previously arrested for prostitution during dinner with a top DOJ official in Moscow, to work for Justice Department management.

- Convincing Congress to cancel "Brilliant Pebbles," the trillion dollar plan for a next generation of America's Star Wars anti-ballistic missile defence system, after proving that contractors were being paid 6-7 times for the same research cosmetically camouflaged by new titles and cover pages; that tests results claiming success had been a fraud; and that the future space-based interceptors would burn up in the earth's atmosphere hundreds of miles above peak height for targeted nuclear missiles.

- Reducing from four days to two hours the amount of time racially-profiled minority women going through US Customs could be stopped on suspicion of drug smuggling, strip-searched and held incommunicado for hospital laboratory tests, without access to a lawyer or even permission to contact family, in the absence of any evidence that they had engaged in wrongdoing.

- Exposing accurate data about possible public exposure to radiation around the Hanford, Washington nuclear waste reservation, where Department of Energy contractors had admitted an inability to account for 5 000 gallons of radioactive wastes but the true figure was 440 billion gallons.

- Inspiring a public, political and investor backlash that forced conversion from nuclear to coal energy for a power plant that was 97% complete but had been constructed in systematic violation of nuclear safety laws, such as fraudulent substitution of junkyard scrap metal for top-priced, state of the art quality nuclear grade steel, which endangered citizens while charging them for the safest materials money could buy.

- Imposing a new cleanup after the Three Mile Island nuclear power accident, after exposure how systematic illegality risked triggering a complete meltdown that could have forced long-term evacuation of Philadelphia, New York City and Washington, D.C. To illustrate, the corporation planned to remove the reactor vessel head with a polar crane whose breaks and electrical system had been totally destroyed in the partial meltdown but had not been tested after repairs to see if it would hold weight. The reactor vessel head was 170 tons of radioactive rubble left from the core after the first accident.

- Bearing witness with testimony that led to the cancellation of toxic incinerators dumping poisons like dioxin, arsenic, mercury and heavy metals into public areas such as church and school yards. This practice of making a profit by poisoning the public had been sustained through falsified records that fraudulently reported all pollution was within legal limits.

- Forcing abandonment of plans to replace government meat inspection with corporate "honour systems" for products with the federal seal of approval as wholesome – plans that could have made food poisoning outbreaks the rule rather than the exception.[49]

## Negatives

While US whistleblower protection laws have been effective catalysts for exposure of bureaucratic misconduct, the fundamental irony is that they have undermined protection against retaliation. The overall premise for US whistleblower laws is chaos. Unlike the consistent set of rules for all corporate and government workers relying on British and South African whistleblower statutes, the unstructured growth of US whistleblower law is saturated with arbitrary inconsistencies and contradictions. For example, corporate workers are covered for dissent within their workplace,[50] while federal government workers are not.[51]

The bottom line is the laws' track record, however. On balance, in practice US statutory whistleblower laws have been Trojan horses, creating more retaliation victims than they helped achieve justice. This is true for two reasons. One is that passage of legal rights persuades more individuals to speak

---

[49] Anti Corruption Briefing, supra note 39, at 4-6. Files and supporting details for all examples except the FBI crime laboratory can be found at the Government Accountability Project. Another US NGO, the National Whistleblower Center, has files for the FBI case. The Center's website is www.whistleblowers.org.

[50] *Mackowiak v. United Nuclear Systems*, 735 F.2d 1159 (9th Cir. 1984).

[51] Infra notes 73-4.

out, risking harassment. The second is that in practice the system has been rigged so that realistically it routinely endorses retaliation challenged by victims. While growing pains are inevitable, US whistleblower law has been suffering them for nearly 25 years since the initial 1978 passage of statutory rights.[52]

As illustrated by the frustrating evolution of civil service law for federal government workers, there can be little credible debate about the negative bottom line. Between passage of the 1978 statute and enactment of the WPA of 1989, employees only won four decisions on the merits[53] out of some 2 000 cases filed.[54] Fear of retaliation nearly doubled, from 19-37%, as the explanation why would-be whistleblowers remained silent in the law's first four years of operation, from 1979-1983.[55] Referencing that track record, Senator Levin conceded prior to the initial August 1988 unanimous Senate passage of the WPA: "These statistics are a clear sign that the system has not worked as intended and needs to be improved."[56] Senator Charles Grassley, who has become known as the conscience of the Senate for whistleblowers, put the track record in perspective when the legislation was unanimously passed again after joint House-Senate negotiations: "The Government still hands out the same prizes to whistleblowers – harassment, demotion, transfer and discharge."[57]

The WPA had a twice unanimous mandate. In October 1988 each chamber unanimously approved the changes.[58] President Reagan, however, pocket vetoed the law after Congress adjourned.[59] In 1989 the new Congress promptly acted unanimously to approve a stronger version of the law, which new President Bush did not veto.[60]

But the law still did not work. In 1994 Congress amended the law, because matters had gone from bad to worse. As the House of Representatives committee noted in its report on the bill: "Unfortunately, while the Whistleblower Protection Act is the strongest free speech law that exists on

---

[52] Supra note 3.

[53] The term refers to cases where a ruling was issued deciding whether an employee's rights were violated, compared to those decided for procedural reasons or settled.

[54] Devine and Aplin, *Abuse of Authority: The Office of the Special Counsel and Whistleblower Protection*, 4 Antioch Law Journal 23n.111 (Summer 1986). (Abuse of Authority.)

[55] Supra note.

[56] 134 Cong. Rec. 10638 (1988).

[57] 134 Cong. Rec. S15337 (daily ed., October 7, 1988).

[58] 134 Cong. Rec. H9464 (daily ed. Oct. 4, 1988); 134 Cong. Rec. S15,337 (daily ed. Oct. 7, 1988).

[59] *Memorandum of Disapproval on a Bill Concerning Whistleblower Protection*, Pres. Pub. Papers 1391-92 (Oct. 26, 1988).

[60] 135 Cong. Rec. S2805 (daily ed. Mar. 16, 1989). Id., at H754 (daily ed. Mar 21, 1989).

paper, it has been a counterproductive disaster in practice. The WPA has created new reprisal victims at a far greater pace than it is protecting them."[61]

While the 1994 amendments overturned virtually all hostile legal precedents, the pattern of futility persists. Between passage of the 1994 amendments and September 2002, whistleblowers lost 74 of 75 decisions on the merits at the Federal Circuit Court of Appeals, which has a monopoly on judicial review of administrative decisions.[62] After the Merit Systems Protection Board ruled in favour of whistleblowers on the merits in 36% of rulings from 1995 to May 1999, the Board succumbed to steadily accumulating court reversals, and its record plummeted to 2-20 to the end of 2002.[63]

The causes for sustained frustration are no mystery. The first is a gap between rhetoric and reality by political leaders. While no institutional chief opposes rights for whistleblowers in principle, few will tolerate them in practice. The WPA's birth is a classic illustration. Typical of the unlimited rhetorical support whistleblowers have received in the abstract were the 1981 remarks of President Reagan, who expressed his wish to make it clear that his Administration assured protection and proper investigation of allegations "to every whistleblower in the Federal Government".[64]

At the moment of truth, however, political rhetoric proved cheap. The President changed his tune after Congress left town for the elections, and took a sharp turn from his earlier unqualified enthusiasm: "Enactment of s508 would have redesigned the whistleblower protection process so that employees who are not genuine whistleblowers could manipulate the process to their advantage simply to delay or avoid appropriate adverse personnel actions."[65]

The causes for this schizophrenia are no mystery. The fragility of paper rights begins with the informal relief that federal government whistleblowers must seek as a prerequisite to trigger due process options. Under civil service law, employees first must file their cases with the US Office of Special Counsel (OSC), which investigates and decides whether to seek corrective action for the complainant in order to defend merit system principles. Envisioned as

---

[61] H.R. Rep. 103-769, 103d Cong., 2d Sess. 12 (1994) The House Report referenced Merit Systems Protection Board ("MSPB") survey findings "that, by a 60-23 margin, employees do not believe their rights will help them, and fear of reprisal remains as strong a reason why would-be whistleblowers remain silent as in 1983." Id., at 13, citing the Board's 1983 survey. Supra n.45.

[62] August 19, 2002 memorandum from Tom Devine to staff of Senator Robert Byrd, analysing trends in Federal Circuit Court of Appeals precedents (available at Government Accountability Project).

[63] May 14, 2003 memorandum from Tom Devine to congressional staff, analysing case law trends under the Whistleblower Protection Act (available at Government Accountability Project).

[64] Quoted in "MSPB Recommends Agency 'Outreach' Efforts to Encourage Whistleblowing," Government Employee Relations Report, Nov. 2, 1981, at 9368.

[65] Memorandum of Disapproval, supra note 59.

a sort of no-cost whistleblower's big brother, for sustained periods the OSC in practice acted like a Big Brother in the Orwellian sense. To illustrate, during the 1980s Special Counsel Alex Kozinski taught courses to federal managers how to fire whistleblowers without getting caught by his agency. He even went so far as to tutor federal managers on how to amend their proposed actions against employees in pending cases, in order to camouflage retaliation.[66]

A refreshing exception was the 1998-2003 administration of Special Counsel Elaine Kaplan, a long time employee rights advocate who worked effectively to turn the Office into a credible good government agency while she headed the unit. The new approach is unlikely to stick, however. Scott Bloch, the Bush Administration's nominee to succeed Ms Kaplan, does not have any experience in federal personnel law.

Federal whistleblowers surviving the informal stage do not receive normal access to the courts. Instead of jury trials available to corporate workers under the Sarbanes-Oxley law, they must have their cases heard by subsidiary administrative judges at an administrative forum, the Merit Systems Protection Board (MSPB). The system of administrative civil service hearings was never designed for major public policy disputes involving high stakes, national consequences and active congressional oversight. The administrative judges who hear the cases have no judicial independence and know they can be treated like whistleblowers if they rule for those challenging politically powerful government officials.[67] As a result, they treat significant whistleblower disputes like poison ivy. The administrative process has consistently been a black hole for cases with national impact, the most significant reason to have a whistleblower law. Decisions are regularly not finalised for years; one case just received a decision after 11 years.[68] In a significant environmental dispute involving millions of dollars in corporate timber theft, five Forest Service employees had to wait eight years for their day in administrative court.[69]

Nor do federal workers even have access to normal judicial appellate review of MSPB decisions. They can only appeal to one court, the Federal Circuit Court of Appeals, unlike normal appeals to one of the 12 circuit courts of appeal or the D.C. Circuit, where there is a healthy mix of perspectives. Unfortunately, at the Federal Circuit the only consistent perspective has

---

[66] Abuse of Authority, supra note 54 generally, and at 27-28, nn. 137-38.

[67] Similar institutional conflicts of interest afflict state whistleblower statutes, which as a rule also are implemented through administrative boards. To illustrate, research by the Arizona conference of the American Association of University Professors revealed that over a three-year period in Arizona, whistleblowers lost 53 of 55 cases. http://aaupaz.org (whistleblower legislation page).

[68] *White v. Department of Air Force*, MSPB No. DE-1221-92-0491-M-4 (slip opinion, Sept, 11. 2003).

[69] *Keefer v. Department of Agriculture*, 92 MSPR 476 (2002).

been hostility to whistleblower rights, with a track record of consistently shooting down any administrative rulings they manage to win.[70] As six members of Congress wrote to their colleagues before introducing WPA amendments, "due to judicial activism, the protections guaranteed to whistleblowers within the statutory language have been erased".[71]

The combined effect of two Federal Circuit doctrines has made it nearly impossible for whistleblowers to prevail. The first is loopholes, which have left the law akin to Swiss cheese that is nearly all holes. Although the WPA on paper protects "any"[72] lawful disclosure evidencing serious misconduct, in practice the Federal Circuit has translated that to mean "almost never". To illustrate, the Federal Circuit has ruled that "any" disclosure does not include those to suspected wrongdoers, co-workers, supervisors,[73] those made in the course of carrying out job duties,[74] those challenging policies instead of personal misconduct, even if the policies are illegal or institutional gross mismanagement,[75] and any disclosure of alleged misconduct unless the whistleblower is the first to raise the issue.[76] This latter loophole means that if you are not the Christopher Columbus who discovers a scandal, you must proceed without free speech rights – disqualifying from protection for dissent against ingrained corruption or testimony supporting the disclosure of the pioneer whistleblower on an issue.

Whistleblowers who survive the gauntlet of jurisdictional technicalities are the lucky ones. The statutory test for entitlement to protection is that the employee discloses information he or she reasonably believes is evidence of listed misconduct.[77] The Federal Circuit has made that test impossible to pass. It held that to have a reasonable belief, an employee must first overcome the presumption that the government "acts correctly, fairly, in good faith and in accordance with the law" by "irrefragable proof".[78] The dictionary defines "irrefragable" as "uncontestable, incontrovertible, undeniable or incapable of being overthrown".[79] It is far easier to put a criminal in jail than for a whistleblower to demonstrate mere eligibility for reprisal protection.

---

[70] <u>Supra</u> note __.

[71] Dear Colleague letter from Representatives Morella, Davis, Gilman, Harmon, Kucinich and Wynn (July 6, 2001).

[72] 5 USC 2302(b)(8).

[73] *Horton v. Department of the Navy*, 66 F.3d 279 (1995).

[74] *Willis v. Department of Agriculture*, 141 F.3d 1139 (1998).

[75] *LaChance v. White*, 174 F.3d 1378 (1999).

[76] *Meuwissen v. Department of Interior*, 234 F.3d 9 (2000).

[77] 5 USC 2302(b)(8).

[78] *LaChance*, 174 F.3d at 1381.

[79] *Webster's Deluxe Unabridged Dictionary* (Second Ed., 1979).

In short, this court with a monopoly on initial appellate judicial review has made a mockery of the free speech law passed by Congress. Because there is no opportunity for disagreement between differing courts of appeals, the Supreme Court has never heard a WPA case.

The most fundamental loophole for government national security whistleblowers is the absence of independent due process rights for actions to deny or remove an employee's security clearance, a back door way to fire employees in a context where they cannot defend themselves. Clearances are a functional prerequisite for employment among three million government or government contract employees. Loss of clearance not only means indirect termination but also makes blacklisting inevitable, because it means the employee's loyalty to the nation cannot be trusted. Since a 1988 Supreme Court decision,[80] the only basis for appeal of clearance decisions is if an agency violates its own procedural rules. Judgment calls about trustworthiness are beyond outside legal challenge. This built-in conflict of interest means an institution that normally is the adverse party in a retaliation case instead serves as judge and jury.

The results have been surreal. Security clearance actions routinely are used to remove whistleblowers from their jobs when they dissent against lax security, by branding them as untrustworthy. Employees regularly are not informed of their alleged misconduct for three years. An illustrative recent example involved national security whistleblower Linda Lewis, a Department of Agriculture employee protesting the lack of planning for biochemical terrorist attacks on the food supply. She was assigned to work at her home for 2 ½ years without duties while waiting for the hearing, which lasted 90 minutes. After the hearing, she still had not been told the specific charges against her. She was not allowed to confront her accusers, or call witnesses of her own. The "Presiding Official" of the proceeding might as well have been a delivery boy. He had no authority to make findings of fact, conclusions of law, or even recommendations on the case. He could only forward the transcript to a three-person panel who upheld revocation of Ms Lewis' clearance without comment, and without ever seeing her. Ms Lewis experienced a system akin to Kafka's Trial, only it is a 21$^{st}$ century reality, not a 19$^{th}$ century fiction.[81]

Ms Lewis' experience is not unique. Senior Department of Justice policy analyst Martin (Mick) Andersen blew the whistle on leaks of classified documents that were being used as political patronage. Within days, he was told that the Top Secret security clearance he had been using for over a year had never existed. Without access to classified information, he could not do any

---

[80] *Navy v. Egan*, 484 U.S. 518 (1988).

[81] Byrd memorandum, <u>supra</u> note __.

work. Instead, he was reassigned without duties to a storage area *for classified documents*, where he spent his days reading the biography of George Washington and the history of America's Civil War.[82]

Similarly, Department of Energy engineer Chris Steele blew the whistle on the government's failure to even have a plan against suicide airplane attacks into nuclear weapons research and production facilities at the Los Alamos Laboratory, a year after the 9/11 World Trade Center tragedy. His clearance, too, was yanked without explanation.[83] Richard Levernier, the Department of Energy's top expert on security and safeguards, got the same treatment when he dissented against failure to act on repeated findings of systematic security breakdowns for nuclear weapons facilities and transportation. For example, he challenged the adequacy of plans to fight terrorists attacking nuclear facilities that were limited to catching them on the way out, with no contingency for suicide squads who might not be planning to leave a nuclear plant they came to blow up.[84]

Pending legislation to amend the WPA would fill the due process vacuum for whistleblowers whose security clearances are yanked.[85] But since 9/11 a tidal wave of national security secrecy rules and proposals threatens to wash away whistleblower rights. The phenomenon is ironic, since the pattern of post 9/11 whistleblowers repeatedly have demonstrated how unchecked secrecy can threaten national security by covering up government breakdowns that sustain vulnerability to terrorism.

The new hybrid secrecy categories are a microcosm for this intensified threat to accountability.[86] The first initiative to be implemented is called Critical Infrastructure Information (CII). The threat comes from provisions in the post 9/11 Patriot Act[87] and the 2002 Homeland Security Act.[88] Section 214 of the Homeland Security Act bans disclosures of voluntarily supplied critical infrastructure information. Section 214(f) imposes termination and criminal liability of up to a year in prison for disclosures. This removes WPA coverage, which does not include general release of information whose disclosure is "specifically prohibited by statute…"[89]

---

[82] Memorandum from Tom Devine to House Judiciary Committee, September 18, 2000 (available at Government Accountability Project).

[83] "Safeguarding America's Deadliest Weapons," *Bridging the GAP* 1-2 (Government Accountability Project, Spring 2003), www.whistleblower.org.

[84] *Amicus curiae* brief from Government Accountability Project to US Office of Special Counsel (Dec, 17, 2001) (available at Government Accountability Project).

[85] S. 1358, section 5.

[86] Supra note 17 and accompanying text.

[87] Pub. L. No. 107-56, 116 Stat. 272 (2001). (USA Patriot Act.)

[88] Pub. L. No. 107-26, 116 Stat. 2135 (2002).

[89] 5 USC 2302(b)(8)(B).

The scope of the loophole, however, is enormous due to the Patriot Act's definition of "critical infrastructure" – anything whose incapacity or destruction "would have a debilitating impact on security, national economic security, national public health or safety, or any combination of those matters".[90] That arguably means anything. The scope of criminal liability is far broader than the Official Secrets Act for more sensitive classified information, twice rejected by Congress in 2000 and 2001.

The impact removes the WPA's soul by criminalising what traditionally has been the most highly regarded, significant whistleblowing – dissent against government collusion with corporate misconduct. Since Congress first created the whistleblower statute in 1978, this scenario has been recognised as exactly when and why we need whistleblower protection the most. Indeed, section 214(f) establishes criminal penalties for disclosing CII about threats to "public health or safety," precisely what the law has protected since 1978, disclosures evidencing a "substantial and specific danger to public health or safety".[91]

Ironically, this loophole could have a particularly devastating impact on national security whistleblowers, whose disclosures of government mismanagement, negligence and collusion with contractors or regulated industries have played a major role in shaping the congressional agenda for post-9/11 oversight. Eight examples from GAP's 2002 docket illustrate how the flow of information vital for national security oversight could dry up. Without advance permission from CII suppliers, they would have risked criminal liability by disclosing:

- Repeated, uncorrected Federal Aviation Authority collusion with air carrier security breakdowns that left airports unnecessarily vulnerable;

- Ingrained, neglectful collusion with contractors at Department of Energy (DOE) nuclear weapons laboratories that sustained security and safeguards systems so fragile they consistently were defeated in mock attacks by government undercover agents when the time of attack was known and the fake intruders had to operate within traffic rules and occupational safety regulations.

- DOE collusion with contractors at nuclear weapons facilities to conceal long-term leaks of radiation and illegal failure to adequately contain radiation and other toxic materials.

- Customs Service collusion with regulated air carriers not to inspect transport systems and commercial cargo, creating a major smuggling loophole.

---

[90] USA Patriot Act, supra note __, section 1016(e).

[91] 5 USC 2302(b)(8).

- Immigration and Naturalization Service mismanagement of contractors for visa and related fact-finding duties, again creating vulnerability to those illegally trying to enter the country.

- Environmental Protection Agency collusion with long-term contamination of air and drinking water supplies from inadequate Superfund cleanups, and related environmental illegality.

- USDA mismanagement, abuse of authority and industry collusion that allows contaminated meat and poultry to be approved for US military personnel.

- Federal Emergency Management Agency conferences with contractors, with more emphasis on entertainment than evacuation plans or strategies against bioterroism, resulting in approval of systems unable to withstand professional scrutiny.[92]

An even more draconian secrecy initiative is on the horizon. The concept is called "Sensitive But Unclassified" (SBU), and the Justice Department is preparing regulations to implement this new secrecy category. While agencies will have discretion to define the term inconsistently, the Department of Energy's approach is representative: "Information for which disclosure, loss, alteration, or destruction could adversely affect national security or governmental interests".[93] In other words, like CII, it could mean virtually anything.

This open-ended secrecy category would apply to all federal, state or local employees, as well as any corporate workers who have access to SBU information – potentially anyone. The government plans to enforce the ban on releasing this information through nondisclosure agreements as a job prerequisite. In the event of a leaks investigation, those who have signed the gag order also agree to sign an affidavit that they did not release the information. This would subject any whistleblower to criminal prosecution for remaining anonymous. Completing the Catch 22, those who "confess" face liquidated, or preset, damages predicted to exceed $100 000 – regardless of circumstances or whether national security actually is harmed. Property such as the whistleblower's home could be seized for enforcement, to be released at the end of the legal process if the employee is found innocent.[94]

---

[92] Memorandum from Tom Devine to congressional staff, "Impact of Critical Infrastructure Information" on Whistleblower Protection Act (February 13, 2003) (available at Government Accountability Project).

[93] Congressional Research Service Report for Congress, *"Sensitive but Unclassified' and Other Federal Security Controls on Scientific and Technical Information: History and Current Controversy,"* (April 2, 2003), at 15.

[94] Jeffrey Smith and Scott Armstrong, *Sensitive Homeland Security Information: Appropriate Protection or Overreaction?* (Annenberg Public Policy Center, 2003) (also available at Government Accountability Project). Mr Smith is former General Counsel for the US Central Intelligence Agency. Mr Armstrong is founder of the National Security Archives, a US nongovernmental organisation that created a library of information the government has sought to conceal. In addition to academic research, their analysis is based on repeated interviews and briefings from Department of Justice officials preparing regulations for Sensitive But Unclassified Information.

In short, the fate of US government whistleblowers is caught between intensive, flatly conflicting political pressures: popular acclaim and a surge of lip service laws on the one hand, compared to a government secrecy campaign of unprecedented severity since the McCarthy era in the 1950s and legal rights little better than window dressing for an empty house.

# Lessons learned about whistleblowing

The US experience with whistleblowers has provided ample opportunity for lessons learned, both negative and positive. The first principle for those advocating whistleblower rights should be the same as with the medical profession: "First do no harm". The duty of whistleblower rights advocates everywhere is to share these lessons learned.

## The facts of life

*Whistleblower protection laws help individuals to challenge abuses of power, not reinforce them.* In nations with a history of totalitarian oppression, whistleblowers are viewed with suspicion akin to those who inform on their neighbours to the government, and whistleblower laws are seen as encouragement for that type of betrayal. While understandable, that fear cannot withstand scrutiny. In a dictatorship, there is no need to protect those who act as informants. They are protected and rewarded by the same repressive institutional mechanisms used to suppress freedom. Whistleblower laws do not become necessary or relevant until individuals dissent against institutional abuses of authority.

*Life will never be the same.* Regardless of the outcome, the decision whether to speak out or remain a silent observer is a life defining choice. Whistleblowers are individuals at the intersection of valid but conflicting values. We like team players and find cynical troublemakers and naysayers to be distasteful. But we also admire rugged individualists and have contempt for bureaucratic sheep. Similarly, no one wants to be viewed as a squealer or tattletale. A common synonym for informant is "rat". But we have equal contempt for those who look the other way, do not want to get involved or make a conscious choice to see nothing. They personify voluntarily choosing the shallow "see no evil, hear no evil, speak no evil" substitute for humanity – leaving their values without eyes, ears or mouth.

Transparency triggers another valid contradiction. Any citizen in a former dictatorship cherishes the right to privacy. But a cornerstone of democracy is accountability through the public's right to know. Would-be whistleblowers have to choose.

The most difficult choices force would-be whistleblowers to answer the question: loyalty to whom? For almost all of us, the top loyalty is to our family. Getting fired threatens our capacity to support our children and other loved ones. The common slogan not to bite the hand that feeds you is both a cultural norm and sometimes a necessity for economic survival. Similarly, there is loyalty to our co-workers, who may be among our best friends, and often feel as defensive or threatened as the whistleblower's institutional target. Loss of family and friends are common consequences for breaching this loyalty. But what about loyalty to our communities, which can be victimised by corruption? Should we remain silent and passively join cover-ups that could kill our neighbours through contaminated food or a poisoned environment? What about loyalty to the law, and to our nation? The latter is called patriotism.

It is easy to pay lip service to values when there is no risk. Would-be whistleblowers must decide which choice is true to themselves, when keeping quiet may deny their humanity but speaking out risks everything dear to their lives, if not life itself.

*Don't take the harassment personally; it's only business.* The forms of harassment are limited only by the imagination. But the existence and intensity of reprisal are normally predictable, and at a certain point come into play no matter how diplomatic or gracious the whistleblower. In this context, retaliation is not a reflection of evil behaviour, but rather the institutional equivalent of animal instinct: eliminate the threat. There is a direct linear relationship between the intensity of retaliation and the perceived seriousness of the threat from dissent. Long-term social relationships and close personal friendships that took years to solidify frequently vanish despite personal regrets. A whistleblower's best chance for acceptance is persuasively convincing targeted institutions or officials that over the long term it is in their best interest to value and listen, rather than to silence or eliminate the messenger.

## Making a difference

*In a free society, nothing is more powerful than the truth.* As seen from the examples listed above, whistleblowers prove that point repeatedly. When used strategically the truth can overwhelm power based on conventional resources, unless it is a secret. Then it can be dangerous to know too much.

*Whistleblowers are a test of organisational maturity.* Free speech for whistleblowers is the freedom to warn, as often as it is the freedom to protest. There is little room for rational debate that whistleblowers should be a valuable resource for organisations. They are the early warning signal to nip problems in the bud and prevent avoidable disasters. Otherwise, organisational leaders may not even know about problems before they are reduced to damage control. While acting on warnings may be a painful, bitter pill in the short term, it is in the organisation's long-term interests to listen, and to establish safe channels of communication for the free flow of information. Organisational reactions to whistleblowers are indices of institutional maturity.

*More can be accomplished through consensus than conflict.* There almost never are real winners in a "win-lose" dynamic of whistleblower conflict. Even when a whistleblower prevails and imposes accountability or stops imminent misconduct, the "victory" generally creates an intensified backlash and determination to prevail over time, while clamping down so others don't think they can get away with the same thing. By far the most effective way for whistleblowers to achieve change with the least pain is to persuade institutional audiences that they are trying to act in the organisation's best interest, and that their insights are valuable in achieving that goal. The most significant contributions occur when synergy replaces conflict. This approach is not always an option, such as when too much liability has been incurred, or the organisation is acting in bad faith or is otherwise committed to a cover up. But whenever possible, it should be the first option.

## The role of law

*At best, the potential of whistleblower laws is to be effective as a last resort.* Perhaps the composite lesson learned from the US experience is a universal application of the axiom that there seldom are winners in a win-lose dynamic. No matter how effective the law, even winning a trial can be counterproductive. The most that normally can be accomplished is vindication and financial compensation. It is highly difficult to go home and continue to work for an employer whom an employee has just defeated in a lawsuit. The whistleblower will be subjected to greater scrutiny, and held to higher standards than were successfully endured for disclosing misconduct in the first place. To illustrate, from 1979 until passage of the WPA of 1989, only four whistleblowers prevailed on the merits under civil service law. Two were promptly fired again after their legal victories.[95]

*Institutional leadership is more significant for whistleblower protection than legal rights.* When an institutional chief establishes an unqualified policy of "zero tolerance

---

[95] *Anderson v. Dept. of Agriculture*, 82 FMSR 5043 (1982); *Plaskett v. D.H.H.S.*, 82 FMSR 5095 (1982).

for retaliation," it prevents exponentially more reprisals than the most effective legal system can stop through draining, time-consuming litigation. Leadership defines the environment of an organisation and creates expectations for behavioural norms. It structurally precludes the problem of post-litigation backlashes for whistleblowers who "win" because they don't have to. It sets an example to appreciate whistleblowers as an early warning resource, instead of reacting to them like a threat. Institutional leadership can set the pace for effective training, so that managers are aware of legal lines that must be respected. Only institutional leadership can establish patterns of rewarding whistleblowers for sticking their necks out. Institutional leaders do not have to wait for legislation to establish legitimate systems of redress. Nearly anything in a law can be duplicated through alternative dispute resolution, from redress for alleged harassment to assessment and corrective action on problems or public policy misconduct challenged by a whistleblower's disclosure. This dynamic maximises the free flow of information. More people act on their values, and blow the whistle when necessary, in a safe environment. When differing views are not tolerated, the rule is to be cynically detached as a survival mechanism. Profiles in courage are the exception, not the rule.

*Tactics are more significant than laws.* It takes all the strategic savvy and hard work of a political or legislative campaign to commit the truth, and then both to survive and make a difference. When a diplomatic consensus is unrealistic, the only other choice besides filing suit or giving up is to out-Machiavelli the Machiavellians by beating the bureaucracy at its own games. Recognising that legal rights are not a credible option for federal workers, in the fall of 2002 GAP and two other organisations authored *The Art of Anonymous Activism: Serving the Public While Surviving Public Service.*[96] As a general rule, remaining anonymous as long as possible inherently means preventing retaliation during that interim, which sustains access to evidence that may dry up once the dissenter is perceived as a threat. Sooner or later, however, at some point in most cases there is no alternative to bearing witness and making the record directly. At that point, the best insurance policy is solidarity, ranging from peers at work to the public that is benefitting. Isolation is a functional death sentence. Solidarity from other workers means supporting witnesses about harassment, and accumulating evidence of public policy misconduct that can turn an initial trickle of disclosures into an evidentiary avalanche that can't be stopped. The lesson here is that a lawsuit seldom should be used in isolation. To be effective, it should be part of a legal campaign until the public surrounds the bureaucracy that previously had surrounded the isolated whistleblower.

---

[96] GAP, Project on Government Oversight and Public Employees for Environmental Responsibility, (Fund for Constitutional Government, 2002).

*The best laws are those that combine doing well with doing good.* There is nothing inherently wrong with self-interest, a primary motivating factor for nearly all of society's functions. Simultaneously serving self-interest and the public interest is the best "win-win" combination. The genius of the False Claims Act is that it merges the two concepts, which explains why it is the most effective law in history for whistleblowers to make a difference through litigation.

# Lessons learned about whistleblower laws: Checklist for effective protection

The common thread of the US experience is that, while whistleblower protection laws are increasingly popular, in many cases the rights have been largely symbolic and therefore counterproductive. Employees have risked retaliation thinking they had genuine protection, when in reality there was no realistic chance they could maintain their careers. In those instances, acting on rights contained in whistleblower laws has meant the near-certainty that a legal forum would formally endorse the retaliation, leaving the careers of reprisal victims far more prejudiced than if no whistleblower protection law had been in place at all. Review of the track records for these and prior laws over the last 25 years has revealed numerous lessons learned, which have steadily been solved on the federal level through amendments to correct mistakes and close loopholes.

GAP labels token laws as "cardboard shields," because anyone relying on them is sure to die professionally. We view genuine whistleblower laws as "metal shields," behind which an employee has a fighting chance to survive professionally. The checklist of 21 criteria below reflects GAP's 25 years of lessons learned on the difference. All the minimum concepts exist in various employee protection statutes currently on the books in the US, illustrating the high points of the legal roller coaster for American whistleblowers.

## Scope of coverage

*"No loopholes" protected speech.* Protected whistleblowing should cover "any" disclosure that would be accepted in a legal forum as evidence of significant misconduct or would assist in carrying out legitimate law enforcement functions. There can be no loopholes for form, context or audience, unless release of the information is specifically prohibited by statute. In that circumstance, disclosures should still be protected if made to representatives of

institutional leadership, or to designated law enforcement or legislative offices.

*Realistic scope of subject matter.* Whistleblower laws should cover disclosures of any illegality, gross waste, mismanagement, abuse of authority, substantial and specific danger to public health or safety, as well as any other information that assists in implementing or enforcing the law or achieving its purpose.

*Duty to disclose illegality.* This provision helps switch the whistleblowing context from a personal initiative for conflict, to a public service duty to bear witness.

*Right not to violate the law.* This provision is fundamental to stop faits-accompli and in some cases prevent the need for whistleblowing. Significantly, however, an employee who refuses to obey an order on grounds that it is illegal must proceed at his or her own risk, assuming vulnerability to discipline if a court subsequently determines the order would not have required illegality.

*Protection for the full scope of activity that leads to harassment.* The law should cover all common scenarios that could have a chilling effect on responsible exercise of free speech rights. Representative scenarios include employees who are perceived as whistleblowers, even if mistaken (to guard against guilt by association), and employees who are "about to" make a disclosure (to preclude preemptive strikes to circumvent statutory protection). These indirect contexts often can have the most significant potential to lock in secrecy by silencing employees.

*Coverage for all employees performing public service functions.* Coverage should extend to all employees who are challenging betrayals of the public trust, whether the employer is public or private. Public whistleblower statutes should protect all who are paid with taxpayer funds to carry out government functions, including employees of government contractors or corporations.

*Coverage for confidential disclosures.* To maximise the flow of information necessary for accountability, protected channels must be available for those who choose to make anonymous disclosures. As the WPA sponsors recognised, denying this option creates a severe chilling effect.

*Protection for the full scope of harassment.* The forms of harassment are limited only by the imagination. As a result, it is necessary to ban any discrimination taken because of protected activity, whether active such as termination, or passive such as refusal to promote or provide training. The prohibition must cover recommendations as well as the official act of discrimination, to guard against managers who "don't want to know" why subordinates have targeted employees for an action.

*Anti-gag order provision.* Any whistleblower law must include a ban on "gag orders" through an employer's rules, policies or nondisclosure agreements that would otherwise override free speech rights and impose prior restraint.

*Prominent posting of rights.* As a practical matter whistleblowers are not protected by any law if they do not know it exists. Whistleblower rights, along with the duty to disclose illegality, must be posted prominently in any workplace.

## Forum

The setting to adjudicate a whistleblower's rights must be free from institutionalised conflict of interest. The records of administrative boards and grievances have been so unfavourable that as a rule laws adjudicated in these settings are Trojan horses. Two settings have a track record of giving whistleblowers a fair day in court.

*Right to a jury trial.* This option institutionalises normal judicial due process rights, the same available for citizens generally who are aggrieved by illegality or abuse of power. Most significantly, it means that whistleblowers will be judged by a jury of peers from the citizens whom they purport to defend.

*Option for alternative disputes resolution with an arbitrator selected by mutual consent.* Arbitration can be an expedited, less costly forum for whistleblowers, if the decision-maker is selected by mutual consent through a "strike" process.

## Rules to prevail

*Modern burdens of proof.* The federal WPA of 1989 overhauled antiquated, unreasonable burdens of proof that had made it hopelessly unrealistic for whistleblowers to prevail when defending their rights.

The current standard, which since 1989 has been adopted consistently in federal laws, is that a whistleblower established a *prima facie* case of violation by establishing through a preponderance of the evidence that protected conduct was a "contributing factor" in challenged discrimination. The discrimination does not have to involve retaliation, which could require personal hostility, but only need occur "because of" the whistleblowing. Once a prima facie case has been made, the burden of proof shifts to the employer to demonstrate by clear and convincing evidence that it would have taken the same action for independent, legitimate reasons in the absence of protected activity.

Since the federal government switched the burden of proof in whistleblower laws, the rate to prevail on the merits has increased from 1-5% annually, which institutionalises a chilling effect, to 25-33%, which gives whistleblowers a fighting chance to successfully defend themselves.

*Realistic statute of limitations.* Although some laws require employees to act within 30-60 days or waive their rights, most whistleblowers are not even aware of their rights within that time frame. A one-year statute of limitations is consistent with common law rights and has proved functional.

## Relief for whistleblowers who win

*Full scope of consequences.* If a whistleblower prevails, the relief must be comprehensive to cover all the direct, indirect and future consequences of the reprisal.

*Interim relief.* Even after winning a hearing or trial, an unemployed whistleblower could go bankrupt waiting for completion of an appeals process that frequently drags on for years. Relief should be awarded during the interim for employees who prevail after their day in court. Awards of back salary would be conditional, to be returned if the initial decision is overturned subsequently.

*Attorney fees.* Attorney fees should be available for all who substantially prevail. Otherwise whistleblowers could not afford to assert their rights, or even to win. The fees should be awarded if the whistleblower obtains the relief sought, whether or not it is directly from the legal order issued in the litigation. Otherwise, employers can and have unilaterally surrendered outside the scope of the forum and avoided fees by declaring that the whistleblower's lawsuit was irrelevant to the result. Employees can be ruined by that type of victory since attorney fees not uncommonly reach five to six figures.

*Transfer preference.* While it is unrealistic to expect a whistleblower to go back to work for a boss whom he or she has just defeated in a lawsuit, the problem is not hopeless. In order to prevent repetitive reprisals that cancel the law's impact, those who prevail must have a strong transfer preference for any realistic chance at a fresh start after winning.

*Personal accountability for wrongdoers.* To deter repetitive violations, it also is indispensable that those responsible for whistleblower reprisal must be held accountable. Otherwise, managers have nothing to lose by doing the dirty work of harassment. The worst that will happen is that they won't get away with it, and they may well be rewarded informally for trying. The most effective option to prevent retaliation is personally liability for punitive damages by those found responsible for violating whistleblower laws. Another option is to allow whistleblowers to counterclaim for disciplinary action, including termination. The most superficial is to make compliance with the whistleblower law a critical element in every manager's performance appraisal, and for decision-makers in reprisal cases to refer responsible officials for investigation to determine if sanctions are appropriate for violating this element.

*Laws that are additive, not substitutive.* Because of some recent court decisions, legislatures that pass whistleblower laws must specify they are not substitutes that cancel out pre-existing constitutional or common law rights. Otherwise, the new law risks being an inferior substitute and significant retreat.

## Making a difference

*Action against wrongdoing exposed by whistleblowing disclosures.* As discussed above, federal studies repeatedly have confirmed that the primary reason would-be whistleblowers remain silent is *not* fear of retaliation. It is that they will not make a difference.[97] Otherwise, there is no point in risking harassment. An effective whistleblower law should have provision to channel reasonable disclosures of misconduct for appropriate legislative or executive investigation, whether or not retaliation occurs. Wherever possible, a third party free from conflict of interest should assess charges and recommend corrective action.

Whistleblower rights protect freedom of speech to dissent where it matters most: the front lines where institutions either serve or betray the public. On balance, the US has been a pioneer for this new paradigm, both in terms of establishing legal protection, making a difference and shifting cultural norms. But the most significant contribution may be from the US' inability to match rhetoric with reality through genuine, enforceable legal rights. Hopefully, blowing the whistle on US failures will help to prevent the same mistakes from being repeated globally.

---

[97] <u>Supra</u> note 45.

# WHISTLEBLOWING –
# THE UK EXPERIENCE

*By Anna Myers*

The British approach to whistleblowing – focusing on organisational account-ability and individual responsibility – has proved far more successful than any of its original campaigners could have predicted a decade ago. In this short time, the term "whistleblower" has evolved from a pejorative epithet mean-ing "snitch" or "traitor" to one conjuring the image of a responsible (and brave) employee. All government departments, local authorities and every hospital in the country should have an internal whistleblowing policy. Regula-tors in the private, public and voluntary sectors are beginning to promote whistleblowing as part of a risk-based approach to regulation.[1] Almost every worker in the UK, no matter the industry or position, is protected from unfair treatment at work for public interest whistleblowing.

Despite this, it has been a quiet revolution. Since its inception in 1993, Public Concern at Work (PCaW) – the charity behind much of the work done on whistleblowing in the UK – has offered confidential legal advice free of charge to any worker with a concern about malpractice in the workplace. Yet the charity remains relatively unknown among the general public. The Public Interest Disclosure Act (PIDA), also known as the "whistleblowers charter", which is now five years old, was passed with little fanfare or govern-ment publicity. Endorsed by business, professional bodies and unions, the new law lacked (somewhat ironically) the necessary controversy to make a good story. Some would argue that however subtle its development, whistleblowing has helped change the way we think and the way we do busi-ness in the UK.

## Background to the Public Interest Disclosure Act

By the early 1990s, a series of disasters and tragedies had shaken the public's confidence in many of the institutions and companies traditionally trusted in Britain. In 1987 a ferry owned by the British company, P&O, capsized off the

---

[1]  For example the Audit Commission and the Financial Services Authority.

coast of Zeebrugge, killing 193 people, including many children. In the summer of 1988, the Piper Alpha oil platform exploded 110 miles off the north coast of Scotland killing 167 people. Later that same year, 35 people died and 500 people were injured when a crowded commuter train plowed into a stationary train at Clapham Junction in London. In 1991, three social services employees working in residential care facilities for children were convicted of the assault and sexual abuse of children over a 13-year period. In July 1991, investigations into the collapse of the Bank of Credit and Commerce International (BCCI) uncovered fraud estimated at over £2 billion world-wide that had evaded exposure for 19 years.

In each of these cases, public inquiries were established to uncover what went wrong and learn lessons for the future. In each case, it was discovered that staff knew of serious problems and either turned a blind eye, were too scared to speak up or tried to raise their concerns but to little effect.

## Say nothing

The Cullen Report identified the causes of the explosion on the Piper Alpha oil rig and found that workers who knew about these serious safety issues had not wanted "to put their continued employment in jeopardy through raising a safety issue that might embarrass management".[2] The Hidden Inquiry into the Clapham Junction train crash revealed that a supervisor had noticed loose wiring a few months prior to the collision but did nothing because he "did not want to rock the boat".[3] Faulty wiring was found to be the cause of the crash. The inquiry into the collapse of BCCI headed by Lord Justice Bingham revealed an autocratic environment in which no one dared to speak up.[4]

## Falling on deaf ears

The Kirkwood Inquiry into the assault and sexual abuse of children in Leicestershire County children's homes found that at least 30 concerns had been raised about Frank Beck (director of the homes) and his colleagues by staff, children and others. No effective action was taken. Andrew Kirkwood QC found "[t]he pressures on middle and junior care staff not to be seen to 'rock

---

[2]  The Public Inquiry into the Piper Alpha Disaster, November 1990, HSO Cm 1310.

[3]  Investigation into the Clapham Junction Railway Accident, November 1989, HMSO Cm 820.

[4]  Inquiry into the Supervision of the Bank of Credit and Commerce International, 22 October, 1992, HMSO.

the boat' with adverse consequences for themselves made it all the more important to take very seriously (their) concerns".[5] The official inquiry into the capsizing of the ferry, the *Herald of Free Enterprise*, found that on five separate occasions staff had raised concerns about the ferries sailing with their bow doors open. It revealed how staff had suggested that lights could be fitted on the bridge to indicate when the doors had closed. The inquiry found that these messages were lost in middle management and concluded that if they had been given the serious consideration they deserved "this disaster may well have been prevented".[6]

## Accountability in action

In each case there was public condemnation – many felt betrayed that those in control had failed to protect the people they were meant to serve, and anger grew over the apparent lack of "accountability". After the ferry disaster, an attempt was made to prosecute P&O for corporate manslaughter. The case was never put to the jury because there was no evidence that the board of directors – in law "the directing mind and will of the company" – was aware collectively or individually of the danger.[7]

However, in 1994, the first of only five companies to ever be convicted for corporate manslaughter[8] in the UK resulted in the three-year jail term of Peter Kite, the managing director of an "outward bound" activity centre. Although too little too late, the case demonstrated how accountability – explaining one's actions – can determine legal liability. A year earlier, four school children drowned in a canoeing accident off the coast of Dorset while attending the centre. Several months before, an instructor had raised concerns with local management about the centre's poor safety standards. When nothing was done, she wrote to Peter Kite setting out the risks and warning that if safety was not improved he might find himself having to explain to someone why their son or daughter was not coming home. This graphic warning was key to the prosecution as it showed the "directing mind" of the company had notice of serious safety risks. The company was convicted and Peter Kite imprisoned because he had done nothing in response.

---

[5] The Leicestershire Inquiry, February 1993, Leicestershire County Council.

[6] Court inquiry, Department of Transport, Ct No 8074, 1987, HMSO.

[7] *HL Bolton (Engineering) Co. Ltd. v. TJ Graham & Sons Ltd.* [1957] 1 QB 159, 172 per Denning LJ.

[8] The Centre for Corporate Accountability has campaigned hard to have the law on corporate manslaughter changed to ensure more companies can be held legally liable for work-related deaths. For more information about their work, visit their website on www.corporateaccountability.org

## The voice

In 1993, PCaW was launched "to tackle whistleblowing". Many of those behind the new organisation, including its present Director, Guy Dehn, had strong legal, consumer protection and policy backgrounds.[9] The aim was to respond to the alarm bell that was ringing loud and clear in the wake of these public inquiries; that tragedies, fraud and scandals can be avoided if the legitimate concerns of employees are heeded. The goal was to help whistleblowers speak up without fear and to encourage employers to listen with intent.

The independent charity's first response was to set up a confidential legal helpline to advise anyone with a concern about malpractice, risk or danger at work. The practical advice, provided on a lawyer-client basis, is to enable a genuine whistleblower to communicate the concern responsibly and to the right people so that a serious problem can be investigated and effectively addressed. Crucial to making whistleblowing work – and key to the charity's remit – is to educate employers, policy-makers and the public on the importance and value of whistleblowing to promote accountability and responsibility in the modern workplace; in effect good management and good governance.

This approach is what Lord Borrie termed "a home-grown solution to a wide-spread problem".[10] By encouraging employers to recognise their self-interest in promoting whistleblowing to their staff, the greater their ability to avert harm and protect their own future. Otherwise, those in charge – no matter how responsible – may not hear of a problem until it is too late and the damage is done. Alternatively, they may only learn of a problem when external authorities intervene, or the media start asking probing and difficult questions. Responsible employers, this approach assumes, will want to learn of any potential problem before they are bumped into managing a crisis without ever having known there was a risk.

## The endorsement

Allegations of corruption and sleaze in government prompted Prime Minister John Major to set up the Committee on Standards in Public Life in 1995.

---

[9] Guy Dehn, a practising barrister and former legal officer of the National Consumer Council, set up PCaW with the help and guidance of *inter alia* Lord Borrie QC (former Director-General of Fair Trading), the Rt. Hon. Lord Oliver of Aylmerton, Ross Cranston QC MP (lately the Solicitor General), Maurice Frankel (Director of the Campaign for Freedom of Information) and Marlene Winfield (a health policy analyst).

[10] Sir Gordon Borrie QC, (1996), "Business Ethics and Accountability" in *Four Windows on Whistleblowing*, Public Concern at Work (ed.) London.

The Committee was chaired by Lord Nolan, one of the UK's most senior judges, and was charged to examine issues of conduct of public office holders and public bodies.

In the context of addressing the effects of a culture of silence in the public sector, the Committee observed:

> *Placing staff in a position where they feel driven to approach the media to ventilate concerns is unsatisfactory both for the staff member and the organisation. We observed that it was far better for systems to be put in place which encouraged staff to raise worries within the organisation, yet allowed recourse to the parent department where necessary.[11]*

In its reports, the Nolan Committee endorsed PCaW's approach to whistleblowing, particularly its emphasis on internal communication. Not only did the Committee recommend revising the civil service rules to allow for the confidential reporting of concerns,[12] it set out what it considered the essential elements of an effective internal reporting system.[13] This sensible guidance continues to be followed by public bodies and private companies alike.[14]

## The legislators

The first attempt to provide a legislative framework for public interest whistleblowing was initiated by Dr Tony Wright MP in a ten-minute rule bill in 1995. The following year, Don Touhig MP introduced a private member's bill drafted by PCaW and the Campaign for Freedom of Information. Although unsuccessful, the Bill was supported by the Rt. Hon Tony Blair MP who – as leader of the opposition – pledged that a future government of his would introduce similar legislation. In 1997 Richard Shepherd MP introduced another private member's bill and it was this that was led onto the statute books by Ian McCartney MP, a Minister in the Department of Trade and Industry. Once again, PCaW was closely involved in the formulation of the Act and was asked to consult with key stakeholders on the detail of its provisions.

---

[11] UK Committee on Standards in Public Life, Second Report, May 1996, page 22.

[12] UK Committee on Standards in Public Life, First Report, May 1995, page 59.

[13] UK Committee on Standards in Public Life, Second Report, May 1996, page 22 and Third Report, July 1997, page 49. These include: a) a clear statement that malpractice is taken seriously in the organisation and an indication of the sorts of matters regarded as malpractice; b) respect for the confidentiality of staff raising concerns if they wish, and an opportunity to raise concerns outside the line management structure; c) access to independent advice; d) penalties for making false and malicious allegations; e) and an indication of the proper way concerns may be raised outside the organisation if necessary.

[14] The Nolan Committee recommendations are incorporated into the Model Policy contained in PCaW's Whistleblowing Policy Pack and used by employers throughout the UK and internationally.

# Public Interest Disclosure Act

PIDA is part of UK employment law.[15] It is designed to address a key barrier to raising concerns in the workplace – the fear of compromising one's employment and career. Most employment rights balance the interests of employers with the interests of the individual worker. PIDA is different in that it balances the interests of employers to maintain the control and direction of their business with the wider public interest to stop wrongdoing and protect society at large – be it customers, vulnerable individuals, taxpayers or workers.

PIDA builds on the common law principle that there "is no confidence as to the disclosure of iniquity".[16] For over 150 years, the courts have consistently held that there is no obligation on an employee to keep information secret if it relates to such misconduct on the part of the employer or fellow employees that there is a public interest in its disclosure. The law recognises the public interest in maintaining confidence but it also recognises a countervailing, and at times overriding, public interest in disclosure. Clearly information about criminal activity, fraud or a potential health and safety danger would be included in the category of information which it is in the public interest to disclose.[17] Over time the category has been extended to fit situations where the malpractice disclosed is of such a nature that the person receiving it is justified. One logical recipient, outside the workplace – other than the police in cases of crime or serious danger – would be the relevant regulating body charged with ensuring minimum standards of conduct and practice in a particular sector, area of work or industry.

PIDA shifts the debate from one that primarily focuses on the motivation of the whistleblower to one that focuses on the nature of the information and the appropriate recipient for it.[18] Guiding the flow of information through the responsible and accountable structures already in place, PIDA does not require anyone to blow the whistle nor does it set out what must happen with the information once the whistle is blown. As one respected observer noted "a society that leaves nothing to an individual or an individual organisation's own sense of what is right and moral and ethical would no longer be a free society".[19]

---

[15] Section 103A, Employment Rights Act 1996. The section was added as from 2 July 1999.

[16] *Gartside v. Outram* [1856] 26 LJ Ch 113, 114,116 per Wood VC.

[17] Section 43B of PIDA sets out the types of information that "qualify" under PIDA and are capable of being protected. It includes information about criminal acts, health and safety risks, environmental dangers, a breach of a legal obligation, potential miscarriages of justice and a cover-up of any of these. A potential breach or failure to comply with a legal obligation would include *inter alia* statutory, contractual, administrative or common law obligations. For further explanation see annotated guide on CD Rom accompanying this book at 15-18.

[18] It is important to note that all the information that "qualifies" under PIDA is subject to its provisions whether or not it is confidential.

[19] Sir Gordon Borrie QC, (1996) "Business Ethics and Accountability" in *Four Windows on Whistleblowing*, Public Concern at Work (ed.) London at 2.

# PIDA's key provisions

The importance of encouraging public interest whistleblowing is underlined by the facts that compensation is unlimited and that a dismissal for making a protected disclosure is deemed to be automatically unfair. This shifts the legal burden to the employer to prove that the dismissal was a fair one.[20] In claims of victimisation short of dismissal, the employer must show the ground on which he subjected the whistleblower to a detriment.[21] PIDA provides a quick resolution to an unfair dismissal through its provision for interim relief[22] and some would argue the overall advantage to PIDA being part of UK employment law is that it allows access to a tribunal system designed to facilitate a quick, non-legalistic resolution of disputes.[23]

## Who is covered?

All workers in the UK are covered by the legislation whether they are employed in the public, private or voluntary sectors. The usual restrictions concerning length of employment and upper age limit do not apply[24] and, unlike most employment protection, PIDA covers workers as well as employees.[25] A recent amendment to PIDA extends its protection to police officers[26] but it continues to exclude serving members of the armed forces and the security services.[27]

## Internal and regulatory disclosures

PIDA's framework for public interest whistleblowing is through a tiered disclosure regime. This means the Act promotes internal communication of information and establishes safe alternatives outside the workplace. The shifting

---

[20] See explanatory note to s. 5 of the annotated guide to PIDA at 46-47 on CD Rom accompanying this book and also at www.whistleblowing.org.uk.

[21] See sections 2 and 3 of the annotated guide to PIDA on CD Rom at 42-44.

[22] Section 9 to PIDA, see the annotated guide on CD Rom at 51, allows a whistleblower to seek an order for reinstatement within seven days of dismissal. If granted and the employer refuses to reinstate, the whistleblower's salary will continue until the date of the full hearing.

[23] The employment tribunal system is not without its critics; that it is too accessible to employees with trivial complaints or that it favours employers, particularly those who can afford legal representation. Some argue that lawyers have formalised the process and prolong disputes to negotiate settlements or pressure the other party to withdraw.

[24] Section 7 PIDA, see the annotated guide on CD Rom at 49.

[25] Section 43K ERA. This means PIDA covers most individuals in work whether contractors, trainees, agency staff or homeworkers. It does not cover volunteers or the genuinely self-employed.

[26] Section 37 of the Police Reform Act 2002. See notes to s. 43KA of guide to PIDA on Cd Rom at 40.

[27] For a full explanation of this exclusion see guide on CD Rom at 53.

public perception of whistleblowing – from an act of treachery to one of loyalty – is promoted by the way the term "disclosure" is used in PIDA. Most would not consider an internal communication of information as a disclosure in the traditional sense. However, by making the protection most readily available to those who raise their concerns with their employer (or the person legally responsible) – and by calling this a "disclosure" – PIDA reinforces the importance of internal lines of accountability. The Act also reinforces ministerial accountability by treating a disclosure to the sponsoring department from staff working in non-departmental government bodies – such as nurses in a National Health Service (NHS) hospital – the same as an internal disclosure. The requirement on the individual whistleblower in these instances is, essentially, an honest and reasonable suspicion of malpractice.[28] This means the whistleblower does not have to be right to be protected.

The most appropriate port of call outside the workplace is the statutory agency charged to regulate and promote minimum standards of conduct in that sector or industry. PIDA gives the key regulators – identified through secondary legislation – specific status as a recipient for information.[29] There is no requirement on the whistleblower to have raised the concern internally first before disclosing it to a "prescribed" regulator. The additional requirement on the whistleblower is to reasonably believe the information falls within the remit of the regulating body they contact and to have some evidence to substantiate the concern.[30] Again, there is no requirement on the whistleblowers to prove they are right in their concern.

## Wider disclosures

Outside this framework of internal and regulatory disclosures, it is up to the worker to decide where to raise a concern. It is here that the protection is less easily available.[31] In effect, this is where the tribunal has to examine and determine the appropriate balance between the public interest and the interest

---

[28] Section 43B PIDA, "any disclosure of information which, in the reasonable belief of the worker making the disclosure, tends to show…". See guide to PIDA on CD Rom (*ref note 20, supra*) at 15.

[29] See s. 43F PIDA, in the annotated guide on CD Rom at 25. The regulation was amended (October 2003) to include new bodies either not included or not existing when the original regulation was drafted. Examples of "prescribed persons" are the Audit Commission (local government and NHS finances), the Health and Safety Executive (workplace safety and accident investigation), the Charity Commission (charitable registration and governance) and the National Care Standards Commission (care homes and facilities). Most of the separate financial services regulators are now subsumed under a single regulator, the Financial Services Authority. An up-to-date list of "prescribed persons" for the UK and Northern Ireland can be found at http://www.pcaw.co.uk/legislation/legislation.html

[30] See s. 43F PIDA, in the annotated guide on CD Rom at 25.

[31] See s. 43G PIDA, in the annotated guide on CD Rom at 28-33.

of the employer. If, for instance, a worker told his or her local paper that she or he suspected wrongdoing in her or his workplace and was dismissed because the story was printed, this disclosure would be viewed as a wider one in a claim for unfair dismissal. The tribunal would first have to determine whether the worker passed a threshold test[32] and, if so, whether the disclosure was reasonable in all the circumstances. Clearly this is a higher test on the whistleblower. Additionally, the whistleblower would lose the protection of PIDA if he or she personally gained from the disclosure – if, for example, the local paper had paid the whistleblower for his or her story.

In determining the reasonableness of the disclosure, the tribunal has to have regard to the identity of the recipient of the information, the seriousness of the concern and whether the malpractice is continuing. If the concern had already been raised with the employer or a prescribed regulator, the tribunal has to take into account their response, if any. In a wider disclosure the risk of a breach of confidentiality owed by the employer to a third party (e.g. doctor-patient or banker-client) is greater and any such breach will also be considered. Finally, and importantly for employers, the tribunal will look at whether the worker complied or should have complied with any internal whistleblowing policy.

UK employers are beginning to understand the true implications of this last point as a whistleblowing policy can reduce the risk that wider disclosures will be protected. However, it will not be enough to introduce such a policy if reasonable steps are not taken to promote it to the workforce.[33] Disclosures of exceptionally serious matters, although they must be made reasonably and not for personal gain, will not be held to exactly the same conditions as less serious public disclosures.[34]

## Legal advice

PIDA protects a disclosure made in the course of seeking legal advice.[35] As there is no good faith or "honesty" requirement, this provision allows an individual who is intending to disclose information solely for some ulterior motive or leverage to safely obtain advice that such conduct jeopardises the

---

[32] The whistleblower has to meet one of three threshold tests before the tribunal examines the reasonableness of the external disclosure. These are that a) at the time of disclosure s/he reasonably believed s/he would be victimised if s/he raised it internally or with a prescribed regulator b) at the time of disclosure, there was no relevant prescribed regulator and s/he reasonably believed there would be a cover-up or c) s/he raised substantially the same matter internally or with a prescribed regulator.

[33] See *Kay v. Northumberland Healthcare NHS Trust*, case summaries on the CD Rom at 13.

[34] See s. 43H PIDA, in the annotated guide on CD Rom at 35.

[35] Seeking advice from PCaW's helpline is protected under PIDA.

protection in PIDA.[36] Reaffirming the principle of legal professional privilege, a lawyer who learns of a concern during the course of giving legal advice cannot – on his or her own volition – make a protected disclosure.[37]

## Remedies

As tribunals are loathe to order reinstatement in cases where the dispute and dismissal has undermined the employment relationship, compensation for financial losses is the usual remedy for unfair dismissal.[38] In the UK there is generally no reward for whistleblowing. However, as the statutory limit in employment law (currently some £55 000) does not apply in PIDA cases, compensation for financial loss can still result in high awards, particularly if the whistleblower was a high earner or where it proves difficult or impossible for the whistleblower to find alternative work.[39] In the first three years of PIDA, the average award was £107 117.[40] In cases of victimisation – detriment short of dismissal – the guiding principle for compensation is what is just and equitable in the circumstances.

## The law in action

On the downside, while the public continues to hear mostly of whistleblowing through high-profile cases involving the victimisation and unfair dismissal of a genuine whistleblower, it can give a negative impression about the improving culture in the workplace. Commentators also point out that the practice of some employment lawyers to tack a PIDA claim to an employment dispute which has little or nothing to do with whistleblowing – to negotiate settlements or avoid the usual qualifying period – does little to promote PIDA as a force for positive change.

---

[36] See s. 43D PIDA, in the annotated guide on CD Rom at 22.

[37] See s. 43B PIDA, in the annotated guide on CD Rom at 15.

[38] One exception under PIDA is the case of *Stevens v. Conwy County Borough Council (September 2001)*. After a full hearing, the tribunal ordered the reinstatement of Mr Stevens – a fitness instructor – who had lost his job after raising concerns that an externally-provided life-saving course fell far below what was contracted.

[39] See the case of *Bhatia v. SRA* (at 6 of case summaries on CD Rom) where the applicant was awarded £805 000 in large part compensating him for the loss of a particularly valuable commission. In *Fernandes v. Netcom* (at 11 of case summaries) the applicant was compensated for six year's loss of earnings to the age of retirement which resulted in an award of £293 000.

[40] See case summaries (at 2 on the CD Rom and at www.whistleblowing.org.uk).

In the first three years of PIDA, over 1 200 claims were lodged by employees alleging victimisation for whistleblowing.[41] Tribunals reached full decisions in 152 cases. Of those cases, over half of the claimants lost. Fifty percent of the successful claimants won under PIDA and the other half won under other employment or discrimination law. The vast majority of claims (over two-thirds) brought under PIDA are settled or withdrawn without any public hearing. As the public has no access to the details of the claims, there is no way of knowing what issues these cases raised and whether or how serious the malpractice was.

Because this policy undermined PIDA, PCaW brought a successful challenge in the High Court in 2000 to the decision to keep secret the details of such claims. The charity argued that it needed to know the gist of the malpractice and of how and why individuals claimed they were victimised in order to review how PIDA was working in practice. The government decided not to appeal the High Court decision but instead – and in rushed and secret circumstances – decided to change the regulations and thus ensured no details, other than the names and addresses of the parties, are presently available on the public register of claims.[42] This increases the risk that individuals and/or their lawyers will use PIDA to trade the public interest in exchange for a favourable out-of court settlement that agrees that the concern that the malpractice is kept out of the public domain. PCaW is campaigning to reverse these regulations governing the public register and so check this misuse of the legislation.

Key to the long-term value of PIDA is that the cases – whether highlighting serious malpractice or outrageous victimisation – clearly separate the message from the messenger. It is still early days for PIDA and though no law is perfect, the tribunals appear to be doing just that and applying the provisions in a robust and purposive way. Interestingly, since PIDA came into force there have been only a handful of cases against the NHS – where whistleblowing awareness work has been done – and none involved disclosures of serious patient safety issues.[43] A possible conclusion is that serious safety issues are now being raised and addressed locally. Outside the courts, the British workplace is showing signs of changing and many agree that PIDA has played a role in promoting and underpinning this shift in culture.

---

[41]  See Introduction to case summaries on CD Rom.

[42]  PCaW has complained to the Parliamentary Ombudsman that the regulations were the result of a series of mistakes and misunderstandings such as to be maladministration.

[43]  The highest profile PIDA claim relating to the NHS in the four years since commencement is being brought by the financial director of a hospital, claiming dismissal for blowing the whistle on the massaging of government-set target figures. It is noteworthy that there has been no suggestion that the junior member of staff who blew the whistle to the financial director was victimised in any way.

# The culture of the workplace

If, as whistleblowing campaigners argue, one of PIDA's true values lies in its declaratory effect, then the idea of this law is to "transform the image of the good faith whistleblower from industrial troublemaker to the embodiment of what it means to be a concerned citizen".[44] The reality is that measures like PIDA challenge the silence and secrecy that have imbued UK institutional life. Viewed as a tool to promote a positive shift in the culture of the workplace – rather than as a weapon to strike at Britain's employers – measuring PIDA's effect is less science than art. This section reviews some of the main influences on the workplace, particularly since PIDA was implemented, to determine what, if anything, has changed.

## Regulators and regulation

The traditional response to disasters and scandals – as outlined at the beginning of this chapter – is to implement new laws and regulations to try to ensure it never happens again. Very few can argue sensibly against an overhaul of a system or an industry that so clearly failed to protect the public. But necessary or desirable as many of these new rules are, it does mean that well-run organisations can find themselves bearing the burden of changes necessitated by their irresponsible competitors. It is also the fact that when so many of these disasters were enabled by, or rooted in, communication breakdowns there is no certainty that improvements in the structure of regulation, inspection and audit can solve that underlying problem, in the way that PIDA attempts to do.

In 1998 the Audit Commission – the body regulating local authority and NHS finance and standards – saw the value of promoting whistleblowing as part of its fraud prevention and detection programme. It sent pamphlets to all local authority employees setting out what to do if they suspected fraud, their legal rights under PIDA, and how they could report concerns through the Commission's confidential hotline.[45] A few years later, this work appears to be paying off. In 2000-2001, the value of reported fraud decreased significantly for the first time since this information was gathered. At the same time, the Treasury noted an increase in the number of whistleblowing

---

[44] Gobert, James & Maurice Punch, (January 2000), "Whistleblowers, the Public Interest, and the Public Interest Disclosure Act 1998" 63 *Modern Law Review* 54.

[45] Audit Scotland is following a similar approach and is working with PCaW's Scottish office to promote whistleblowing in Scotland.

mechanisms and reported that developments in corporate governance were helping to create an environment in which fraud is considered as part of a wider set of risks.[46]

In 2002 – prior to the financial scandals at Enron and WorldCom that shook corporate America – the UK's Financial Services Authority (FSA) issued a policy statement recommending that all the companies it regulates implement whistleblowing policies for their staff. This UK "super-regulator" made it clear that staff should be told they can blow the whistle to the FSA directly.[47] In July 2003 the Financial Reporting Council published its Combined Code on Corporate Governance. The Code includes a new provision on whistleblowing that favours the open and confidential reporting of concerns promoted by PIDA over the anonymous reporting that features in the US Sarbanes-Oxley law (the American legislative response to Enron).[48] The Combined Code makes it clear that responsibility for ensuring that staff can raise concerns about any risk should rest at board level and, in particular, with the Audit Committee.[49] Restating the responsibility for managing corporate risk and ensuring proper governance and controls in this way is likely to push whistleblowing up the corporate agenda in Britain and focus minds on what may have been until now a cursory exercise in policy writing.

Whistleblowing as a means to combat fraud in the public and private sectors has also been understood and promoted as part of counter fraud procedures. Similarly, whistleblowing has been accepted and promoted as a means to protect patients in the NHS. Described in more detail below, recent work by the Commission for Health Improvement (CHI)[50] in conducting clinical governance reviews, and practical tools being sent by the Department of Health to NHS employers, are helping to imbed a culture of open reporting of concerns.

In other key sectors, however, whistleblowing has yet to be championed and few regulators are taking positive steps to promote and support the organisations they regulate to address it properly. For example, little or nothing

---

[46] HM Treasury, (January 2002), *2000-2001 Fraud Report*.

[47] FSA, (April 2002), "Whistleblowing, the FSA & the financial services industry: feedback on CP101 and made text".

[48] The Corporate and Criminal Fraud Accountability Act, 2002, Public Law Number 107-204 (otherwise known as the Sarbanes-Oxley law). The Act is limited to corporate whistleblowing and genuine whistleblowers can be rewarded and compensated. In certain circumstances, those who victimise a genuine whistleblower can be criminally prosecuted.

[49] See the full text of C.3.4 of the Combined Code at www.frc.org.uk/publications The Code applies to all listed companies in the UK and will be in force from November 2004.

[50] The CHI is the independent inspection body for the NHS set up in 2000. It conducts clinical governance reviews of every hospital trust (acute care, mental health) in England every four years. It also investigates serious service failures and from April 2004 it takes over the inspection of private and voluntary health care as well.

has been done in the voluntary sector, construction or manufacturing industries generally, and no concerted effort has been made to reach small or medium-sized companies against whom the majority of claims at employment tribunals are brought. Despite the number of reports into harrowing cases of abuse of children in care,[51] for example, little has been done effectively in the sector to promote whistleblowing to safeguard children and others in care.[52]

## Employers

While organisations like PCaW are explaining to employers why it is in their own interests to promote whistleblowing to their staff, the challenge for all employers in the UK is to make whistleblowing work in real practical terms. A survey in 2002 found that half of the randomly selected respondent organisations (both public and private) had a whistleblowing policy.[53] This signals that organisations are taking the issue seriously at some level – whether it is to protect themselves against claims under PIDA or to demonstrate good governance.

However, for it to succeed in the workplace, whistleblowing needs to be properly understood as a risk management and governance issue. Many in the UK – employers and employees – fail to understand the difference between whistleblowing (bearing witness) and a grievance (seeking personal redress) and this fundamental failure will slow the pace of positive change. The confusion has remained despite guidance from the UK's statutory arbitration and advisory institute.[54] Following lobbying by PCaW, government and parliament amended new primary legislation on statutory grievance procedures – due to come into force in 2004 – to help clarify the difference.[55]

---

[51] Inquiries into serious cases of child abuse have repeatedly recommended local authorities and care providers implement and support whistleblowing and reporting polices (the Warnock Report, 1992; the Utting Report, 1997; the Waterhouse Report, 2000). Most recently Lord Laming stated in his report into the torture and death of 12-year-old Victoria Climbié: "Never again should people in senior positions be free to claim – as they did in this Inquiry – ignorance of what was happening to children." (The Victoria Climbié Inquiry, January 2003, Cm 5730, para. 1.42 at 8.)

[52] National Minimum Care Standards now require most care providers to establish clear whistleblowing procedures but without further guidance on how to do it. The National Care Standards Commission who regulates the sector has been designated a "prescribed person" under PIDA see *supra*, at 29. The Children's Commissioner for Wales – now prescribed under PIDA – recently published a report ("Telling Concerns") reviewing the operation of complaints, advocacy and whistleblowing mechanisms in Welsh local authorities. The review found little had been done on whistleblowing and now part of the Commissioner's focus is improving practice to protect children. For more information and a copy of the report, visit www.childcomwales.org.uk

[53] Industrial Society, (2002) "Whistleblowing", No. 93 Managing Best Practice. More information about the Work Foundation (formerly the Industrial Society) can be found at www.theworkfoundation.com

[54] Advisory Conciliation and Arbitration Service (ACAS) Code of Practice on Disciplinary and Grievance Procedures, September 2000 at 18, para. 47.

[55] The effect of the new law will depend in part on detailed regulations yet to be finalised and in part on the education and information campaign the government has promised will accompany them.

## Public sector employers

The first concerted attempt by a UK employer to address whistleblowing took place in 1993 when the Department of Health sent whistleblowing guidance to all hospital trusts. The NHS is the largest employer in the UK and while the approach was cautious, it was a welcome development. In 1997 the new government reminded hospital trusts of the need to have effective local procedures following the Nolan Committee recommendations and in anticipation of the new whistleblowing law. When PIDA came into force in 1999, all NHS trusts were given a compliance toolkit[56] and were told to implement whistleblowing policies.[57]

The CHI – after conducting its first 175 clinical governance reviews of hospitals in England – reported that many staff still fear reprisals if they report things going wrong.[58] However, a survey of NHS workers conducted in the spring of 2003 revealed that though half did not know if their hospital trust had a whistleblowing policy, a quarter believed the culture for raising concerns in their workplace is better now than it was three years ago. Despite the third of staff reporting unspecified grievances, 90% of those with a concern about patient safety raised it and did so locally.[59]

The NHS may stand apart from other public sector employers in its commitment to whistleblowing but attempts to address the issue have happened elsewhere. The Ministry of Defence set up an internal whistleblowing hotline in 2002 even though PIDA only protects civilian staff, and individual police forces have responded to recommendations that they provide equivalent protection to PIDA to their officers through internal mechanisms.[60] Once the protection for police officers comes into force, and with access to an Independent Police Complaints Commission, it will be important for forces to review their policies.

Government departments are required to have whistleblowing policies in place and the Civil Service Code encourages internal reporting of concerns while allowing for an "appeal" to the Civil Service Commissioners who are independent of government. How effective this approach is in identifying

---

[56] PCaW developed a tailored Whistleblowing Policy Pack for the NHS. It was distributed to 500 NHS trusts in England and Wales.

[57] Health Service Circular 1999/198.

[58] Commission for Health Improvement, (November 2002), "Emerging Themes from 175 Clinical Governance Reviews." A full copy can be found at www.chi.nhs.uk

[59] UNISON-PCaW., (May, 2003), "Is Whistleblowing working in the NHS? The Evidence". The full report can be found at www.pcaw.co.uk

[60] The Association of Chief Police Officers (ACPO), (April, 2001), "Doing the Right Thing: Policy for Professional Standards Reporting".

malpractice and protecting those who report it is not yet known. The emphasis on disclosure in PIDA may sit uncomfortably with a Whitehall culture whose traditional default of secrecy will be hard to remove.[61]

## Private sector employers

From its introduction in the UK, whistleblowing has been more readily accepted by those for whom financial malpractice is a serious risk. Many auditors in large companies and banks, for example, already knew first-hand the value of whistleblowing in detecting financial wrongdoing. This has meant that whistleblowing is often subsumed within anti-fraud policies and traditionally did not stand on its own as a way to try to ensure that information on any risk or wrongdoing could be communicated.

Increased emphasis on business ethics as part of an overall corporate social responsibility agenda means that most global corporations have implemented some form of whistleblowing or reporting procedures. Some of these are linked to external hotline providers[62] and others promote anonymous whistleblowing with varying degrees of success.[63] The focus on whistleblowing as part of broader ethics policies is positive – the only note of caution is that emphasis on codes of conduct and whistleblowing as a staff relations issue may unwittingly limit the range of concerns raised and blur the difference between whistleblowing and grievance.

It would not be far-fetched, in light of past and recent corporate scandals, to assume that robust risk management strategies would be implemented to protect corporate reputation. Whatever the motivation, the reality is that too few UK companies – large and small – promote to their employees a mechanism for signalling problems early and even fewer provide the training or management systems to support that commitment.[64]

---

[61] Though clearly essential to issues of national security, the fact that all civil servants must sign the Official Secrets Act (OSA) may have a chilling effect on disclosure even when the OSA is not applicable. Section 43B(3) clarifies the position with respect to the OSA (see guide on CD Rom at 17).

[62] Commercial hotline providers often combine counselling and other grievance reporting with whistleblowing as part of an overall confidential service to staff. Such a service does not (and cannot) act as an advice line to the whistleblower nor can it investigate or test the validity of the concern.

[63] Enron – once America's seventh largest company – did have a whistleblowing policy that set out how staff could raise concerns and how to do so anonymously. On paper it looked fine but the culture of the organisation – anonymous reporting in any event does little to promote an open and accountable workplace culture – meant it was too little and too late.

[64] A survey of 82 European companies found that fewer than half had a whistleblowing policy and of those that did, few included more than existing state protection. The survey concluded that "whistleblowers are often seen as a problem, rather than part of the solution". Friends Ivory & Sime, (February, 2002 at 8), "The Governance of Bribery and Corruption: A Survey of Current Practice".

In the UK large companies like Argos, Abbey, BP and the Co-operative Group, for example, are taking active measures to ensure their whistleblowing policy is properly understood by management and has the confidence of staff. While smaller and medium-sized companies may still fail to recognise the value of whistleblowing for them, moves by UK regulators, the new Combined Code for Corporate Governance and European anti-corruption laws are making it increasingly difficulty to ignore.

## Media

Traditionally, the only "whistleblowing" cases to hit the headlines have been those where it has all gone very badly wrong – the boat has sunk or the whistleblower has lost everything. The sensational story focusing on the damage, martyrdom or motivation of the whistleblower has done little to reassure the public that whistleblowing is a safe and acceptable part of daily work. Part of the problem lies in the traditional view – rejected by the Nolan Committee – that whistleblowing is only about external disclosures.

Despite the dearth of positive whistleblowing stories, the shift in the perception of whistleblowing was made dramatically apparent in the *Time* magazine feature naming three American whistleblowers "Persons of the Year".[65] All three raised their concerns internally, none of the three was dismissed from their jobs and all three viewed their disclosures as an act of loyalty both to their employers and to the public. While the UK approach recognises this reality and does not promote the media as the first port of call, public disclosures and the role of the media is recognised as an essential basis of PIDA as it is the ultimate and fail safe system of accountability in a democracy. It is hoped that in time this approach will help meet the criticisms that the media often mistakes its own interest with the public interest[66] and that media interest in the "person behind the story" can obfuscate and diminish the message, shifting the focus back onto the messenger.

---

[65] *Time* magazine, December 30, 2002/January 6 2003. The three women were Cynthia Cooper of WorldCom, Coleen Rowley of the FBI and Sherron Watkins of Enron.

[66] Two recent high-profile cases in the UK raised questions about the media's role as recipients of disclosures. The first was when a number of British newspapers refused to comply with a court order to help reveal the anonymous source who had sent them a false story about Interbrew bidding for South African Breweries, apparently for his own gain by market manipulation. It is notable that European newspapers who had received the same information had declined to run the story. Of greater prominence, the Hutton Inquiry into the suicide of the UK weapons inspector, David Kelly, is raising questions *inter alia* about the conduct of journalists and the use of anonymous sources.

## Government

The Council of Europe – in its report on national anti-corruption strategies – recommended that the UK do more to promote PIDA.[67] Although individual government departments – such as health – have used whistleblowing to improve services and protect the public, the UK government as a whole has done little to actively promote the law since it was passed in 1998. After its strong support for PIDA, this has been a notable failure, which has not helped to promote and protect the public interest, encourage good citizenship or ensure corporate responsibility.

## Conclusion

The UK approach to whistleblowing came from civil society, won support from key interests and government, and is now finding its feet. Although the lack of follow-up support from government means it is some way from reaching its full potential, the fact that civil society still drives this public interest is perhaps a price worth paying. Though PIDA is looked to internationally as a benchmark of public interest whistleblowing, at home it is not clear how widely known or understood the law is by UK citizens. The workplace – as in all capitalist countries – is changing and adapting to new pressures and demands. The current focus – post-Enron – on corporate culture and accountability is coinciding, in the UK at least, with a more general concern about the integrity of information and our ability as citizens and workers to question it or rely on it.

At the same time – whether by default or design – PIDA and the UK approach to whistleblowing is now being examined as never before. On the domestic front, government departments, regulators and individual organisations want to know what whistleblowing is, how it works and how effective it is in helping the right information get to the right place at the right time. How far this examination will lead to a deeper debate within the UK about the merits and value of this civil society response to accountability, governance and openness remains to be seen.

---

[67] Council of Europe (GRECO), (September, 2001 at 23), "Evaluation Report on the United Kingdom".

# THE AUSTRALASIAN PERSPECTIVE

*By Kirsten Trott*

In 1999 and again in 2000, Jeffrey Simpson, a financial services manager at HIH Insurance, raised concerns that the company was in breach of minimum solvency provisions.[1] He was ignored. In March 2001, HIH went into liquidation resulting in the loss of billions of dollars, millions of worthless insurance claims and thousands of jobs lost in Australia's largest corporate collapse.[2] In 2002, federal MP Andrew Theophanous was jailed for bribery, conspiracy and fraud.[3] In 2003, the former Australian ambassador to Cambodia, Tony Kevin, accepted an International Whistleblower of the Year Award after revealing the Australian government's cover-up of the sinking of the SIEV X boat carrying illegal immigrants into Australia.[4]

Year after year preventable scandals occur Down Under. Preventable, because where there are scandals, there is inevitably someone who knows or suspects something is going on. The HIH collapse could have been avoided or minimised if Jeffrey Simpson's concerns had been heeded. Society needs people like Tony Kevin to expose cover-ups. However, it would be better if people, such as staff worried about a corrupt politician, felt safe to come forward so that their concerns could be addressed before the damage was done. But how safe is it to blow the whistle in Australia?

In Australia, as in other countries, there is a cultural reluctance to speak out. Being classed a "dobber" in Australia is a serious insult and "dobbing" is considered a betrayal in a culture where "mateship" is often omnipotent. A 1994 report of the New South Wales Independent Commission Against Corruption demonstrated that the Australian public was fearful of the effects of whistleblowing; 74.1% of the people surveyed agreed with the statement "people who report corruption are likely to suffer for it". The survey also showed, however, that dobbing could be a force for good as 95.6% of people

---

[1]  Saville, M, "Attempts to blow the whistle on HIH 'ignored," *The Age*, 12 July 2002.

[2]  Rankin, R, "HIH inquiry seeks scapegoats for Australia's biggest bankruptcy," see www.wsws.org/articles/2003/jan2003/hih-j10.shtml

[3]  Australian Associated Press, "Theophanous starts jail term," see http://news.ninemsn.com.au/National/story_28157.asp

[4]  See http://www.refugeeaction.org/policy/kevin3.htm

surveyed disagreed with the statement that "people who report corruption are just troublemakers".[5]

This chapter considers the approach that Australasian legislatures have taken to whistleblowing.[6] It focuses particularly on how the legislation aims at promoting whistleblowing as a means to deter, detect and address wrongdoing. As there is a dearth of case law, the chapter is based on the legislation, with both primary and secondary research.[7] Readers wishing to consider sociological critiques of whistleblowing will find much in the work of, and bibliographies compiled by, Australian academics William de Maria and Brian Martin.[8]

# Background to whistleblowing laws in Australasia

Australia is a federation comprising of six states and two territories. For historical and consequently constitutional reasons, states legislate for their own peace, order and good government whilst the federal legislature, known as the Commonwealth, legislates on specific matters prescribed by the Australian Constitution (for example foreign affairs, the Commonwealth Public Service, industrial relations disputes extending beyond any one state, and international or interstate trade of commerce and trading or financial corporations[9]). The Commonwealth has devolved power to the territories to legislate on matters relevant to them. By contrast, New Zealand has one central legislature.

Both Australia and New Zealand are common law countries with highly developed jurisprudence relating to issues such as employment and industrial relations, defamation, tort and public interest immunity.

---

[5] Lewis, D, (1996) "Employment protection for whistleblowers: on what principles should Australian legislation be based?" 9 AJLL135. For further statistics on whistleblower reprisals see De Maria & Jan, "Eating its own: the whistleblower's organisation in vendetta mode," *Australian Journal of Social Issues,* 32(1) 37-59, 1997.

[6] New Zealand, the Australian Commonwealth, Australian states South Australia, New South Wales, Queensland, Western Australia, Tasmania, Victoria and the Australian Capital Territory.

[7] Primary research has been conducted on the laws of Western Australia, Tasmania, Victoria and the Commonwealth. However, for the jurisdictions of New South Wales, New Zealand, South Australia, Queensland and the Australian Capital Territory, this work draws heavily on Lewis D, "Whistleblowing at work: on what principles should legislation be based?" *Industrial Law Journal,* Vol 40, No 2, June 2001 169-193, (Oxford, Oxford University Press for the Industrial Law Society) (hereinafter referred to as "Lewis ILJ") and Lewis D, "Employment protection for whistleblowers: on what principles should Australian legislation be based?". (1996) 9 AJLL135, (hereinafter referred to as "Lewis AJLL").

[8] William De Maria's whistleblowing bibliography is located at http://www.uow.edu.au/arts/sts/bmartin/dissent/documents/DeMaria_bib.html and Martin's "Suppression of Dissent" website can be found at http://www.uow.edu.au/arts/sts/bmartin/dissent/ Information on the whistleblower's campaigning and support group, Whistleblowers Australia, can be found in this book, see Part 4, pg 194, and also at http://www.whistleblowers.org.au/

[9] See section 51 of the Australian Constitution.

Legislation to protect whistleblowers was first introduced in South Australia in 1993 and by July 2003, New Zealand and all Australian jurisdictions except the Northern Territory and the Commonwealth had enacted legislation. Since the formation in the mid-1990s of the Australian Federal Government Senate Select Committee on Public Interest Whistleblowing (SSCOPIW) and the consequent Senate Select Committee on Unresolved Whistleblowing Concerns (SSCOUWC) the issue has been before federal parliament. Despite recommendations from these committees about whether and how whistleblowing should be the subject of Commonwealth legislation,[10] no legislation has as yet been passed, leaving the majority of Commonwealth public sector workers without whistleblower protection. Whilst the recommendations of these committees may have influenced some state legislators, enacting laws in the interim, the current Commonwealth private member's bill[11] appears to be based on the Australian Capital Territory law.[12] There have also been recommendations that the Northern Territory introduce legislation.[13]

In addition to specific whistleblowing statutes, there is a spattering of whistleblowing provisions in legislation and codes of conduct pertaining to Commonwealth public servants,[14] health and safety,[15] competition[16] and corruption.[17] There is also a provision of Commonwealth employment law, which makes it invalid for employment to be terminated if one of the reasons is "the filing of a complaint, or the participation in proceedings, against an employer involving alleged violation of laws or regulations or recourse to competent administrative authorities".[18]

---

[10] Lewis, D AJLL op cit.

[11] The Parliament of the Commonwealth of Australia, Public Interest Disclosure (Protection of Whistleblowers) Bill 2002.

[12] Murray, A, Public Interest Disclosure (Protection of Whistleblowers) Bill 2002, Second Reading Speech, 11 December 2002. See http://parlinfoweb.aph.gov.au/piweb/view_document.aspx Senator Murray also states that the bill attempts to address comments made by the Senate Finance and Public Administration Legislation Committee (Sept 2002) in regard to an earlier whistleblowing bill.

[13] Northern Territory Law Reform Committee, "Report on Whistleblowers Legislation," Report no 26, December 2002, see www.nt.gov.au/justice/docs/lawmake/whistleblowers.pdf

[14] "Public Service Regulations 1935," guidelines on official conduct of Commonwealth Public Servants, (See Lewis AJLL op cit), Public Service Act 1999, see Whitton Howard, "Submission to the Senate and Public Administration Legislation Committee Inquiry into the Public Interest Disclosure Bill 2001," (May 2002) and Murray, A op cit.

[15] Section 21(1) Occupational Health & Safety (Commonwealth Employment) Act 1991 (See Lewis AJLL op cit).

[16] Section 162A Trade Practices Act 1979, see Bhojani, S, "Should whistleblowing be encouraged and is it?" Presented to Transparency International Australia's conference, "Whistleblowing: Betrayal or Public Duty," 6 August 2002, Sydney.

[17] Section 11, New South Wales Independent Commission Against Corruption Act 1988 (New South Wales), see Lewis AJLL op cit, Anti-corruption Commission Act 1988 (Western Australia) see Hon Jim McGinty, Whistleblowers Protection Bill 2002, Second Reading Speech, March 20, 2002.

[18] Section 170CK (2)(e) Workplace Relations Act 1996. See Lewis AJLL for discussion but note the change in legislative provision. See *Hogan v Employment National (Administration) Pty Ltd* (2002) NSWIRComm 313, for examination of whistleblowing under Commonwealth employment law.

Whilst these provisions provide some limited protection to whistleblowers, specific whistleblowing legislation goes further. Such legislation not only provides guidance on how to raise concerns, and get redress or apply sanctions if victimised for doing so, it has a strong declaratory effect. It should also raise awareness that it is safe, acceptable and valuable to blow the whistle on public interest concerns.

## What concerns are Australasians encouraged to raise?

It is striking that, just like the US, until recently Australasian whistleblowing legislation predominately focused on the public sector. In New South Wales, Tasmania and Queensland, disclosures must be by a public official.[19] However in the Australian Capital Territory, South Australia, Western Australia, New Zealand, Victoria and the Commonwealth anyone can blow the whistle on public sector wrongdoing[20] or on reprisals taken against a whistleblower.

Given the high incidence of privatisation in Australia in the 1990s,[21] most jurisdictions have extended their legislation to include state-owned companies and Western Australia and Tasmania legislation extends to the conduct of public sector contractors.[22]

Other than public sector wrongdoing, concerns about substantial risk to the environment[23] and public health and safety are protected in some jurisdictions.[24] More generally, it is only South Australia and New Zealand that have not ignored concerns of those in the private sector and legislation covers

---

[19] New South Wales Protected Disclosure Act 1994, s8, Tasmania Public Interest Disclosures Act 2002, s6(1), Queensland Whistleblowers Protection Act 1994, s8.

[20] Australian Capital Territory Public Interest Disclosure Act 1994, s15(1), South Australia Whistleblowers Protection Act 1993, s5, Western Australia Public Interest Disclosure Act 2003, s5(1), New Zealand Protected Disclosures Act 2000, s3, Victoria Whistleblowers Protection Act 2001, s5, Public Interest Disclosure (Protection of Whistleblowers) Bill 2002 (Commonwealth) s14(1).

[21] De Maria, W, (2002), "Common law – common mistakes. The dismal failure of whistleblowing laws in Australia New Zealand, South Africa and the United Kingdom," Centre for Public Administration, The University of Queensland.

[22] Tasmania Public Interest Disclosures Act 2002, s3, Western Australia Public Interest Disclosure Act 2003, s3.

[23] Australian Capital Territory Public Interest Disclosure Act 1994, s3, Queensland Whistleblowers Protection Act 1994, s9(3), South Australia Whistleblowers Protection Act 1993, s4, Public Interest Disclosure (Protection of Whistleblowers) Bill 2002 (Commonwealth) s4, New Zealand Protected Disclosures Act 2000, s3 and Lewis ILJ op cit at 174.

[24] South Australia Whistleblowers Protection Act 1993 s4, Queensland Whistleblowers Protection Act 1994 s9 (relating to the health and safety of someone with a disability only), New Zealand Protected Disclosures Act 2000, s3, Lewis ILJ op cit at 175.

[25] Lewis ILJ op cit at 175, New Zealand Protected Disclosures Act 2000, s3, South Australia Whistleblowers Protection Act 1993 s4.

concerns about illegality.[25] As South Australia was the first Australian state to enact legislation, it is unfortunate that other Australian jurisdictions have not yet followed its lead.[26] This is especially the case since private sector coverage was recommended by the SSCOPIW[27] and, as Whitton comments, this existing extension to the private sector does not appear to have been abused.[28]

For constitutional reasons the Commonwealth cannot legislate for the private sector generally.[29] However use of the corporations and industrial relations powers[30] and state co-operation could enable much effective coverage. Whereas the US government swiftly legislated for private sector whistleblowers in the Sarbanes-Oxley Act 2002 following the Enron and WorldCom disasters, the Australian Commonwealth government has dragged its feet following the HIH collapse. After calls from Australian media,[31] lobby groups,[32] regulators[33] and politicians[34] for legislation to extend to the private sector, the government has stated that it will allow company employees to raise concerns with the Australian Securities and Investments Commission (ASIC)[35] in its new corporate governance measures (Corporate Law Economic Reform Package [CLERP9]). This approach begs the question as to why the very same employees should not be protected for reporting concerns to other private sector regulators, such as those regulating competition law, pensions and insurance.

With or without legislative protection, the private sector seems keen to embrace the issue. Numerous consultancy firms have begun to offer whistleblowing hotlines,[36] Australian Standard AS8004 on whistleblowing protection programmes for entities as part of its corporate governance series

---

[26] The recommendations of the Northern Territory Law Reform Committee suggest taking the approach of the Tasmanian and Victorian legislatures. However they have specified that the class of persons to be protected should be "any person" as in the South Australian legislation. Northern Territory Law Reform Committee Report on Whistleblowers Legislation, op cit.

[27] Lewis AJLL op cit.

[28] Whitton, H, op cit.

[29] Lewis AJLL op cit.

[30] Ss51(xx) and 51(xxxv) of the Australian Constitution.

[31] Roberts, C, "Dobbers get rights," *Business Review Weekly,* July 3-9 2003.

[32] Transparency International Australia's submission on "Corporate Law Economic Reform Program CLERP9: Corporate Disclosure Whistleblower Protection," November 2002.

[33] See comments of David Knott, Chairman of the ASIC, at 40 in Gilligan G, "Whistleblowing initiatives – are they merely secrecy games and/or blowing in the wind?" *The Company Lawyer,* Vol 24 (2003) No 2, 37 – 40.

[34] Murray, A, op cit.

[35] Gilligan, G, op cit at 40. Transparency International Australia has argued that it would be unfortunate if the ASIC was the only regulator to which company employees were able to raise concerns, as this would unnecessarily narrow the range of concerns raised and the type of malpractice uncovered. Transparency International op cit.

[36] Hepworth, A, "Dobbing becomes big business," *The Weekend Australian Financial Review,* September 6-7, 2003 pg 4.

has been introduced[37] and the Professional Standards Council is encouraging professional associations to include whistleblowing systems as part of its codes of ethical conduct.[38]

# With whom can concerns be raised?

In a culture where speaking out has strong social disincentives, laws seeking to encourage whistleblowers to come forward need to make it easy and safe for people to do so. However whistleblowing is not just a means to detect wrongdoing, but also a means to make society more accountable. For this reason, many jurisdictions world-wide recognise that whistleblowing should follow the lines of accountability, from within an organisation to its regulators, to the government and to the public. Where there are public resources and reputations at stake, whistleblowers must also be responsible for their actions.

## Mandatory whistleblowing procedures

Tasmanian, Western Australian, Victorian, New Zealand, Australian Capital Territory legislation and the Commonwealth Bill make it mandatory for public sector bodies to establish procedures encouraging employees to make disclosures by explaining employee rights and setting out disclosure routes.[39] In Queensland, a public authority must put procedures in place to protect its officers against reprisals, but not necessarily to facilitate disclosures.[40] Most legislation prescribes how the procedures should be promoted and be accessible to staff. Only in Victoria are public authorities provided with model disclosure procedures, reporting structures and registers of records, as well as detailed guidance on how to comply with the Act, collate and publish statistics and receive, assess and investigate disclosures.[41]

---

[37] www.standards.com.au

[38] Professional Standards Council Report, "Whistleblowing in the professions – where does a disclosure model fit?" See www.lawlink.nsw.gov.au/psc.nsf/pages/rep_whistle _where

[39] Tasmania Public Interest Disclosures Act 2002, s60, Western Australia Public Interest Disclosure Act 2003, s23, Victoria Whistleblowers Protection Act 2001, s68, New Zealand Protected Disclosures Act 2000, s11, Australian Capital Territory Public Interest Disclosure Act 1994, s10, Public Interest Disclosure (Protection of Whistleblowers) Bill 2002 (Commonwealth) s12.

[40] Queensland Whistleblowers Protection Act 1994 s44.

[41] Victoria Whistleblowers Protection Act 2001, ombudsman's guidelines, November 2001 see http:// www.ombudsman.vic.gov.au/downloads/whistle.pdf

In New South Wales and Queensland if a public agency has a whistleblowing policy, as in Victoria and Tasmania, the public official must make his/her disclosure in accordance with that policy.[42]

Generally, in Australian jurisdictions, protected disclosures can be made to either the head of the public body where the wrongdoing is occurring or to specified regulatory or supervisory public agencies, which commonly includes an ombudsman. In many jurisdictions disclosures about a specific type of wrongdoing must be made to the corresponding or appropriate body dealing with that type of wrongdoing, in order to be protected. In South Australia, the provision is slightly wider as a disclosure is protected if it is made to a person to whom it is, in the circumstances of the case, reasonable and appropriate to make the disclosure. This includes, but is not restricted to, an appropriate authority as defined in the Act.[43]

## New Zealand's tiered disclosure regime

New Zealand has a four-tiered disclosure regime and, unlike some of their Australian counterparts, New Zealand whistleblowers cannot choose whether to raise concerns internally or externally but must follow the regime.

Under the regime, employees must blow the whistle in accordance with their employer's internal whistleblowing procedures, which are mandatory for public sector organisations.[44] The Act provides exceptions to this (for example if there is no policy in the private sector) enabling concerns to be raised directly with the head of the employer's organisation.[45]

If the matter is urgent, the head of the organisation is involved or no action has been taken after 20 days, the whistleblower may raise his or her concerns with a specified authority (including a private sector professional body, which has power to discipline its members[46]). If there is no appropriate authority or the authority has declined to investigate, failed to take action following an investigation or failed to make progress on the issue within a reasonable time the whistleblower can make the disclosure to a Minister of the Crown or, if in relation to a public body, the ombudsman.[47]

---

[42] New South Wales Protected Disclosures Act 1994 s14 and Lewis ILJ at 179 and 184, Tasmania Protected Disclosure Act 2002 s 7(6)(b), Victoria Whistleblowers Protection Act 2001 s6 (6)(b).

[43] South Australia Whistleblowers Protection Act 1993 s5.

[44] Ibid.

[45] Ibid.

[46] New Zealand Protected Disclosure Act 2000 s6-10 and s3.

[47] Ibid.

With its tiered regime, the New Zealand law is similar to the UK law. There is a clear preference for internal disclosures and, if the message is not addressed, employees are free to go to the next level, thereby ensuring organisational accountability. Unlike the UK law, the New Zealand law does not provide for disclosures to the media.[48]

## Media disclosures

As the public is the last line of accountability, it is essential that whistleblowers are protected for raising concerns publicly when there has been a failure by regulators or government to deal with the issue, or where the issue is exceptionally serious. The Western Australian legislature is particularly fearful of the media as the law expressly states that a whistleblower loses protection if s/he publicly reveals information contained in the disclosure other than that permitted.[49]

Only the New South Wales law allows disclosure to the media or to an MP and the Act mandates onerous conditions. There, before a whistleblower can make such a disclosure, s/he must believe it to be "substantially true" and make the disclosure to an authority or agency. This agency or authority must, within six months, have either decided not to investigate or failed to complete an investigation, failed to recommend action be taken or to inform the whistleblower whether or not they would be investigating.[50] The six months grace provided to the authorities and agencies hinders the practical application of this important initiative by making it ineffective as a tool to detect and resolve urgent public interest concerns and making other concerns unattractive to the press as old news.

As a private sector employee, Jeffrey Simpson was not covered by whistleblowing laws when he sensibly raised his concerns about HIH with the Institute of Chartered Accountants and then with Australian Prudential Regulation Authority (the pensions regulator), both of whom ignored him.[51] The HIH collapse might have been avoided had they known that he could safely raise his concerns with an MP or the public through the media.

---

[48] UK Public Interest Disclosure Act 199 s43G.

[49] Western Australia Public Interest Disclosure Act 2003 s17.

[50] New South Wales Protected Disclosures Act 1994, s19 and Lewis ILJ 180.

[51] Saville, M, op cit.

# Protections for those raising concerns

Australasian legislatures have provided whistleblowers with a range of protections to encourage them to come forward with concerns.

## Whistleblower immunity

Whistleblowers in all jurisdictions are immune from civil and criminal liability for having made protected disclosures.[52] In most jurisdictions, whistleblowers are also afforded immunity from obligations of confidentiality. Depending on the jurisdiction, immunity can extend to specific legislative provisions relating to confidentiality, common law actions for breach of confidence and relevant oaths or rules of practice.

## Downside of the sectoral approach

In *AG Australia Holdings Ltd v Burton & Anor*,[53] Mr Burton's ex-employer, GIO, sought an injunction to stop him providing further information to solicitors acting for company shareholders in a class action against GIO for breaches of corporations and trade practices law. GIO claimed that confidentiality provisions in Mr Burton's employment contract prevented him, as an ex-employee, from supplying information that the solicitors claimed was evidence of wrongdoing. The Supreme Court of New South Wales's decision focused on the issue of whether it was against public policy to enforce the confidentiality obligations. In considering whether the whistleblowing legislation relieved Mr Burton of his confidentiality obligations, the court held that the New South Wales whistleblowing law could be of no assistance as it only related to "public officials". The Court also held, "that parliaments have, comparatively recently, enacted legislation to permit whistleblowing but have not made it extend to someone in the situation of Mr Burton, is an indication that there is no public policy which prohibits the enforcement of confidentiality obligations which GIO here seeks to enforce".[54] The injunction was granted.

---

[52] Tasmania Public Interest Disclosures Act 2002, s16, Western Australia Public Interest Disclosure Act 2003, s13, Victoria Whistleblowers Protection Act 2001, s14, New Zealand Protected Disclosures Act 2000, s18, Australian Capital Territory Public Interest Disclosure Act 1994 s35, Public Interest Disclosure (Protection of Whistleblowers) Bill 2002 (Cth) s36, South Australia Whistleblowers Protection Act 1993 s5, Queensland Whistleblowers Protection Act 1994 s39(1), New South Wales Protected Disclosures Act 1994 s21.

[53] (2002) NSWSC 170.

[54] Ibid, Campbell, J, at paragraph 170.

## Defamation

Under the Commonwealth Bill and the Queensland, New South Wales and Victoria Acts, the defence of absolute privilege, in relation to defamation proceedings, is afforded to people who have made disclosures in the prescribed ways according to the legislation.[55] Under the Australian Capital Territory law, the lesser defence of qualified privilege is provided.[56]

The most real and serious risk of defamation is for a media disclosure. As (other than in New South Wales) disclosures can only be protected if they are made to the employer or to government bodies such protection is of limited legal significance (as it would attract qualified privilege anyway). However, it does provide practical and important reassurance to a whistleblower should someone wish to deter him or her by raising the risk of defamation.

## The identity of the whistleblower

One question often posed in relation to whistleblowing is whether a whistleblower's managers or colleagues will find out that the information came from him/her.[57] This is recognised in the Australasian schemes.

It is an offence to reveal information that is the subject of, or received as a result of, a protected disclosure under the Commonwealth Bill and the Queensland, Western Australian, Victorian, Australian Capital Territory and Tasmanian Acts.[58] Exceptions to this typically allow for the reporting of the substance of the disclosure and the manner and outcome of its investigation to enable effective oversight. In contrast New South Wales, South Australia and New Zealand laws focus only on keeping the identity of the whistleblower confidential. The New Zealand, New South Welsh and Western Australian laws state that information that might identify the whistleblower must not be revealed without his/her consent, unless it is essential:

- For the disclosure to be properly investigated;
- Having regards to the principles of natural justice; or

---

[55] New South Wales Protected Disclosures Act 1994 s21, Victoria Whistleblowers Protection Act 2001, s17, Public Interest Disclosure (Protection of Whistleblowers) Bill 2002 (Cth) s36 (3), Queensland Whistleblowers Protection Act 1994 s39(2), Lewis ILJ at 187.

[56] Australian Capital Territory Public Interest Disclosure Act 1994, s35.

[57] Author's own experience as legal advisor working on Public Concern at Work's helpline.

[58] Public Interest Disclosure (Protection of Whistleblowers) Bill 2002 (Commonwealth) s34, Queensland Whistleblowers Protection Act 1994 s55, Victoria Whistleblowers Protection Act 2001, s22, Western Australia Public Interest Disclosure Act 2003, s16, Australian Capital Territory Public Interest Disclosure Act 1994, s33, Tasmania Protected Disclosure Act 2002 s23.

- To effectively investigate the wrongdoing alleged.[59]

New Zealand has an additional exception – where the whistleblower's identity can be revealed without consent if it is in order to prevent serious risk to public health and safety or the environment.[60]

In Western Australia there are requirements for the person proposing to disclose the identity of the whistleblower to notify the whistleblower of that intention.

Information contained in protected disclosures, or which could reveal the identity of the whistleblower or the person against whom a disclosure has been made, are exempt from freedom of information laws in Western Australia, New Zealand, New South Wales, Tasmania and Victoria.[61]

## Whistleblower support and feedback

Recognising the fears whistleblowers may have in coming forward, some jurisdictions have legislated to ensure information and support are provided to the whistleblower. Under the New Zealand law, once an employee contacts the office of the ombudsman to make a disclosure, they must be provided with information about the Act, how to make a disclosure under it and the protection that it affords.[62] In the Australian Capital Territory Act and in the Commonwealth Bill, information must be provided to the whistleblower if the disclosure concerns unlawful reprisals against the whistleblower.[63] The Victorian ombudsman's guidelines suggest that authorities provide a whistleblower welfare manager to liaise with and support the whistleblower, as part of their internal procedures[64] and, like the Commonwealth Bill, that whistleblowers be provided with counselling if requested.[65]

---

[59] New South Wales Protected Disclosures Act 1994, s22, New Zealand Protected Disclosure Act 2000, s19, Western Australia Public Interest Disclosure Act 2003, s16, South Australia Whistleblowers Protection Act 1993 s7, Lewis ILJ at 186.

[60] New Zealand Protected Disclosure Act 2000, s19.

[61] Tasmania Protected Disclosure Act 2002 s 92, Victoria Whistleblowers Protection Act 2001, s109, New Zealand Protected Disclosure Act 2000 s19, Western Australia Public Interest Disclosure Act 2003, Schedule 1, New South Wales Freedom of Information Act, Schedule 1, 20(d). Also see *Purcell v Ombudsman* (2002) VCAT 842 and *Wallschutzky v Department of Education* (2002) NSWCC 52.

[62] New Zealand Protected Disclosure Act 2000, s15.

[63] Australian Capital Territory Public Interest Disclosure Act 1994, s26, Lewis ILJ at 185, Public Interest Disclosure (Protection of Whistleblowers) Bill 2002 (Cth) s27(1).

[64] Victoria Whistleblowers Protection Act 2001, ombudsman's guidelines, op cit.

[65] Public Interest Disclosure (Protection of Whistleblowers) Bill 2002 (Commonwealth) s27(1),

## Rewards

No Australasian jurisdiction offers financial rewards to whistleblowers,[66] although there have been calls by academics and regulators to introduce such incentives[67] which already exist in the US.[68]

# Exceptions and caveats

## Wrongdoing by the whistleblower

Whilst whistleblowers are provided with immunity for what they disclose (see above), this does not pertain to any involvement which the whistleblower may have had in the wrongdoing. In all jurisdictions other than South Australia, New Zealand and New South Wales, the statutes specifically state that a whistleblower's liability for his or her own conduct is unaffected by the legislation.[69]

## Legal professional privilege

New Zealand, Australian Capital Territory, Western Australian, Victorian, Tasmanian laws and the Commonwealth Bill specifically state that nothing in the legislation authorises the disclosure of information that is subject to legal professional privilege.[70] The other jurisdictions do not refer to the issue at all. However in Queensland and New South Wales an obligation of confidentiality by way of oath, rule of law or practice does not apply to disclosures under the Acts.[71] Arguably, this provision could apply to legally privileged information, in the absence of a specific preservation of that right.

---

[66] The argument was rejected by the SSCOPIW. See Lewis AJLL.

[67] See comments of K Sawyer in Wells, R, "Greater protection and anonymity urged for whistleblowers," *The Age*, 1 August 2003, see http://www.theage.com.au?text?articles/2003/07/31/1059480481158.htm and "Fels says whistleblowers should be financially rewarded," *ABC Online*, 31 July 2003, see http:/www.abc.net.au/news/justin/weekly/newsnat-31jul2003-37.htm

[68] Public Concern at Work, *The Whistleblower*, Issue 3, July 2003.

[69] Tasmania Public Interest Disclosures Act 2002, s18, Western Australia Public Interest Disclosure Act 2003, s6, Victoria Whistleblowers Protection Act 2001, s17, Australian Capital Territory Public Interest Disclosure Act 1994 s36, Public Interest Disclosure (Protection of Whistleblowers) Bill 2002 (Commonwealth) s37, Queensland Whistleblowers Protection Act 1994 s40.

[70] Tasmania Public Interest Disclosures Act 2002, s11, Western Australia Public Interest Disclosure Act 2003, s5(6), Victoria Whistleblowers Protection Act 2001, s10(2), New Zealand Protected Disclosures Act 2000, s22, Australian Capital Territory Public Interest Disclosure Act 1994 s8, Public Interest Disclosure (Protection of Whistleblowers) Bill 2002 (Cth) s10.

[71] New South Wales Protected Disclosures Act 1994 s21 and Queensland Whistleblowers Protection Act 1994, s39.

The preservation of legal professional privilege in the Australasian laws is interesting given the arguments voiced in the US and UK, following the Enron and WorldCom disasters. These arguments recognise that lawyers who know of malpractice need to fulfil both their ethical duties as officers of the court and their duties to their client.[72]

## The frivolous, malicious or reckless whistleblower

Only Queensland explicitly requires whistleblowers to have an honest belief that the information they disclose tends to show the conduct or danger alleged[73] the same as the UK's test "in good faith". In all jurisdictions except New South Wales, the whistleblower is required to have reasonable grounds for his or her belief about wrongdoing[74] and anyone who knowingly or recklessly discloses false or misleading information will commit an offence in any of the Australian jurisdictions (but merely lose protection in New Zealand).[75] Such an offence is certainly a strong disincentive to raise not only malicious concerns but also concerns that prove to be inaccurate. So there is a real risk that it will work against the public interest if the threat of prosecution means that whistleblowers decline to raise concerns where they only have a suspicion.

Under the New Zealand law, the whistleblower must wish to disclose the information so that it can be investigated and wish the disclosure to be protected.[76] In South Australia, if a whistleblower cannot determine the truth of the information it is enough that the information is of such significance to

---

[72] In the UK, Public Concern at Work is lobbying for the Public Interest Disclosure Act 1998 to be amended so that lawyers can raise concerns about privileged information if in doing so they do not breach privilege. Public Concern at Work, "In the public interest'," legal professional privilege description: response to a consultation on the legal profession by the Lord Chancellor's department, December 2002, see www.pcaw.co.uk In the US, proposed Securities and Exchange Commission regulations under the US Sarbanes-Oxley Act 2002 requiring lawyers to make a "noisy withdrawal" if their clients do not heed their concerns have caused heated debate (Qualters, S, "Proposed SEC regs may turn attorneys into whistleblowers," *Boston Business Journal*, February 2003). Consequent amendments to client confidentiality rules by the American Bar Association offer a softer approach to the issue, Ames J, "Corporate lawyers face burden as ABA raises stakes in battle to report crime," *The Law Society Gazette*, (UK) 100/31, 14 August 2003 pg 6.

[73] Queensland Whistleblowers Protection Act 1994 s14(2) and Lewis ILJ at 175.

[74] Public Interest Disclosure (Protection of Whistleblowers) Bill 2002 (Cth) s4, Queensland Whistleblowers Protection Act 1994 s14(2), Victoria Whistleblowers Protection Act 2001, s5, Western Australia Public Interest Disclosure Act 2003, s5, Australian Capital Territory Public Interest Disclosure Act 1994, s3, Tasmania Protected Disclosure Act 2002 s6, New Zealand Protected Disclosure Act 2000 s6, South Australia Whistleblowers Protection Act 1993 s5(2).

[75] Public Interest Disclosure (Protection of Whistleblowers) Bill 2002 (Cth) s35, Queensland Whistleblowers Protection Act 1994 s56, Victoria Whistleblowers Protection Act 2001, s106, Western Australia Public Interest Disclosure Act 2003, s24, Australian Capital Territory Public Interest Disclosure Act 1994, s34, Tasmania Protected Disclosure Act 2002 s87, New Zealand Protected Disclosure Act 2000 s20, South Australia Whistleblowers Protection Act 1993 s10, New South Wales Protected Disclosures Act 1994 s28.

[76] New Zealand Protected Disclosure Act 2000 s6.

warrant investigation.[77] In New South Wales, protection is lost if the disclosure was made in order to avoid disciplinary action.[78]

In New South Wales whistleblowers lose protection,[79] and under the Commonwealth Bill privilege from defamation, if the disclosure is frivolous or vexatious.[80] Under the Commonwealth Bill privilege is also lost if any of the grounds for which an authority may decline to investigate are met (see below).[81]

## Anonymous disclosures

Despite the obvious practical difficulties of protecting an unknown person, the legislation in all jurisdictions protects anonymous disclosures. The Commonwealth Bill limits the agencies to which anonymous disclosures can be made and requires the person making the anonymous disclosure to identify themselves to the head of the agency they disclose to and request confidentiality,[82] thereby making the disclosure a confidential one rather than an anonymous one.

## Case study

The difficulties with anonymous disclosures were dramatically demonstrated in Australia when in December 2001 the Australian Competition Consumer Commission (ACCC) received an anonymous letter, on green paper, about price-fixing.[83] Needing further details before it could investigate, the ACCC placed advertisements in all Australian weekend papers asking for the author of the green note, whom it thought was an oil company employee, to come forward.[84] As a result the whistleblower's husband contacted the ACCC and a short time later the ACCC received another letter with more substantial information and some documentation. However this information was still insufficient and further advertisements were placed.[85] Although the

---

[77] South Australia Whistleblowers Protection Act 1993 s5(2).

[78] New South Wales Protected Disclosures Act 1994 s18.

[79] Lewis ILJ at 175.

[80] Public Interest Disclosure (Protection of Whistleblowers) Bill 2002 (Commonwealth) s36(4).

[81] Ibid.

[82] Public Interest Disclosure (Protection of Whistleblowers) Bill 2002 s15(3).

[83] Morris, L, "Whistleblower keeps a low profile," *The Age*, 25 April 2002, see www.theage.com.au/articles/2002/04/24/1019441264055.html

[84] Ibid.

[85] Ede, C, "Mystery woman sparks inquiry," see http://www.news.com.au/common/story_page/0,4057,4195402%5E421,00.html

whistleblower did not reply, the ACCC commenced investigations into possible collusion by three multinational oil companies in setting petrol prices.[86] Presumably frustrated at the ACCC's inaction (the ACCC were unable to inform her of their decision to investigate), the whistleblower sent a copy of her second letter to a newspaper.[87] At the ACCC's request, the newspaper agreed to hold off on publishing the letter, but the ACCC had to act fast in conducting Australia's biggest corporate raid and investigation. This would usually have taken place secretly, but these events made it public.[88] One of the companies raided, Caltex, threatened legal action against the ACCC for reputational damage caused by the adverse publicity,[89] claiming that the whistleblower never existed and that their information was a hoax.[90] The investigation was finally dropped in March 2003 because of lack of evidence.[91]

If the whistleblower had felt protected and safe enough to raise concerns with a regulator like the ACCC confidentially, rather than anonymously, the outcome could have been very different. Not only would the ACCC have been able to obtain quality information from her, thereby forming a more solid basis for its decision to investigate, but also the investigation could have taken place without the publicity. The ACCC would also have been able to keep the whistleblower informed of its plans. In addition, the ACCC would have been able to defend claims that the whistleblower was a hoax having assessed whether the information came from a reliable source. If the whistleblower wrote the green letter because she wanted something done, she largely failed because of her anonymity. With the right legislative safeguards, the ACCC would have been able to do its job and, as it was in their interests to do, keep the whistleblower's identity confidential.

## Dealing with the message

Whistleblowing achieves little if it is not a means to address wrongdoing, as

- People generally raise concerns in order for something to be done;[92]

---

[86] Ede, C, "Mystery woman sparks inquiry," see http://www.news.com.au/common/story_page/0,4057,4195402%5E421,00.html

[87] Ibid.

[88] "ACCC drops petrol price fixing probe," *Australian Associated Press*, 28 March 2003, see http://news.ninemsn.com.au/Business/story_47131.asp

[89] Moore A, "Lessons from HIH," transcript of interview with Dick Warburton, Chairman of Caltex, *Business Sunday*, 20 April 2003, see http://sgp1.paddington.ninemsn.com.au/businesssunday/Interviews/stories/story_1830.asp

[90] Epstein R, "Caltex begins court action against ACCC," *ABC Online*, 15 November 2002, see http://www.abc.net.au/am/s727362.htm

[91] Bachelard, M, Crawford B and Marris S, "ACCC petrol backdown," *The Sunday Mail*, (Queensland), 29 March 2003.

[92] Author's own experience as legal advisor working on Public Concern at Work's helpline.

- People decline to blow the whistle because they lack trust in authorities to "do the right thing" with their allegations;[93] and

- Whistleblowers feel aggrieved by authorities that fail to conduct adequate and timely investigations into their claims.[94]

Several Australian legislatures have sought to mandate and regulate investigations into the suspected wrongdoing disclosed and evaluate the way concerns are investigated and remedied.

## Duty to investigate

There are two approaches taken by the jurisdictions to the issue of investigation (discounting South Australia where the issue of investigation is not mentioned). In Queensland, New South Wales and New Zealand there is no express duty to investigate, but it is implied within the respective legislative frameworks that an authority will do so once notified of suspected wrongdoing. In these jurisdictions (as in the UK and South Africa) normal principles of accountability are relied upon. If an investigation is not commenced within the specified time, in New South Wales the whistleblower can go to the media or to an MP[95] and in New Zealand the whistleblower can go to a Minister of the Crown or, if the malpractice relates to the public sector, the ombudsman.[96]

Legislation in Western Australia, Victoria, Tasmania, Australian Capital Territory and proposed in the Commonwealth Bill, imposes on authorities a duty to investigate whistleblower concerns[97] but with the right to decline to investigate in certain circumstances. In these jurisdictions, and also in New South Wales, where there is no such duty, authorities can decline to investigate if it is determined that the disclosure was frivolous or vexatious.[98] In the

---

[93] De Maria, W, "Unshielding the Shadow Culture," *Queensland Whistleblower Study Result Release One*, the University of Queensland, April 1994.

[94] De Maria (2002) op cit at 15 refers to research by Gorta & Forell, "Layers of decision: linking social definitions of corruption and willingness to take action," *Crime Law & Social Change*, 23 315-343, 1995 and Zipparo, L, "Factors which deter public officials from reporting corruption," *Crime Law & Social Change*, 30, 273-287, 1999.

[95] New South Wales Protected Disclosures Act 1994 s19.

[96] New Zealand Protected Disclosure Act 2000 s10.

[97] Public Interest Disclosure (Protection of Whistleblowers) Bill 2002 (Commonwealth) s18, Victoria Whistleblowers Protection Act 2001, s39, 72, 84, Western Australia Public Interest Disclosure Act 2003, s8, Australian Capital Territory Public Interest Disclosure Act 1994, s19, Tasmania Protected Disclosure Act 2002 ss39, 63.

[98] Public Interest Disclosure (Protection of Whistleblowers) Bill 2002 (Commonwealth) s18, Victoria Whistleblowers Protection Act 2001, s40, Western Australia Public Interest Disclosure Act 2003, s8, Australian Capital Territory Public Interest Disclosure Act 1994, s17, Tasmania Protected Disclosure Act 2002 s40, 64, New South Wales Protected Disclosures Act 1994 s16.

Commonwealth Bill and in Western Australian, Tasmanian and Victorian legislation an investigation into a public interest disclosure may also be declined
if the disclosure:

- Is trivial;

- Is misconceived or lacking in substance;

- Has already been adequately dealt with; or

- Concerns an issue, which has been determined by a court or tribunal.[99]

An authority may decline to investigate the concern if, under the Australian Capital Territory's legislation, the whistleblower remains anonymous[100]
and under the Tasmanian and Victorian Acts, the whistleblower had known
of the disclosure for more than 12 months and cannot give a satisfactory
explanation for the delay in making the disclosure.[101]

All jurisdictions, except South Australia, minimise the risk inherent in
prescribing a limited number of recipients for the disclosure by specifically
allowing authorities receiving disclosures to refer that disclosure to another
authority, if more appropriate.[102]

## Checks, balances and feedback

Legislating for the investigation of whistleblower concerns requires a balancing of the public interest in the detection of wrongdoing and ensuring proper
allocation of public resources.

South Australian and Western Australian whistleblowers lose protection
for their disclosures if they refuse, without reasonable excuse, to assist with
an investigation into their disclosure.[103]

Under the Victorian and Tasmanian legislation, which is explained below, it is an offence to:

- Obstruct, hinder, resist or obstruct the ombudsman in relation to the
  exercise of his powers;

---

[99] Public Interest Disclosure (Protection of Whistleblowers) Bill 2002 s18, Tasmania Protected Disclosure Act 2002 ss40, 64. Victoria Whistleblowers Protection Act 2001 s40, Western Australia Public Interest Disclosure Act 2003 s8.

[100] Lewis op cit at 186. Australian Capital Territory Public Interest Disclosure Act 1994, s16.

[101] Tasmania Protected Disclosure Act 2002 ss40, 64(d), Victoria Whistleblowers Protection Act 2001 s40(1)(b).

[102] Public Interest Disclosure (Protection of Whistleblowers) Bill 2002 (Commonwealth) s20, Queensland Whistleblowers Protection Act 1994 s 28, Victoria Whistleblowers Protection Act 2001,ss41-44, 96, Australian Capital Territory Public Interest Disclosure Act 1994, ss18, 20, Tasmania Protected Disclosure Act 2002, ss41, 42, 78, New South Wales Protected Disclosures Act 1994, ss25, 26, Western Australia Public Interest Disclosure Act 2003 s9, New Zealand Protected Disclosure Act 2000 s16.

[103] South Australia Whistleblower Protection Act 1993, s6, Western Australia Public Interest Disclosure Act 2003 s17.

- Refuse to comply with a lawful requirement of the ombudsman without a lawful excuse; or

- Give false or misleading information to the ombudsman during an investigation.[104]

Australian legislatures (not New Zealand) have required authorities (in the Commonwealth and Australian Capital Territory on the request of the whistleblower) receiving disclosures to give feedback to the whistleblower by notifying him or her of:

- A decision not to investigate the issue;

- A decision to refer the matter to another body to investigate; or

- The outcome of any investigation which took place.[105]

## Tasmania and Victoria – investigating the 'public interest'

Tasmania and Victoria have adopted a unique two-tiered approach to the investigation of concerns, which seeks to ensure that public resources are spent on investigating public interest concerns and not private grievances. Once there has been a protected disclosure, the body receiving the disclosure (either the ombudsman itself or the public body) must determine whether the disclosure is a public interest disclosure.[106] Decisions must be made within specified time limits[107] and the whistleblower has a right to have the decision reviewed by the ombudsman,[108] or to make a complaint about the ombudsman under legislation pertaining to ombudsman powers and standards.[109] If either the review or the complaint is successful, and it is held to be a public interest disclosure, the ombudsman must investigate it or refer the matter back to the public body, or to another appropriate body for them to investigate.[110]

---

[104] Tasmania Protected Disclosure Act 2002 s54, Victoria Whistleblowers Protection Act 2001 s60.

[105] Public Interest Disclosure (Protection of Whistleblowers) Bill 2002 (Commonwealth) s23, Queensland Whistleblowers Protection Act 1994 s32, Victoria Whistleblowers Protection Act 2001, s67, 95, Australian Capital Territory Public Interest Disclosure Act 1994, s23 Tasmania Protected Disclosure Act 2002, s59, 77, New South Wales Protected Disclosures Act 1994, s27, Western Australia Public Interest Disclosure Act 2003 s10, South Australia Whistleblowers Protection Act 1993 s8.

[106] Tasmania Protected Disclosure Act 2002 ss30, 33, 79, Victoria Whistleblowers Protection Act 2001 ss24, 28, 33, 97.

[107] Tasmania Protected Disclosure Act 2002 ss31, 34, 35, 80, Victoria Whistleblowers Protection Act 2001 ss25, 27, 29, 30, 34, 35, 98.

[108] Tasmania Protected Disclosure Act 2002 ss35-37, Victoria Whistleblowers Protection Act 2001 ss30-32, 34, 35.

[109] Tasmania Protected Disclosure Act 2002 ss32, Victoria Whistleblowers Protection Act 2001 ss27.

[110] Tasmania Protected Disclosure Act 2002 ss37-39, 41, 42, Victoria Whistleblowers Protection Act 2001 ss37, 39, 41 – 44.

The ombudsman's powers of investigation, the evidentiary rules to which s/he must adhere and the manner in which s/he must report the findings of completed investigations are detailed in the legislation.[111]

## Oversight and response to investigations

In all jurisdictions it is usual for public authorities to report to a functionary such as an ombudsman who oversees its investigation or decision not to investigate. Under the Commonwealth Bill and Victorian, Tasmanian, Australian Capital Territory and Western Australian laws, if an investigation shows that the wrongdoing disclosed was taking place, the authority in question is required to take appropriate steps to prevent the conduct from recurring and to remedy any harm.[112] These steps typically include referring the matter to a higher authority or taking disciplinary action against the person involved in the misconduct. In Victoria and Tasmania, the ombudsman must also report to parliament if he feels that the authority has taken insufficient steps in response to his recommendations.[113]

## Monitoring

In all jurisdictions other than New South Wales and South Australia, annual reports to parliament about the number, content and investigation of disclosures are required.[114] New Zealand and Western Australia require the legislation to be reviewed by a minister, within two and three years respectively of the introduction of the Act and the review must be reported to parliament.[115] In New South Wales a parliamentary committee must review the Act every two years,[116] however unfortunately these reviews are not available on the Internet.

---

[111] Tasmania Protected Disclosure Act 2002 Part 6, Division 3 and s56, 71, Victoria Whistleblowers Protection Act 2001 Division 3 and s63.

[112] Tasmania Protected Disclosure Act 2002 s75, Victoria Whistleblowers Protection Act 2001 s81, Public Interest Disclosure (Protection of Whistleblowers) Bill 2002 (Commonwealth) s22, Australian Capital Territory Public Interest Disclosure Act 1994, s22, Western Australia Public Interest Disclosure Act 2003 s9.

[113] Tasmania Protected Disclosure Act 2002 s58, Victoria Whistleblowers Protection Act 2001 s66.

[114] Public Interest Disclosure (Protection of Whistleblowers) Bill 2002 (Commonwealth) 13, Queensland Whistleblowers Protection Act 1994 ss30, 31, Victoria Whistleblowers Protection Act 2001,ss102, 104, Australian Capital Territory Public Interest Disclosure Act 1994, s11, Tasmania Protected Disclosure Act 2002, ss84, 86, Western Australia Public Interest Disclosure Act 2003 s22, New Zealand Protected Disclosure Act 2000 s16.

[115] New Zealand Protected Disclosure Act 2000 s24, Western Australia Public Interest Disclosure Act 2003, s27.

[116] New South Wales Protected Disclosures Act 1994, s32.

# Remedies and sanctions

Whilst the legislation provides that whistleblowers cannot be sued for raising concerns, many potential whistleblowers will be more worried about their personal position, typically that they might lose their job.

## Reprisals against the whistleblower

With the exception of New Zealand and South Australia, all jurisdictions make it a criminal offence to take reprisals against a whistleblower.[117] In New Zealand, a whistleblower will have a right to take a grievance under relevant employment law or to seek redress under the Human Rights Act.[118] In South Australia and Western Australia, actions can be taken under equal opportunity legislation[119].

All jurisdictions other than New South Wales and New Zealand attempt to prevent reprisals by making it a tort and providing actions in damages to whistleblowers.[120] Whistleblowers can seek injunctive relief against reprisals in all jurisdictions except New Zealand, South Australia, Western Australia and New South Wales[121] with some jurisdictions enabling whistleblowers to seek injunctions through state agencies who may be required to provide undertakings as to costs on behalf of the whistleblower.[122]

In Australian jurisdictions the types of detrimental action proscribed includes actions causing:

*   Injury;
*   Loss or damage;

---

[117] Public Interest Disclosure (Protection of Whistleblowers) Bill 2002 (Cth) s26, Queensland Whistleblowers Protection Act 1994 s42, Victoria Whistleblowers Protection Act 2001, s18, Australian Capital Territory Public Interest Disclosure Act 1994, s25, Tasmania Protected Disclosure Act 2002, s19, Western Australia Public Interest Disclosure Act 2003 s14, New South Wales Protected Disclosures Act 1994, s20.

[118] New Zealand Protected Disclosure Act 2000 ss17, 25.

[119] Western Australia Public Interest Disclosure Act 2003 s15(4), South Australia Whistleblower Protection Act 1993, s9.

[120] Public Interest Disclosure (Protection of Whistleblowers) Bill 2002 (Commonwealth) s30, Queensland Whistleblowers Protection Act 1994 s43, Victoria Whistleblowers Protection Act 2001, s19, Australian Capital Territory Public Interest Disclosure Act 1994, s29, Tasmania Protected Disclosure Act 2002, s20, Western Australia Public Interest Disclosure Act 2003 s15(1)(2), South Australia Whistleblower Protection Act 1993 s9(2).

[121] Public Interest Disclosure (Protection of Whistleblowers) Bill 2002 (Commonwealth) s32, Queensland Whistleblowers Protection Act 1994 ss47-49, 52, Victoria Whistleblowers Protection Act 2001, ss20, 21, Australian Capital Territory Public Interest Disclosure Act 1994, ss30, 31 Tasmania Protected Disclosure Act 2002, ss21, 22.

[122] Public Interest Disclosure (Protection of Whistleblowers) Bill 2002 (Commonwealth) ss32, 33, Australian Capital Territory Public Interest Disclosure Act 1994 s32, Queensland Whistleblowers Protection Act 1994, s54.

- Intimidation or harassment and discrimination; and

- Disadvantage or adverse treatment in relation to a person's employment, career, profession, trade or business, including disciplinary action.[123]

The Queensland law also includes threats of detriment and financial loss from detriment,[124] whereas the South Australia law includes the threat of reprisal.[125] In New Zealand, a reprisal is anything amounting to a personal grievance under employment law.[126]

Public service employees under the Commonwealth Bill and the Australian Capital Territory and Queensland laws can apply to be relocated if there is a danger of reprisals and it is seen as the only practical way of removing or substantially removing the danger. Relocation is prohibited without the whistleblower's consent.[127]

## Evaluation and assessment

### Awareness, case law and prosecutions

The practical success of the Australasian whistleblowing schemes is a series of unanswered questions. Sawyer states that there has not been a single prosecution (for either victimisation of a whistleblower, the revealing of confidential information relating to a whistleblower or a disclosure, or for a false, misleading or reckless disclosure) under any Australian whistleblowing act and the author's own research supports this finding.[128] Sawyer extrapolates from this that whistleblowers are not using the legislation because it is never enforced.[129] The possible reasons for this are infinite. Is it that the threat of criminal sanctions is working as a sufficient deterrent to victimising

---

[123] Public Interest Disclosure (Protection of Whistleblowers) Bill 2002 (Commonwealth) s4, Queensland Whistleblowers Protection Act 1994 schedule 5, Victoria Whistleblowers Protection Act 2001, s18(2), Australian Capital Territory Public Interest Disclosure Act 1994, s3, Tasmania Protected Disclosure Act 2002, s19(2), Western Australia Public Interest Disclosure Act 2003 s3, South Australia Whistleblower Protection Act 1993 s9(4).

[124] Queensland Whistleblowers Protection Act 1994 schedule 5, definition of detriment.

[125] South Australia Whistleblower Protection Act 1993 s9(4)(d).

[126] New Zealand Protected Disclosure Act 2000 s17.

[127] Lewis op cit at 188 and Public Interest Disclosure (Protection of Whistleblowers) Bill 2002 (Commonwealth) s28, Australian Capital Territory Public Interest Disclosure Act 1994, s27, Queensland Whistleblowers Protection Act 1994, s46.

[128] The author would like to thank Jason Quah and Dianne Donati of Corrs Chambers Westgarth Lawyers Australia for their valuable assistance in researching whistleblowing case law.

[129] Sawyer, K, "Lets Encourage Whistleblowers," *The Age*, January 13 2003, see www.theage.com.au/articles/2003/01/12/1041990177705.html

whistleblowers? Is it that there is a lack of awareness of, or trust in, the legislation among prospective whistleblowers? Perhaps whistleblowers are not using the legislation because they are afraid that they will go to jail if their suspicion of wrongdoing turns out to be false?

Although there are some indications that the legislation has encouraged people to speak up, as yet the number of disclosures remains low[130] and media reports certainly do not indicate that the legislation has worked well.

Although there have been no prosecutions, there is a limited amount of case law deriving from the whistleblowing statutes. The author was able to isolate seven such cases. Two of these cases were ill brought with the relevant courts stating that one plaintiff was not a whistleblower[131] and the other was vexatious.[132] One case involved a defamation defendant attempting to use the whistleblowing law as a defence – it was held that the defamatory statement was not a public interest disclosure.[133] The other four cases involved whistleblowers who were taking actions against their employers for reprisals. In two of those cases, both of which provide a good analysis of the relevant laws, it was held that the employees were not dismissed because of their protected disclosures.[134] The other two cases focused on whether the whistleblowers' employers could be held vicariously liable for reprisals from colleagues.[135]

For a more complete analysis of case law, the relevant decisions of lower courts and tribunals in Australia and New Zealand should be researched. In addition, research as to the levels of awareness of the legislation, and into why tort actions and prosecutions are not being pursued, is essential and preferably should take place before further legislation is enacted.

## National whistleblowing scheme – future development?

The Australian approach has been criticised for being too "fragmented and diverse".[136] There have been calls for a national whistleblowing act to cover all Australian jurisdictions and the introduction of an independent national

---

[130] See comments by Rosemary Barker, Protected Disclosure Co-ordinator within the Victorian Department of Human Services in Roberts, C, op cit.

[131] *Pelechowski v NSW Land and Housing Corp* (1999) FCA 1110.

[132] *King v SA Psychological Board* (1998) SASC 6621 and related case *Sutton and Anor v State of South Australia* (unreported), Supreme Court of South Australia, BC9605980, 2 December 1996.

[133] *Morgan v Mallard* No SCCIV-00-970 (2001) SASC 364.

[134] *Berry v Ryan* (2001) ACTSC 11 and *Education Queensland v Vidler* (2000) QIRComm 52.

[135] *Howard v State of Queensland* (2000) QCA 223, *Reeves-Board v Queensland University of Technology* (2001) QSC 314.

[136] Sawyer K, op cit 13 January 2003.

public interest disclosure agency to receive and investigate disclosures.[137] In 2002, De Maria argued: "An independent authority with disclosure reception, investigatory and educative powers is vital because it … gives the statute a clear stand alone identity by encasing it in an administrative home."[138]

The Victorian, Tasmanian and Western Australian laws have gone some way to meeting this goal, giving responsibility for monitoring and promoting the legislation to the independent bodies, the ombudsmen and the Commissioner for Public Sector Standards respectively. Such responsibility includes receiving and investigating concerns and establishing guidelines for public authorities within the auspices of the Acts. In Western Australia, the Commissioner is also required to establish a code setting out the minimum standards of conduct and integrity of those who may receive disclosures.

These bodies have some advantages over a newly constituted authority in that, apart from the absence of set-up costs, they have existing expertise and resources to investigate concerns, including politically sensitive concerns. These bodies are respected by government and other senior players and can refer investigations to public authorities and regulators, thus reinforcing accountability and overseeing it. However, their ability and suitability to deal with concerns from the private sector is unclear. Whether potential whistleblowers have sufficient confidence in these bodies is yet to be seen and the schemes would benefit from research on this point.

Whilst some whistleblowers might have more confidence in a newly formed public interest agency, many others may question not only its independence but its virtue. Such an agency calls into question the role of the media in the whistleblowing scheme and also risks undermining normal lines of accountability and duplicating the role of existing bodies. In the light of the practical experience of Australian whistleblowers of state bodies described above, there are real questions whether a new state agency will add to the problem rather than provide a solution to it.

## Why look to Australasia for guidance on whistleblowing?

One reason for considering Australasia's approach to whistleblowing is that, in a sense, it is a ready-made comparative law study. The eight legislatures have introduced different regimes to address the same issues and within eight

---

[137] Sawyer K, op cit, De Maria, (2002), op cit at 13, Lewis AJLL.

[138] De Maria, W, (2002) op cit at 13.

jurisdictions of substantially the same culture. New Zealand has a different approach again for what some would argue is not an extremely different culture. Not only is the legislation in each jurisdiction different, but each has attempted to progress and improve by building on the experience of the others. This is particularly demonstrated in the way issues such as the investigation and monitoring of whistleblower concerns have been integrated. Unfortunately, many of the states have copied each other's mistakes and ignored some of the best of the early laws (for example South Australia's extension of the law to the private sector and New South Wales inclusion of media disclosures).

There is plenty of whistleblowing activity in the pipeline in Australasia as future developments include:

- The proposed passage of the Commonwealth Bill;

- Production of guidelines from the Western Australia and Tasmania Commissioner and ombudsman respectively;

- Biennial reviews of the New Zealand and New South Wales Acts;

- Likely introduction of whistleblowing legislation in the Northern Territory; and

- Application of corporate governance regulations relating to whistleblowing in the private sector.

These developments should bring fresh debate and increase awareness of the importance and value of whistleblowing as a means to a more accountable culture. However research should sensibly be undertaken into how these array of schemes work individually and collectively, not only to encourage and protect whistleblowers but so as to deter and deal with malpractice.

In Australia, anti-authoritarianism has been romanticised since the days of the Eureka Stockade and through national heroes such as Ned Kelly. Mateship, and hence loyalty, is among the highest of "aussie values" and the default is to give whistleblowers and wrongdoers alike a "fair go". In this culture there is no doubt that whistleblowing is a challenging phenomenon. This challenge is balanced with Australia's knowledge that in order to be considered a real player in the developed world, as it is so desperate to be, nothing less than good governance in both private and public sectors will do. Unfortunately, the Commonwealth government's hesitancy to pass whistleblowing legislation, the illogical limitation that legislation is limited to the public sector and the absence of a protected avenue to bring serious concerns or cover-ups to the attention of the public means that Australia is missing a trick.

# THE SOUTH AFRICAN EXPERIENCE

*By Mukelani Dimba, Lorraine Stober and Bill Thomson*

Whistles were only blown on sports fields – sports fields that were designated white and black. This was a segregation that extended to all spheres of life in South Africa, dictating where people could live, play, relax, worship, study and even work. The apartheid system had engineered a society that ensured white domination over black, where the white minority elite benefited substantially at great cost to the black majority and to society as a whole. Part of the apartheid government's apparatus of repression included the development of a sophisticated spy network, successfully infiltrating every sector of society. The "mass democratic movement" was a main target. Communities, trade unions, NGOs and individuals were watched closely, and a culture formed where people did not know who could and could not be trusted.

In recent years allegations of apartheid era spies have increasingly surfaced, fingering once trusted human rights lawyers, academics and other respected members of society. Fellow workers, students, union officials, neighbours and even family members fell prey to the monetary rewards dangled in front of them by apartheid officials. Against a backdrop of poverty and high unemployment, some of the "carrots" were just too enticing to resist. Fear of being watched and reported on dominated every meeting and gathering, rooms were bugged and telephones tapped, not only by the sophisticated spy network of the ruling regime, but also by private sector business, as no stone was left unturned to ensure that any challenge to the "system" was stopped in its tracks.

People who reported on others were referred to as *impimpis* and if caught or even suspected of informing faced an often gruesome public death in front of other members of their society, as an example of behaviour that would not be tolerated. Given the *impimpi* era and childhood lessons that it is not good to "tell tales", research has showed that one of the key obstacles in the fight against corruption is the reluctance of individuals to "speak out" against corrupt activities.

In addition to the abuse of public power, South Africa's private sector was notoriously unaccountable and prone to abuse. Moreover, following a period of extreme oppression from the 1960s onwards, the national government spent the 1970s "wooing" the private business sector to collaborate with it in maintaining the apartheid system. Except for a few dissenting voices, big business largely worked with the government. Many corporations were only too willing to take advantage of the many opportunities that the oppressive apartheid legislation presented them to advance themselves at the expense of black workers.

It is against this historical backdrop that the period of wholesale transformation began in 1994 when South Africa's first democratic elections were held. It was clear from the early stages of negotiations that preceded the founding election that transition to a "New South Africa" was not going to be a half-baked affair but a comprehensive overhaul of the governance system. History had shown how the secrecy that permeated operations of organs of state had fanned the abuse of human rights of a major part of the population. It is the same secrecy and lack of accountability that allowed malpractice and corruption to thrive in the public service, more especially in the former Bantustans.[1]

Accordingly, the Interim Constitution that was negotiated prior to the 1994 election enshrined an aspiration to a "democracy which empowers the people to participate in their governance, and which requires government to account to them for its decisions", a constitution that aspired to an "open and democratic society".[2] Shortly after the historical elections of 1994 and the appointment of Nelson Mandela as head of state, the then Deputy President, Thabo Mbeki, convened a team of senior government officials, academics and administrative law experts to conduct research and make proposals for legislation that would ensure that the government does deliver on the promise of openness, as envisaged in the Interim Constitution.

In 1995 the Task Group on Open Democracy submitted its policy proposals for an Open Democracy Act, where they stated that the Act would:

*recognise that [government] officials' willingness to speak out against corruption, lawbreaking or maladministration in their departments is indispensable to accountable government and efficient administration.[3]*

A protracted process then ensued, and the final draft Bill was finally published in the *Government Gazette* only in October 1997. Among its stated objectives was to:

*provide for the protection of persons disclosing evidence of contraventions of the*

---

[1] Former self-governing territories of black people which were demarcated on an ethnic and tribal basis.

[2] Section 35(1) of the Interim Constitution.

[3] Task Group on Open Democracy, (1995), *Open Democracy Act for South Africa: Policy Proposals*. (Unpublished document.)

*law, serious maladministration or corruption in governmental bodies; and to provide for matters connected therewith.*

The whistleblower protection section of the Bill provided protection to whistleblowers who made "disclosures in good faith about evidence of contravention of the law, corruption, dishonesty and serious maladministration in organs of state or by government officials".[4] However such protection could only be guaranteed if the disclosure was made to the institutions prescribed in the law such as parliamentary committees and committees of provincial legislatures, the Public Protector, the Human Rights Commission, the Auditor-General and the Attorney-General.[5] The whistleblowers would also enjoy protection in terms of the law if they made a disclosure to the media under special circumstances.

The glaring flaw in the Bill was that it only applied to the public sector and therefore could not offer the same protection to potential whistleblowers in the private sector. This exclusion of the private sector from the application of the provisions of the Bill had all the makings of a fatal flaw in drafting when one considers that corruption is not only a public sector issue, but also an issue that affects the private sector. By their nature corruption and malpractice involve a "two-way street" which is characterised, in their common manifestation, by government or public officials who willingly accept inducements to favourably consider companies in the private sector for government contracts or projects.

There is also a need for the private sector to accept some duty to be accountable to all its stakeholders for the decisions it takes, especially if such decisions will affect people in the external environment. This is even more important as a number of private organisations and companies, as a result of corporatisation, privatisation and outsourcing of public services and assets, have come to exercise power and carry out functions that traditionally fell within the responsibility of the state. This analysis of power relations in post-apartheid South Africa prompted NGOs to start to call for the whistleblowing provisions of the Open Democracy Bill to be extended to the private sector.

The Bill was finally tabled in parliament in July 1998, when a public consultation process also began. Public submissions were received, including that of the Open Democracy Campaign Group, which comprised ten leading NGOs. The campaign group argued that the scope of the whistleblower protection section of the bill needed to include the private sector.

---

4   Section 63(1)(a) of The Open Democracy Bill. 18 October 1997. *Government Gazette* No. 18381. Pretoria.

5   In the South African legal system the function of the Attorney-General is performed by the National Director of Public Prosecutions.

The NGOs' call got an important shot in the arm when the delegates to the 1998 National Anti-Corruption Summit – a multi-sectoral formation comprising business, faith organisations, NGOs, community-based organisations, donors, political parties, academic institutions, the media, labour and government – recognised the efficacy of whistleblowing in combating corruption in the public and private sectors. The Summit captured this spirit in a resolution passed at the end of the deliberations:

> *We therefore resolve to implement the following resolution as the basis of a national strategy to fight corruption: To support the speedy enactment of the Open Democracy Bill[6] to foster greater transparency, whistleblowing and accountability in* all *sectors (emphasis added).*

The same sentiment was repeated in Mbeki's first address to parliament as the newly elected president succeeding Nelson Mandela. Mbeki spoke extensively about the need for a partnership between the government and the people to fight corruption. He also reiterated his government's commitment "to honest, transparent and accountable government and our determination to act against anybody who transgresses these norms".[7] It was in the same address that Mbeki undertook to ensure that the Open Democracy Bill was passed and that there was speedy movement "to ensure the implementation of the provisions relating to the protection of whistleblowers".

Meanwhile, lobbying and advocacy by members of civil society gained momentum. The Institute for Security Studies (ISS) organised a number of seminars on the practical implications and potential effects of the proposed legislation. The ISS – whose work was led by Lala Camerer – made a number of recommendations not only with regard to the technical aspects of whistleblower protection in the Bill but also on conceptual issues around the section itself. Key among its proposals was that the whistleblower protection section should be removed from the legislation dealing with freedom of information and be made separate legislation. The ISS argued that this action would result in whistleblower protection becoming more visible.

The ISS also proposed that the committee look at other legislation and proposals in other jurisdictions that may be relevant to the South African situation, for example the British law, the Public Interest Disclosure Act of 1998. It also supported the call that the whistleblower protection provisions of the Bill should also apply to the private sector.

---

[6] Predecessor of the Promotion of Access to Information Bill and the Protected Disclosures Bill.

[7] Mbeki. T. *Address of the President of the Republic of South Africa, at the Opening of Parliament,* National Assembly, Cape Town, 25 June 1999, see http://www.polity.org.za/html/govdocs/speeches/1999/sp0625.html

In October 1999 the Chairperson of the Justice Committee, Advocate Johnny de Lange, was introduced to Guy Dehn, the Executive Director of the London-based NGO, Public Concern at Work. Dehn was on a visit to South Africa to speak about the work of his organisation. De Lange was interested in the conceptual approach of the British law and soon after he offered the first indication that his committee would re-write the whistleblower protection section of the Bill. He also triggered agreement in the committee that the UK law would be used as the central model when the committee deliberated on the redrafting. As in the UK law, the committee also agreed that the whistleblower protection sections of the Bill should be extended to include the private sector.

In the meantime an initial new whistleblower protection Bill was drafted by Richard Calland of the Institute for Democracy in South Africa (Idasa) and Lala Camerer of ISS, at the invitation of the ANC grouping on the justice committee. Their draft was the basis for the subsequent South African law. It borrowed from the concept behind the British Public Interest Disclosure Act, but sought to adapt it to South African law and society.

Using this draft, the committee then developed a second draft for public comment and deliberation. Even though in terms of the new draft the Act would apply to the private sector as well, one of the major criticisms about the draft was that it only applied to the employer/employee relationship. Calland argued in a later submission to the committee that this limitation would serve to remove from protection a whole range of potential bona fide whistleblowers who should be protected. He cited a number of examples:

- A retired parson who regularly visits a local prison becomes aware of information that the chief warden is responsible for a drug-running scheme in the prison. As a result of disclosing this information, the parson is denied access to the prison or his access is made more difficult by the creation of interminable delays. Damages awarded for the inconvenience would be minimal: this points to the need for a new delict;

- A prisoner makes a disclosure that the prison warders in his section are sexually abusing inmates. Since reports of the prisoner's good behaviour are important for provisions like parole, a prisoner who "blows the whistle" could be easily prejudiced;

- A medical scientist working in a state research agency becomes aware that free vaccinations being given to children are ineffective. Nevertheless having acquired the vaccine at a cheap price and received great publicity for promoting free primary health, the ministry insists on continuing the use of the vaccine. Having raised the issue internally and being met with resistance from the head of the organisation, s/he is unable to operate in this work environment and subsequently resigns over the issue. The head of the institute also happens to be in charge of an academic journal and obstructs publication of the researcher's findings;

- A student conducting cancer treatment tests suspects that his supervisor may be tampering with the results. Disclosing this could affect the student's scholarship application to an overseas university that relies on a positive reference from his supervisor;

- A person applying for a taxi permit becomes aware of corruption in the licensing department. He discloses this information and thereafter finds his application delayed/rejected. He might possibly have a remedy in administrative law to overturn the decision to reject his application. However what heat would the bureaucrat feel without an appropriate civil or criminal sanction?

- A pensioner reports a corrupt bureaucrat in the post office. She suffers detriment when her pension is withheld or delayed by the bureaucrat. The remedy she would have access to is the right to interdict the post office for not giving her pension timeously.

- An individual leaves his/her employment since s/he is unhappy with the way in which ethical issues are dealt with and later comes to apply for a job, a benefit or a contract. S/he suffers detriment because it is not granted since it is known that he or she is a "dangerous trouble maker who blows the whistle".

- A doctor or dentist blows the whistle on corrupt practices either in the department of health over, say, registration practices or on a private pharmaceutical company that is offering kickbacks to medical practitioners who accept and use out of date drugs. He is subsequently marginalised by all the drug suppliers, and can't serve his community.

Despite indications that the ANC component of the committee was sympathetic to this argument, particularly in the light of high unemployment in South Africa (around 40%), the Bill was not amended to included non-employees. However, the committee resolved to invite the South African Law Commission to explore the possibilities and appropriateness of extending the reach of the law.

The Protected Disclosures Act was finally passed by Parliament in mid 2000. The Act offers an alternative to remaining silent by making provision for procedures in terms of which employees in both the public and the private sector who disclose information of unlawful or corrupt conduct by their employers or fellow employees are protected from "occupational detriment". The law sought to encourage honest employees to raise their concerns and report wrongdoing within the workplace without fear. The Act also encourages organisations to put structures in place to enable whistleblowing and, in seeking to protect whistleblowers against any occupational detriment, prescribes the route to follow in the event of a disclosure. While providing organisations and employees with the necessary legal mechanisms to combat fraud, the Act also entrenches the obligation of employers to protect whistleblowers.

The Protected Disclosures Act has its flaws though. The original reservations made by Calland during the Bill's drafting stage that it only applied to employers and employees has proved to be a major shortcoming. Representations have subsequently been made to the South African Law Reform Commission to widen the ambit of the Act to include a wider category of people, including contractors.

Another concern about the Act is the lack of protection that it affords whistleblowers who lose their jobs as a result of their whistleblowing. Where an employee has been dismissed and has qualified for protection in terms of the Act, the compensation is limited to 24 months salary. This is a small amount when considering the "other costs" of whistleblowing to the employee, which can often include protracted and expensive legal proceedings, negative perceptions of the whistleblower by the community and potential employers, not to mention the cost to personal and family life.

Given the tendency in South Africa for one or two large companies to dominate any sector of the economy, many whistleblowers in South Africa have a limited number of companies they can work for. This means that blowing the whistle may mean not working in a particular sector again. Other employment will then be on a significantly more junior level, resulting in loss of earnings over many years. Whistleblowers in the UK under the Public Interest Disclosures Act are able to secure higher settlements in the event of losing their jobs. The attraction of using the Act is also reduced by the existence of "victimisation" as a familiar, pre-existing unfair labour practice. The introduction of the Act did not extend the possible compensation already available under this heading, which has resulted in whistleblowing being treated as similar, or the same as, victimisation.

A major initiative to comply with good governance has come from the public sector. Under the direction of the Public Service Commission, an independent body created by the Constitution to enhance excellence in governance in the public service, workshops took place nationally to train officials on the legislation and to get their input on how best to implement it. Employees at the workshops said that while they were aware of a number of cases of fraud and corruption taking place in the public service, they were too scared to blow the whistle for fear of becoming victims of what the Act referred to as "occupational detriment". Identifying the crime was one thing; blowing the whistle another and their fear of reporting the corruption extended way beyond the workplace, to the protection of their property, their families and their own lives.

This was the experience of Alice Daniels[8] who lives in a large rural town and who noticed that hospital linen and food were being stolen. She was also aware of how it was done and by whom. She telephoned ODAC's helpline and was advised of her rights and obligations in terms of the Protected Disclosures Act and was also advised of the structures within the hospital and the Department of Health with whom she could raise her concerns. She was also advised of a regulatory authority outside the medical environment. She chose not to raise her concerns as in addition to the fear of losing her job she was greatly concerned about her and her family's safety if it was suspected that she blew the whistle.

A number of whistleblowers in South Africa recently have lost their jobs, in spite of often lengthy and costly legal proceedings. With already high levels of unemployment and poverty, risking jobs that are like gold takes a very particular and committed individual. This was the case of Ben Small who worked as a manager at a large organisation. Ben observed that the general manager was responsible for financial irregularities and nepotism. He raised it with his line manager who told him to take it up with the board of directors, which he did. Soon after this he was suspended and charged with misconduct in that, amongst other things, he used the company's resources to access pornography. He applied to the Labour Court for an interim interdict of the disciplinary hearing. Ben argued that he did access pornography but so did many of his colleagues against whom no disciplinary action was taken. He said that the action taken against him was as a result of his blowing the whistle. The interim interdict was granted pending a conciliation hearing at a labour tribunal. This was held and Ben was re-instated only to be slapped with more misconduct charges shortly after his return to work. He was dismissed after a disciplinary hearing at which it was argued that the trust relationship had broken down between Ben and his employer. He intends taking his matter up with the labour court once again. He says that the events have taken a heavy toll on his personal life and have almost financially ruined him.

Employees at the public sector workshops were unanimous in stating that they would welcome a mechanism to expose fraud and corruption in the public service, but that such a mechanism would need to guarantee their confidentiality and, far more importantly, their protection. In furthering its mission to deal with corruption in the public sector, the Public Service Commission also commissioned a further study into the establishment of a national hotline for the public service, and at the time of writing was in the process of establishing it.

---

[8] We use pseudonyms to protect the identity of the whistleblowers involved.

A number of cases show that the South African corporate sector is prone to serious abuses of corporate governance, and witnesses are unable to raise concerns effectively. In 2000 Leisurenet, which ran a very popular group of 85 health gym clubs with approximately 900 000 members and about 5 400 employees, suffered a multi-million rand collapse. Wendy Addison, the Internal Treasurer of Leisurenet, told a commission of inquiry investigating the company's collapse that the directors, Peter Gardener and Rod Mitchell, had used the company as their personal bank. They had charged personal expenses to Leisurenet. They had deceived investors and bankers about the true financial status of the group, cheating investors out of tens of millions of rand. When Addison raised concerns about the company's cash flow and spending proposals, senior executives started excluding her from meetings. After warning Gardener and others that the future of the company was being compromised she felt that there was nothing more that she could do. Unfortunately there were no systems in place at Leisurenet for her concerns to be dealt with.[9]

Sadly the proactive initiatives for fighting corruption in the workplace in the public sector have not been mirrored in the private sector in South Africa where corporate fraud corruption and collapses are being more frequently reported. This is despite the recommendations of the King Report – heralded by many as being one of the best corporate governance documents in the world – which strongly encouraged compliance with the Protected Disclosures Act and advised in favour of the "establishment of easily accessible safe reporting mechanisms, including 'whistleblowing' and other channels for employees". The report also speaks strongly of the need to change organisational cultures to comply with good corporate governance. The corporate sector has had to meet a whole raft of legal compliance responsibilities since 1994, and there is a sense of "legislative fatigue". As the Protected Disclosures Act does not require employers to do anything other than not victimise whistleblowers, few see any urgency or imperative to put in place the sort of whistleblower policies or systems that the law envisages. Few companies are prepared to see the long-term advantage of avoidance rather than cure and therefore few are investing in whistleblowing systems, preferring, if anything, the "cheap fix", false economy of anonymous tip-off hotlines and the like. Proposals being considered by the law commission working group include bolstering the Act by requiring companies above a certain size to put in place a whistleblower policy. Strengthening the provisions dealing with penalties, for example by increasing the compensation awards that can be paid, is also important. Indeed, the recommendations of the law commission, and the

---

9  http://www.iol.co.za/general/news/newsprint.php?art_id=ct20011016212732372L265580&, Moneyweb Digest 19 October 2001.

parliamentary review that will likely follow towards the end of 2004 or early in 2005, will be crucial in refining the Protected Disclosures Act so that it can have optimal impact.

Given the intense history of mistrust and contestation between employers and employees in South Africa, there is a serious question mark about the notion of a shared public interest that underlies the Act. Nevertheless, at a recent conference, a senior trade union leader reaffirmed that there was indeed a common interest between employers and employees in eradicating all forms of workplace fraud and corruption, citing the collapse of organisations and the commensurate loss of jobs and investor confidence which in turn led to even fewer jobs being created and the growth of further crime and corruption in the broader society as a result. He said that there was a common interest in employers and employees coming together and establishing safe reporting mechanisms where employees could confidently and confidentially come forward to report matters that they were concerned about without the fear of reprisal.

Recent whistleblowing cases in South Africa have revealed a pattern. The whistle gets blown, and there is a witch hunt for the whistleblower. This is not altogether surprising when one considers that from an early age children were admonished for telling tales and for informing on one another. This way of thinking has continued to largely dominate the way we think as adults. However in the 2003 Pricewaterhouse-Coopers Global Economic Crime Survey it was found that economic crime in organisations was mainly detected as a result of whistleblowing or tip-offs.

Thus it is far too soon to confidently speculate about the prognosis for the Protected Disclosures Act. One of the biggest challenges in implementing an effective whistleblowing mechanism in South Africa is how to promote a culture of whistleblowing in a society that has come to equate whistleblowing with mistrust and betrayal – the *impimpi* culture. Whistleblowing has been found to be most successful in organisations where there is a culture that encourages openness, transparency and accountability, a culture of ethics that is led from the top and shared throughout the organisation. Without this culture, the risks of blowing the whistle are sometimes too enormous to contemplate.

South Africa is engaged in a transformation from an intolerant, racist and hierarchical society to one in which the values of freedom, openness and tolerance are upheld. As the Constitution recognises, it is critical that as part of that transformation people in and outside the workplace are able to speak up about the wrongs they see done, and be heard. The law is an essential piece in the jigsaw, but clearly should not be seen as a panacea in and of itself. Far more needs to be done, across society, if a new "right to speak" culture is to emerge as a part of the new South Africa.

# THE POSITION IN JAPAN

*By Yukiko Miki*

## Background

In Japan over many years there have been cases of whistleblowing to expose malpractice in the workplace. While the chapter on PISA in Part 4 looks at more recent examples, two particular cases, from more than 20 years ago, have become famous.

One case concerned a newly introduced drug approval application process. In 1980, a pharmaceutical company applied for approval to sell a new high-risk carcinogenic drug. The researchers in charge of the development of the drug blew the whistle at an internal meeting and also brought it to the attention of their employers. When their concerns were ignored they decided to form a trade union to try to stop the selling of the dangerous drug. The employers tried to crush the union; the union chairperson was ordered to take an indefinite business trip that would remove him from the workplace and from the union, union members faced serious harassment and the union was refused recognition. It was only when a newspaper reported the dangers of the new drug that the union began to receive strong support from outside parties, including a support group organised by doctors, consumer groups, groups for victims of medical harm and others. As a result of this process, the company gave up selling the medicine and an agreement was reached between the union and the employers in 1991, which included open discussion between the workers and their employers on any problems relating to in-house products.

Another case involved a worker at a transportation company who blew the whistle on an unauthorised cartel among transportation companies who together maintained artificially high transportation rates. He first approached his superior and another employer, but got no help from them. In fact they instructed him not to say anything about it. His next move was to disclose the information to a newspaper, which reported it in 1974. When the company still did not take appropriate action he reported it to the Fair Trade Commission who conducted an on-the-spot investigation and the cartel was shut down.

However, immediately after the report appeared in the newspaper, the worker was summoned to a hearing by his employer. He and his family were harassed, he was visited at home very late at night and urged to retire by his employer and his elder brother received phone calls putting pressure on him. Moreover, his employer told him that he would never be promoted. Instead he was reassigned, without being given any reason, to work at a so-called educational training institute where, since 1975, he has to work alone every day in a very small office without a telephone. He basically has not been given any work to do, and his salary has been eroded almost to that of a new employee. This situation has continued for more than 25 years.

These cases demonstrate that, although the malpractice may be discontinued as a result of the disclosures, Japanese workers who blow the whistle face real victimisation, notwithstanding strong labour laws providing job security. While they receive support from their families and outside parties, and they themselves believe in social justice and that what they did was right, it would be true to say that it is difficult to blow the whistle without paying the price.

## The difficulty of whistleblowing in Japan

Many whistleblowers' stories in Japan, like those above, confirm to society that whistleblowing can be a tool to halt and correct malpractice and prevent damage and danger to the public. But factors such as the Japanese mentality, the employment system, the labour protection system and corporate responsibility, show the need for a legal system to protect whistleblowers. A whistleblower can either be seen as a betrayer or a hero in pursuit of justice and most workers do not think that they themselves might one day need to blow the whistle on malpractice in the workplace.

Japanese people have a tendency to exclude those who have a different opinion and they dislike tackling conflicts of interest. These tendencies are referred to as "a sense of togetherness," which is regarded as part of the Japanese character. It is also said that a worker's sense of belonging to a company is strong. Most Japanese workers build their careers in a single company where they are employed for their entire working life, working their way through the seniority-based system of promotion. This creates a strong corporate culture. In this way, the company is assured of a worker's loyalty, while the job is secured for the lifetime of the worker.

If the whistle is blown anonymously, in-house or outside, the company will try to identify the source, who will be regarded as a betrayer or an informant. If the source is identified, he or she could be dismissed or redeployed. Sometimes, trivial, unrelated reasons may be given for the dismissal. There are many cases in which a whistleblower or source is forced to retire after being subjected to serious visible and invisible harassment in the workplace.

The Labor Standard Law of Japan requires employers to show rational reason for dismissal. Yet sometimes the whistleblower becomes so stressed that he or she has no other option but voluntary retirement. Given these circumstances, it is more rational to overlook malpractice and avoid conflict in the workplace rather than blow the whistle.

Moreover, many companies offer accommodation at a low price for their workers. This means human relations between the workers in a company can become neighbourhood relations. This discourages workers from raising their concerns. Also, generally, trade unions have not protected victimised whistleblowers. Trade unions in Japan are company unions and it is said that big unions are company-dominated. There is a "sweetheart" contract between a union and the employers.

In Japan, governments have considerable power to regulate business through regulatory laws. This has led to close collaborative relationships developing between companies and administrations. In the past this has resulted in many cases in which companies that have caused serious public damage, such as diseases from environmental pollution, or tragedies resulting from the side effects of drugs, only for it to appear that the company's responsibility is condoned or overlooked by the administrations.

For example, a lecturer at a vocation school disclosed to the regulator that the school was not fulfilling the quota of teachers, which was against the law. But the regulator leaked the name of the whistleblower and as a result he was dismissed. Other examples are given in the chapter on PISA in Part 4. As a result, many in Japan believe that the government first protects business interests, even where the wellbeing or safety of the public is threatened or harmed. Therefore it is unlikely that a potential whistleblower will believe that an administration would treat disclosures of malpractice appropriately and protect the whistleblower's safety.

If whistleblower protection legislation is introduced in Japan without also influencing a change in the culture and environment, it may well prove ineffective, if not meaningless.

# The changing situation surrounding whistleblower protection

Nevertheless, the situation has been changing step by step. The lifetime employment system has been gradually fading and promotion based on merit and ability instead of seniority is being introduced. Also, a large number of workers, many of them middle-aged, have lost their jobs in the name of workforce reduction and as a result a worker's sense of belonging to a particular company is becoming weaker.

In the last ten years, the Japanese economy has fallen into a depression and the public now view dubious and illegal activities by companies, as well as by administrations, in a far more serious light. Terms such as "accountability", "freedom of information", "governance" and "business ethics" are now being used. This was difficult to imagine ten years ago. Social values have shifted to demand a more accountable society. There are many whistleblowing cases underway that are tackling malpractice in companies and administrations and many people in Japan now understand the importance of whistleblowing.

Many listed companies have now set up helplines for workers to raise concerns if they are afraid to disclose the malpractice outside. Corporate culture cannot change at short notice and, in fact, business still shows a very negative attitude to introducing whistleblower protection legislation. However, there is growing recognition that without any legal guarantee of protection, workers may still feel the risk of blowing the whistle is too high.

Civil society in Japan is now interested in the issue of whistleblower protection because it realises the importance of such legislation in protecting lives and safety. In 2002 the citizen network for whistleblower protection was launched to introduce effective whistleblower protection legislation. People from different backgrounds, including consumer groups, environmental groups, doctors, scientists, lawyers, academics, shareholders' ombudsmen, citizen ombudsmen and freedom of information NGOs have come together for one purpose – to promote the common value of whistleblower protection legislation.

A whistleblower protection law (outlined in the chapter on PISA in Part 4) is being drafted and maybe introduced in 2004. How far it inspires or assists the cultural changes that Japanese society and business need if public interest whistleblowing is to work remains to be seen.

# PART 4:

## CIVIL SOCIETY RESPONSES

# THE USA: GOVERNMENT ACCOUNTABILITY PROJECT

*By Tom Devine*

The Government Accountability Project (GAP) is a non-profit, non-partisan tax exempt public interest law firm whose reason to be is helping whistleblowers – those employees who exercise freedom of speech to challenge abuses of power that betray the public trust. The organisation's headquarters are located less than two blocks from the White House in Washington, D.C. It also has an office in Seattle, Washington, primarily to assist whistleblowers at nuclear weapons facilities in general, and the US Department of Energy's Hanford radioactive waste reservation in particular.

GAP was founded in 1977 at a national conference on whistleblowing in Washington, DC. In the beginning we had only one small office with a staff of two. We have grown gradually, but steadily. Now we have a full- or part-time staff of 30, as well as 50 interns and regular volunteers annually, and we have a budget of $1.7 million. GAP receives no government grants. It derives 65% of its income from over 30 different American foundations, 20% from 8 000 individual donors and 15% from legal fees we receive for winning whistleblower cases against the government or corporations.

The ideas behind GAP have their roots in the early 1970s, after Dr Daniel Ellsberg completed a classified study on the secret history of US involvement in Vietnam. When his Pentagon bosses displayed little interest in the facts that they replaced with their big lie approach to history, Ellsburg decided to go public with the truth. He demystified and packaged his information at the Institute for Policy Studies, a Washington, D.C. think-tank, which helped him to distribute what became known as the Pentagon Papers. Although the Nixon Administration threatened criminal prosecution and took all other possible legal steps to prevent publication, the Supreme Court permitted major newspapers to release Mr Ellsberg's disclosure, and it helped change the course of history.

In 1977 the Institute for Policy Studies in Washington organised a national whistleblower conference to recognise and honour employees who felt compelled to disclose important information to the public about secret and questionable governmental activities. We recognise the second day of the

conference as the actual birthday of GAP. On that day conference participants filled out survey forms supporting the creation of a non-government,
independent organisation to provide citizen "truth tellers" with job guidance,
moral support, legal help and assistance in bringing their important corruption concerns into the public light.

Initially GAP primarily served as a hotline for personal support and a
matchmaking service for whistleblowers with kindred spirits and potential
allies in Congress or the media. In 1978, however, GAP testified and campaigned for the enactment of statutory whistleblower free speech rights. Congress enacted the breakthrough in the Civil Service Reform Act of 1978.
Ever since, GAP has extended its initial focus into broad-based legal campaigns helping individual workers make a difference. We represent and coach
them in using free speech rights to turn information into power that thwarts
bureaucratic abuses of power by government and corporate institutions, without becoming martyrs in the process. Our creed is that in a free society nothing is more powerful than the truth. We limit our formal legal representation
to whistleblowers covered by US laws, due to lack of professional credentials
and experience to practice in other legal systems.

Much of GAP's service to whistleblowers is carried out through an ambitious intern and apprenticeship programme. The hub is a law school clinic
founded in 1979, initially with the Antioch School of Law and now with the
University of District of Columbia School of Law. Students actively assist in
providing representation to legally indigent whistleblowers, under the supervision of GAP attorneys who are adjunct clinical law professors. Over 500
students have participated in the clinic, which has been equally significant as
a training ground for a new generation of free speech activist lawyers. A
plurality of GAP's staff attorneys was trained through the legal clinic.

The magic word for our strategy in helping whistleblowers is solidarity.
We represent them in legal campaigns, rather than mere lawsuits. Litigation in
isolation is hostile territory for those challenging the status quo. As a rule, the
courts are designed to preserve the status quo, and whistleblowers are challenging it. Further, even if this bias is overcome, lawsuits tend to be drawn
out and expensive.

The goal of legal campaigns is to break the cycles of isolation and secrecy that sustain abuses of power, by sharing the whistleblower's knowledge
with all the elements of society that should be benefitting from it. When we
effectively establish those links, society ends up surrounding the bureaucracy
that had surrounded the whistleblower. Over and over again, the solidarity
strategy has proved the core premise for our work with whistleblowers: We
repeat, in a free society, there is nothing more powerful than the truth.

This formula has worked to stop three nuclear power plants from completion that were accidents waiting to happen, depriving powerful multinational corporations such as the Bechtel Corporation of more than ten billion dollars in income. Three times it has stopped the Department of Agriculture from deregulating government-approved food. It has forced the shutdown of toxic incinerators that burned poisons like arsenic, polychlorinated biphenyls or PCBs, lead and mercury in the air around churches and schoolyards. In 1991, it sparked the cancellation of all funding for the next generation of the Star Wars anti-ballistic missile project. A survey of GAP's recent casework can be found at our website, www.whistleblower.org.

GAP wears four hats in carrying out this mission. The first is to defend whistleblowers against retaliation. As a public interest legal organisation, we represent employees of government and corporations who have, or want to raise, concerns about serious problems within their agencies or companies. We offer our legal services if the problem is serious enough and the employee is committed to seeking reform. In this capacity we have represented over 1 000 whistleblowers since 1978 and provided a lesser level of legal support for an additional 1 000 individuals with whistleblower concerns.

Secondly, we design and carry out effective campaigns, most often national in scope, to publicise and force change on issues of concern for the general public, policy-makers and key decision-makers. Our legal campaigns typically link up whistleblowers with the media; relevant national, state and local legislatures; competing government agencies with jurisdiction; academic experts; and, most significant, affected societal constituencies. Before launching any full-blown campaign, however, we first conduct a rigorous preliminary investigation to determine the credibility of the allegations, and then design a campaign that will lead to significant reform. We make sure the alleged problem is credible and real and then ensure that its exposure will lead to significant reform. Additionally, if appropriate, we first try to resolve problems internally, even before launching any effort outside the particular institution that is the focus of our attention. We estimate that we have helped an additional 1 000 whistleblowers raise their concerns beyond the 2 000 clients and others mentioned previously.

Thirdly, we work to enact, strengthen and monitor the effectiveness of free speech laws protecting whistleblowers. We draft both model and actual legislation for federal, state and local governments as well as for international NGOs, governments or other bodies. We have led the campaigns to pass nearly every major national whistleblower law protecting government and corporate employees in the US. We also help government agencies and companies develop and implement analogous internal policies.

Fourthly, we serve as experts on the phenomenon of whistleblowing, authoring books, law reviews and academic articles, while serving as commentators on free speech issues at conferences and in the media. This role complements our service as clinical law school professors. Examples of GAP's books on lessons learned are *Courage Without Martyrdom: A Whistleblower's Survival Guide* and *The Art of Anonymous Activism.*

Whether organising legal solidarity campaigns for individuals or campaigning for stronger whistleblower laws, a prerequisite to making a difference is constantly organising support coalitions. For example, in representing a Star Wars scientist, we channelled his evidence to a coalition led by the Federation of American Scientists, the Union of Concerned Scientists and the Project on Military Procurement. Helping government inspectors challenge contaminated meat and poultry, we funnel their evidence to a coalition led by the Consumer Federation of America, National Consumers League, the Center for Science in the Public Interest and Ralph Nader's Public Citizen organisation. Whistleblower rights campaigns involve core groups of good government organisations such as Common Cause, the Project on Government Oversight and the National Taxpayers Union, as well as broad grassroots networks of hundreds of civil rights, environmental, labour and civic organisations.

GAP has expanded free speech advocacy to the international level for two reasons. Initially we responded to initiatives from kindred spirits in Britain's Public Concern at Work, which sought GAP's counsel when it began and later directed volunteer staff to help us develop an international programme. This trend was reinforced by the US State Department, which has directed hundreds of visitors from over 50 countries to our offices for briefings on why freedom of speech for whistleblowers is a cornerstone of civil society.

More fundamentally, the convergence of globalisation and associated anti-corruption campaigns has created a compelling necessity to expand the scope of our work. For better or worse, globalisation is a basic paradigm shift. It may mean the effective end of many national regulatory programmes and laws created to check corporate abuses of power. That means whistleblowers are needed more than ever to expose institutions that take advantage of this. Anti-corruption campaigns, designed to maintain market stability, cannot work effectively without protection for those who bear witness. This has created the rare scenario where whistleblower rights are in the self-interest of established status quo institutions. At the same time, any paradigm shift is a time of turmoil and transition, which means the chance to break out of ingrained patterns exists. With effective advocacy, whistleblower rights can be institutionalised as a cornerstone of accountability.

There are signs that the system is responding. Besides the country-by-country progress summarised in this book, international organisations are keeping pace. In 2000 the Organization of American States approved a model whistleblower law to implement its Inter-American Convention Against Corruption. In December 2003 the US Congress passed a law requiring biannual progress reports from the US Treasury Department to congressional oversight committees on implementation of whistleblower laws at international financial institutions such as the World Bank, Asian Development Bank and Inter-American Development Bank.

Throughout this process, NGOs like GAP and others can make a critical difference through advocacy to institutionalise whistleblower protection in principle and sustained oversight to make sure the new rights are genuine metal shields behind which the courageous have a fighting chance to defend themselves. Otherwise, so-called new rights can be illusory, false advertising for cardboard shields that trap the naive. Whistleblower protection is at a global crossroads, and NGOs have a unique opportunity to make a difference.

## Summary of GAP docket

GAP helps to ensure government and corporate accountability by bringing together whistleblowers' inside information and expertise with concerned citizens, policy-makers and the media. After months of development, in 2003 GAP launched two major initiatives: a Corporate Accountability Campaign and, in the international arena, an International Financial Institution Accountability Campaign. For the next two years these new efforts will augment and extend our traditional work on nuclear oversight, national security, food safety, environmental enforcement, worker health and safety and freedom for all citizens to warn about hazards and dangers.

### Corporate Accountability Campaign

GAP launched this new campaign based upon our successful development of the whistleblower provisions of the new Corporate Accountability Act (the Sarbanes-Oxley Act of 2002). With these legal protections, we now have the most significant leverage ever to defend whistleblowers, advocate for corporate accountability and fully implement sweeping corporate reform. The Campaign includes public education, litigation to shape the courts' interpretation of the law, investigation of substantive allegations of wrongdoing at companies or industries with ties to other GAP public interest campaigns and further refinement of national policy and law.

We will write, publish and disseminate educational materials such as handbooks and flyers about the new law for employees and "best practices" and training material for corporations describing a process for evaluating the effectiveness of corporate whistleblower protections. We will engage in a broad public relations and media effort around the law.

Since the law provides an opportunity for jury trials we are actively evaluating new whistleblower cases to see if they meet the criteria for litigating under Sarbanes-Oxley and monitoring all cases before the Department of Labour. The law also opens up new investigative opportunities for us to target corporate wrongdoing and promote reform on a wide range of issues. We are already experiencing significant opportunities to work with corporate employees from the heavily regulated industries, such as drugs, nuclear weapons, airlines, chemicals, food, oil, gas, coal, timber and mining.

## Multilateral Development Banks Accountability Campaign

As economic globalisation continues apace, GAP has also been increasingly drawn into international work, focusing on those opportunities that might significantly check global abuses of corporate and government power and promote institutional accountability and improved governance. We have launched a campaign to bring greater transparency and more effective oversight to the multilateral development banks.

We are first developing effective partnerships with NGOs whose missions are oversight of the banks to check institutional abuses of power. Simultaneously we will work with selected bank officials or managers who believe that the banks need to carry out internal changes. We plan to conduct a thorough organisational assessment to describe the existing internal mechanisms which employees of multinational institutions can use when they discover wrongdoing. This review would include any employee concerns programme, internal hotlines and formal Inspector General structures, roles and authorities. We are also developing recommendations to promote greater openness, transparency and accountability through comprehensive whistleblower protection. We are already developing these, but they will become even better defined and comprehensive as we gather more information.

The media exposures of corruption scandals are expanding the base of sympathetic congressional staff audiences for multilateral development banks' accountability initiatives. The congressional oversight process offers opportunities to play watchdog, raise public questions, obtain documents from the banks, learn of institutional policies that otherwise would remain shrouded, and promote policy changes to the banks from the most strategic perspective. To the limited extent that we are able, we will also seek to influence the banks through the US Treasury's role over US votes at that institution, as well as seek out supportive executive directors to the World Bank's governing body from Italy, England and Holland, among others.

## Nuclear Oversight Campaign

The Nuclear Oversight Campaign, led by Director Tom Carpenter, seeks to protect and advocate for nuclear whistleblowers and injured workers in the nuclear industries; reduce or eliminate the environmental, safety, health and economic consequences of nuclear weapons operations; secure compensation for nuclear weapons workers injured on the job; and collaborate with Russian citizen groups to help them better address their country's nuclear legacy. We are working on significant environmental, health and safety issues that have surfaced through government and corporate whistleblowers at nuclear facilities, including Hanford (Washington), Pantex (Texas), Lawrence Livermore (California), Los Alamos (New Mexico), Oak Ridge (Tennessee) and the Idaho National Environmental Engineering Laboratories.

Our most prominent nuclear whistleblowers are:

- Chris Steele, the Safety Director at the Los Alamos laboratory, who oversaw all legal requirements to protect workers and the public from radiation releases;

- Matthew Zipoli and Charles Quinones, security officers at Lawrence Livermore national laboratory, who raised serious safety and security vulnerability concerns with the Department of Energy (DOE) following September 11;

- Casey Ruud, who exposed environmental hazards at the Hanford nuclear site;

- Hanford tank farm pipefitters, who refused to install sub-standard values in a waste transport pipe from high-level nuclear waste tanks;

- Hanford quality assurance auditors, who are exposing Bechtel's attempts to derail the quality assurance programme and get rid of the regulations covering the vitrification programme;

- Hanford electricians, who allege that safety lapses at the waste tanks resulted in toxic exposures that caused illnesses and deaths;

- Idaho National Engineering and Environmental Laboratory employees who believe a subcontractor dramatically undercut its quality assurance programme on a critical nuclear project with nuclear safety dangers. We are now conducting a major investigation into the false claim allegations.

GAP's Nuclear Oversight Campaign focuses more than half of its programme resources on the Hanford nuclear site because it is the most contaminated place in the western hemisphere, and it has the largest volumes of radioactive and non-radioactive hazardous wastes in the DOE complex. Our programme there is challenging the administration's abandonment of comprehensive clean-up efforts and its new plans to import new highly radioactive plutonium-laced waste. We are also continuing to challenge the DOE's mismanagement of Hanford's unstable radioactive waste-tanks and its potentially boondoggle vitrification programme to treat the waste.

In addition to launching an extensive media/public education campaign with the help of Environmental Media Services, GAP is making huge investments in building a new citizen initiative for holding DOE accountable. The organising vehicle, the "Hanford Roundtable," resulted from almost two years of work with new voices in Washington and Oregon on Hanford issues, including the Nature Conservancy, the Pacific Coast Federation of Fishermens' Associations, tribal governments and other environmental organisations.

GAP is working closely with Washington State Attorney General Gregoire – the most popular statewide elected official – on the state's role in holding DOE accountable under the Tri-Party Agreement. The state has recently filed suit (after much direct and active encouragement and help from us) to halt the importation of radioactive waste. Bolstering our whistleblower support and coalition activities, we have brought an intense focus on the issue of water resource contamination – both groundwater and surface water. GAP has been carrying out environmental investigations, finding significant, unreported, radioactive and chemical contamination throughout the Hanford site and in and around the Columbia River. We will continue these studies at Hanford.

## Atomic Weapons Workers Compensation Campaign

As part of our national focus we initiated our Atomic Weapons Workers Compensation Campaign in the spring of 2001 to monitor, organise and advocate around the implementation of the Energy Employees Occupational Illness Compensation Program of 2000. This is the first federal worker compensation entitlement programme in over three decades. GAP has seen the fruits of its advocacy work, led by senior policy analyst Richard Miller, play out in blocking anti-worker regulations, advocating for legislative improvements, gaining appointments and thus allies on the National Institute for Occupational Health and Safety Advisory Board, assuring fidelity to congressional intent at the Department of Labour, forcing negotiations over how the DOE programme is structured, and keeping congressional involvement and engagement at high levels. In the next two years we will hold the Departments of Energy, Health and Human Services, and Labour accountable in implementing the programme; supporting injured worker advocacy groups at DOE sites with information and organising grants; and sustaining local and media efforts to build interest and support for policy changes.

### Russia Project

Lastly, our Nuclear Oversight Campaign is in its fourth year of collaborating with Russian citizen groups on similar issues of nuclear accountability. This year we are bringing a group of scientists to Hanford to conduct environmental research alongside our own retained scientist who will guide the overall study.

## Environmental Enforcement/National Forest Oversight Campaign

### Establishing a permanent, independent Environmental Protection Agency (EPA) ombudsman office

GAP held a "Citizen's Hearing" to broaden support for whistleblowers and grassroots groups and show the need for an independent ombudsman at EPA. The forum allowed concerned citizens and members of Congress to expose the reality behind EPA promises of improved service to resolve community concerns about threats from toxic wastes and Superfund sites, which are uncontrolled sites where hazardous waste is located.

### National Forest Oversight

GAP's forestry programme seeks to ensure better management of our national forests, move the US Forestry Services from single-minded timber production to protecting ecosystems and biodiversity and hold the timber industry legally and environmentally accountable. GAP continues to pursuit a lawsuit involving ten former members of the now defunct Timber Theft Investigations Branch. After years of legal wrangling, we expect to litigate the case in a full hearing during 2004.

## Food Safety Campaign

We are leading a fight by whistleblowing federal meat inspectors, labourers and consumer advocates to preserve the principle of government inspection of meat and poultry. The most recent threat to government inspection is a new programme that replaces federal government inspectors with industry employees for critical inspection functions. This programme of the US Department of Agriculture's (USDA's) Food Safety Inspection Service incorporates these changes as part of a new system called Hazard Analysis Critical Control Points (HACCP). HACCP was phased into meat and poultry plants between 1997 and 2002. With Public Citizen, we issued two major reports in 2000 and 2002 on how HACCP is riddled with systematic breakdowns that allow large quantities of potentially contaminated ground beef to land on supermarket shelves.

GAP has contracted investigator Rick Parks to research how the USDA is making scapegoats of small meat plants and turning a blind eye to the testing failures of large, multinational producers. Parks is currently liaising with a small meat plant whistleblower who has knowledge of large plant abuses and the USDA's lack of effective oversight. He is also investigating plants where food poisoning outbreaks have occurred.

GAP Food Safety Campaign program director, Felicia Nestor, along with Public Citizen, has spearheaded the establishment of the Global Safe Food Coalition. This coalition brings together more than 30 groups on the forefront of various food safety issues, including genetic modification, consumer protection, worker health and safety, family farms and irradiation.

## Freedom to Warn Campaign

This campaign uses whistleblower disclosures to address current threats to the environment, public health and safety and national security, as well as promote policy initiatives for greater openness and transparency to prevent future threats. GAP, led by Legal Director Tom Devine, has sought to ensure that in the rush to improve security following September 11 we do not silence those who would bring to light information about critical national security vulnerabilities.

The campaign's five legislative initiatives are: passing necessary revisions to the Whistleblower Protection Act, including security clearance protections and establishing real federal court judicial review; providing Whistleblower Protection Act protection to employees of the FBI presently exempted from the Act; adding a standard remedy onto a long-established ban against obstructing communications with Congress i.e. the Lloyd-LaFollette Act; extending Sarbanes-Oxley style protections, including jury trials, to employees of the Nuclear Regulatory Commission and the DOE; and passing a permanent anti-gag statute.

Key whistleblower cases that dovetail with our policy agenda include:

- Bogdan Dzakovic and Carrie Hancasky, former agents with the Federal Aviation Administration "Red Team," who conducted covert tests before September 11 to see if airports were secure against terrorists. In exercises where they acted as mock terrorists, they were able to overcome airline carrier security more than 90% of the time at airports around the world, including major terminals in Boston, Washington, D.C., London, England and Frankfurt, Germany. The government ignored their repeated warnings that the defences had no more value than bluffs that maintained the appearance of security, and then grounded them from conducting further tests.

- Mark Hall, a senior Border Patrol agent, who disclosed in Senate testimony that the Canadian border in Michigan was left unguarded in the days after September 11 because all agents had been moved to the Detroit airports for mass detentions of foreign families who were travelling. Mr Hall was stripped of all his duties and files, and his desk moved to the waiting area for people who had been arrested.

- Richard Levernier, the DOE's top expert on safeguards and security for nuclear weapons materials. Similar to the Red Team, he led mock attacks that breached security at nuclear weapons facilities over half the time, despite restrictions on his team that a terrorist never would have to worry about, such as obeying speed limits, stop signs and occupational safety rules on site.

- MIT professor and nuclear engineer Ted Postol, who is exposing the current failures of the new Star Wars anti-missile defence system, which lacks the capacity to distinguish accurately between actual missiles and decoy threats.

- Chris Steele, the DOE's Nuclear Safety Director at the Los Alamos research laboratory where the atomic bomb was developed and continues to act as the hub of nuclear research in the US. He blew the whistle on the failure to have any contingency plans in place for suicide aeroplane attacks into nuclear reactors at Los Alamos a year after September 11, as well as secret nuclear waste dumps on site that neither complied with environmental nor security requirements.

# THE UK:
# PUBLIC CONCERN AT WORK

*By Evelyn Oakley and Anna Myers*

## Background

By the end of the 1980s, public confidence in the ability of British institutions – private or public – to deliver their services safely had suffered. The British public were shocked when it was revealed that children in care had been abused over a 13-year period by those employed to protect them; that serious lapses in safety standards had been common prior to the explosion on a north sea oil rig that killed 167 men and that a top UK insurance company could collapse leaving behind £34 million in unpaid debts.[1] In 1990 the Public Interest Research Centre (PIRC) – through its publishing arm, Social Audit – published the findings of a research project it had conducted into self-regulation and whistleblowing in UK companies.[2] The report was the seed from which the first serious civil society initiative to address whistleblowing in the UK would grow.

One of the report's key findings was that staff often knew of problems or risks but few organisations provided adequate mechanisms for staff to raise their concerns in the workplace. Case studies showed how the absence of such mechanisms often led to misunderstandings, confrontations, victimisation of the employee and adverse publicity if the concern was unnecessarily aired outside the company. In the worst cases – as public inquiries into disasters and scandals demonstrated – genuine opportunities to prevent damage were missed. Launched during a press conference at the Confederation of British Industry in 1990, the CBI's Director-General, Sir John Banham,

---

[1] The police inquiry into the abuse of children in care led to the conviction in 1991 of three men employed by Leicestershire County Council, including the Officer in Charge of Children's Homes, Frank Beck. The Cullen Inquiry not only identified the causes of the explosion on the Piper Alpha oil platform but found that "workers do not want to put their continued employment in jeopardy through raising a safety issue that might embarrass management". After the collapse of the Roger Levitt's Group – a top UK life insurance company – Levitt was charged with fraud worth £90 million but pleaded guilty to a lesser charge and served only 180 hours community service.

[2] The project was supported by the Nuffield Foundation.

recommended the PIRC report, *Minding Your Own Business,* as "essential reading for all corporate managers".

PIRC and others identified the need for an independent body to address accountability in the workplace in the public interest. As originally conceived, a new organisation could advise individuals, help employers, conduct research and promote good practice. The Joseph Rowntree Charitable Trust offered £250 000 start-up funding in the form of a five-year challenge grant.[3]

In 1990 a steering committee[4] was set up and consulted widely to determine what, if any, support existed for such an initiative. The committee spoke to British businesses and professional organisations, corporate executives, lawyers, individual whistleblowers and public interest groups in Britain and the US. The consultation revealed great interest in the issues of organisational accountability and whistleblowing, and support for an independent body to address it – the seed had germinated.

It was decided that the new body would obtain charitable status, incorporate as a limited company and seek designation from the Law Society of England and Wales and the Bar Council as a legal advice centre. As a charity and limited company, the new body could seek and receive the funding it needed and would have an accepted public benefit function. As a designated legal advice centre individuals could seek help in the context of lawyer-client confidentiality. This latter point was extremely important if the new body was to reassure individuals that it was safe to seek advice about their concerns outside the workplace.

Surprisingly, charitable status was initially refused by the Charity Commission on the basis that "such a service would not be in the public interest". After a year of argument and persuasion,[5] charitable status was finally granted in September 1993.[6]

After much consideration, the steering committee chose the name Public Concern at Work[7] (PCaW) and passed the reigns to the charity's new board

---

[3] A challenge grant required the new body to raise a further £250 000 – either in earned income or by securing other charitable funds.

[4] This steering committee included Marlene Winfield, freelance social policy specialist and author of the PIRC report, Maurice Frankel of the Campaign for Freedom of Information, Guy Dehn, Legal Officer of the National Consumer Council (NCC) and Charles Medawar, Director of PIRC.

[5] Advocating for the new charity, Michael Brindle QC and Christopher McCall QC provided invaluable assistance free of charge to persuade the Charity Commission to grant charitable status.

[6] Ironically, soon after this the Chief Charity Commissioner delivered a public address on the future of UK charities and selected PCaW as a model of the new breed of charity that meets and develops the public interest.

[7] The name emphasised the role of the new body to help address public interest concerns that staff – often the first to realise something may be going wrong – learn about at work.

of trustees[8] and Executive Director, Guy Dehn. Throughout its life, the charity relied heavily on the weight and input of its trustees[9] and on the guidance of its advisory council, with members from business, unions, public service, the media and the professions. In October 1993, PCaW – the whistleblowing charity – was officially launched.

Briefly, the charitable objectives of PCaW were and remain:

*To promote ethical standards of conduct and compliance with the law by … relevant organisations in their administration and management, treatment of personnel, health safety and commercial practices and protection of the natural environment.*

The charity strives to meet these objectives through four core activities. These are:

- Offering confidential practical and legal advice to individuals concerned about wrongdoing in the workplace;

- Providing training, guidance and consultancy to employers and other organisations on risk management, governance and whistleblowing;

- Informing and influencing public policy on the responsibility of individuals and the accountability of organisations;

- Working across the community at home and abroad – through schools, groups and the media – to promote whistleblowing and the public interest.

## The work

PCaW – now more than a decade old – is a small organisation with the equivalent of six full-time staff. In 2001, the charity expanded north and has a part-time Scottish Director based in Glasgow. Traditionally, key posts have been filled by lawyers (or those with legal training) as the helpline and maintaining the quality of advice has always been a priority. However, the charity does not litigate and its emphasis on practical advice for individuals, as well as its training, consultancy and policy work, has meant that those working for the charity need broad skills and experience, and the ability to adapt to new challenges.

---

[8]  Chair, Sir Gordon Borrie, former Director General of Fair Trading; Professor Ross Cranston of the London School of Economics; Maurice Frankel, Director of the Campaign for Freedom of Information; Marlene Winfield, social policy advisor; and Mark Mildred, solicitor.

[9]  The board of trustees at the time of writing is chaired by Michael Smyth and includes Gary Brown, Peter Connor, Maurice Frankel, Martin Le Jeune, Carol Sergeant and James Tickell.

This section describes in more detail the work of the charity over the past decade by focusing on its four main activities.

## Helpline

PCaW's helpline is fundamental to its existence. The key feature of the advice is its practical approach. The PCaW lawyers try to help the whistleblower keep or regain a perspective on the situation. By advising whistleblowers how they can best raise a concern and by focusing on how to do so responsibly – either to those in charge or, where necessary, outside the organisation – the aim is to minimise the risk that the messenger will suffer and maximise the chance that any serious concern will be promptly addressed. This means that callers can make an informed decision about what they want to do with the information they have, knowing the risks and opportunities before them. The lawyer-client relationship ensures that callers can speak freely and openly about their concern and discuss the differences or conflicts between the public interest and their own, if there are any. Confidential feedback surveys – now conducted twice a year – have shown a consistently high satisfaction rate among callers over the past decade.[10]

It is also important to note that whereas the helpline has operated since 1993, the UK's Public Interest Disclosure Act – protecting responsible whistleblowing in the workplace – has only been in force since 1999. While the helpline does advise on rights under the Act, its primary role remains to try to ensure that serious public interest concerns are addressed and individual whistleblowers are not victimised. PCaW itself does not run a whistleblowers' support group as this function is met in the UK by another voluntary body, Freedom to Care.

## The Public Interest Disclosure Act

A law to protect whistleblowers was a long-term goal of the charity, but events meant that things moved much more swiftly than we could have imagined. Eighteen months after our launch Dr Tony Wright MP asked us and the Campaign for Freedom of Information to draft a Bill to protect whistleblowers in 1995 as a means to highlight the issue. The Bill received widespread support

---

[10] The helpline has advised over 3 000 clients with public concerns in the past decade. Client recommendation rates have been around 90%.

in and outside Parliament with the result that another Labour MP, Don Touhig, introduced a revised version of the Bill in 1996 after he won a ballot of backbench MPs. While this private member's Bill[11] was given strong support, it did not reach the statute book as it lacked government support. However in the wake of the Arms to Iraq report, Tony Blair pledged that, if elected, his government would legislate on these terms. Immediately after the 1997 election, this opportunity arose as Richard Shepherd, a Tory MP and long term supporter of the Bill won a place in the ballot. He introduced his Public Interest Disclosure Bill with strong support from the Labour Government, led by Ian McCartney MP. PCaW was closely involved in settling the scope and detail of the Bill and was asked by government and Mr Shepherd to consult on it. The Bill was enacted in 1998 after Lord Borrie – our founding chairman – had taken it through the House of Lords.

The Public Interest Disclosure Act (PIDA) is part of UK employment law and was described as one of the most far-reaching whistleblower protection laws in the world.[12] Lord Nolan, former Chair of the Committee on Standards in Public Life,[13] praised it as "skillfully achieving the essential but delicate balance between the public interest and the interests of employers".[14]

The legislation proved a key milestone in the work of PCaW, declaring whistleblowing a legitimate activity and offering legal protection to those in the workplace who speak up on behalf of others. Having achieved this, the charity has taken on the task of monitoring the law in practice and reviewing its operation at home[15] and explaining its approach abroad.

## Consultancy and training

PCaW recognised that raising awareness among employers and encouraging them to promote whistleblowing to their own staff would be the most effective way to change the culture of the workplace. In its first years, PCaW published good practice guidelines which were widely distributed in the public sector. In 1998, prior to PIDA coming into force, PCaW developed a comprehensive whistleblowing "Policy Pack" to enable organisations to

---

[11] A private member's Bill does not emanate from government but rather from individual MPs who win the opportunity (in a special ballot) to propose law on an issue they feel strongly about and which is not currently on the government agenda.

[12] The Act covers most individuals in work in the UK.

[13] Allegations of corruption and sleaze in government prompted then Prime Minister John Major to set up the Committee on Standards in Public Life in 1994 to examine issues of conduct of public office holders and public bodies.

[14] Hansard HL, 5 June 1998, col. 614.

[15] Please see CD Rom accompanying this book for PCaW's annotated guide to PIDA and case summaries produced by PCaW.

establish effective internal whistleblowing mechanisms. At the same time, the Department of Health commissioned PCaW to develop a tailor-made version to distribute to all hospitals in England. In 2003, the Policy Pack was fully updated on CD-ROM and a newly revised version was developed for secondary healthcare providers in England.

PCaW has offered both open and in-house training to regulators, unions and employers on how to implement and promote internal whistleblowing mechanisms (policies) and handle concerns. More recently, the focus has been on in-house training as organisations seek to ensure their senior managers and executive and non-executive directors understand the value of whistleblowing as key to effective risk management and corporate governance. Organisations who wish to embed whistleblowing in an open and accountable workplace culture are requesting bespoke services from PCaW to train officers designated under a whistleblowing policy, develop promotional and guidance materials and help review the effectiveness of these initiatives in the workplace. PCaW does not advise employers on specific whistleblowing cases but rather provides the tools to help ensure organisations handle whistleblowing properly and effectively.

In 2003 the charity launched a helpline subscription[16] for organisations that refer their staff directly to PCaW in their whistleblowing policies. By providing access to independent advice and promoting their own policies, employers are giving their workforce tangible assurance that the organisation is committed to handling concerns responsibly.[17]

As PCaW's expertise has become more widely recognised, its consultancy work has increased and developed. PCaW has worked, and will continue to work, with regulatory bodies, government departments, professional bodies and unions. They all have a significant role to play in making whistleblowing work both by setting a good practice example as employers and by raising awareness in their individual sectors or industries.

## Policy work

The charity also runs a policy and research programme[18] to stimulate debate and inform the decisions of employers and policy-makers. Even before it

---

[16] The helpline subscription is a nominal annual fee – 10 pence – based on the number of employees. PCaW has found that employers who subscribe to the helpline promote it more actively to their staff.

[17] In 1993/4 callers found out about the PCaW helpline from advice agencies and the media. In 2001/2 the largest source of referrals was from the workplace (34%).

[18] PCaW originally undertook this work through short-term staff contracts until, in 1995, the Nuffield Foundation and the Esmée Fairbairn Charitable Trust funded a senior research post for two years.

was officially launched, PCaW was commissioned by the European Parliament to report on the role of whistleblowers in controlling fraud in Europe, and by the Audit Commission to carry out market research and produce a report on fraud and corruption in local government. In its first few years, PCaW produced a series of reports – *Speaking Up by Sector* – that covered, among other things, the defence industry, the police and abuse of vulnerable people in care.

PCaW's public policy work has focused on issues of individual responsibility, organisational accountability, whistleblowing and the law where it believes its perspective would add value. This has included explaining the legal implications of PIDA, as well as responding to government proposals on corporate killing, freedom of information, human rights, protection for police officers, regulation, employment disputes, open justice, corporate governance, standards in public life and the role and public responsibilities of professionals such as lawyers and accountants.[19]

PCaW has established an annual ethics and accountability lecture to promote the issues and bring together different British and international perspectives. The charity's goal is to continue to monitor PIDA, consult on possible changes or improvements where necessary and lobby to ensure that PIDA remains practical and effective. The work of PCaW, the effect of PIDA and the recent public focus on accountability in the wider context of corporate responsibility and democracy means that continuing to try to influence public policy is essential. This wider influence is key to embedding the kind of cultural change – affecting individual responsibility and organisational accountability – that PCaW promotes.


## Community initiatives

Making whistleblowing work in real terms requires a shift in culture – from keeping one's head down to speaking up for the sake of others. When the charity was set up, the term whistleblower was equated with being a "snitch" or a "telltale" and most would not speak out for fear of reprisals by managers or colleagues. As well, the term whistleblower was applied almost exclusively to those who took their concerns outside their workplace – usually to the media and mostly anonymously.

It was one of the early aims of the new body to remove the pejorative sense of the term and to promote whistleblowers as responsible employees

---

[19] More details on PCaW's public policy work can be found at www.whistleblowing.org.uk

and citizens acting in the interests of their organisation and wider community. A timely boost came in 1995, when the Committee for Standards in Public Life endorsed PCaW's approach, particularly its emphasis on internal communication, and called it "whistleblowing".[20]

However, as many people will rightly identify, such views can be instilled early – in the school playground and at home – and continue right through one's education and working life. It is for this reason that PCaW has worked with community and school groups wherever possible. In 2000 PCaW ran a pilot project for sixth form students (16-18-year-olds) to address accountability and social responsibility. In addition, each year PCaW participates in the "Leadership and Team Building Course for Sixth Formers" at an English college. Despite the enthusiastic responses from students and educators, PCaW has not yet been successful in securing funding or support to develop whistleblowing as a part of the citizenship programme in the national curriculum. This remains an important target.

PCaW staff write articles for legal journals, trade magazines and professional briefings and will comment, where appropriate, for the media. Over the years, the charity has produced a number of pamphlets describing its services to different audiences including employers, workers and advice agencies. More recently, the key tool in the charity's public education and awareness programme is its comprehensive website – www.whistleblowing.org.uk. PCaW's biennial reports and newsletters[21] help keep the issues alive and the message relevant.

## Scotland

In 2001 PCaW undertook a six-month pilot project in Scotland to assess the need for its work there. It appeared that despite the activity in England, there was little awareness in Scotland of whistleblowing generally or of PIDA in particular. The need for a presence in Scotland to help tackle these issues in a Scottish context – taking account of legal, governmental and demographic differences – was emphasised by all those contacted during the pilot including whistleblowers, politicians, employers and voluntary groups. The project also identified the peculiar difficulties that can face individuals in smaller, more isolated communities or in deprived areas where jobs are scarce.

---

[20] For more details see Part III, page 101, "Whistleblowing – the UK Experience".

[21] The newsletter is published twice a year and is available in hard copy or in PDF format. As it can be transmitted electronically it has been distributed more widely than other PCaW publications.

The charity secured a two-year grant from the Community Fund (the body which expends a portion of the proceeds of the National Lottery) to cover the salary costs of a Scottish director whose primary function is to promote the issue of responsible whistleblowing as widely as possible in Scotland. PCaW Scotland was officially launched in February 2002,[22] and though still in its infancy, contact with unions, employers and the media have helped to focus minds on the benefits of a positive approach to whistleblowing in Scotland. In particular, PCaW Scotland has worked closely with Audit Scotland – an early supporter of a Scottish presence – to raise awareness in the public sector. In October 2003, PCaW Scotland jointly hosted an international conference on whistleblowing in Edinburgh.[23]

## International work

The UK approach to whistleblowing and the work of PCaW has caught the interest of European policy-makers and international civil society groups over the years. As stated earlier, even before its official launch PCaW was commissioned to do work in Europe. Since then PCaW has worked with the Organisation for Economic Cooperation and Development and been consulted by policy-makers, professional bodies and citizen groups from Nigeria, Lithuania, Ireland, Japan and Germany, amongst others. In particular, PCaW has worked closely with the Open Democracy Advice Centre (ODAC) in South Africa and has shared experience with its counterpart in the US, the Government Accountability Project (GAP).

Although PCaW remains a nationally-based organisation providing services to UK citizens, its contact and experience internationally helps to inform its domestic approach and ensures that whistleblowing and accountability are seen in their wider context. It does not mean, however, that the UK model will be appropriate in all cultures or legal systems but sharing experience can only help strengthen the debate and ensure that issues of accountability are addressed properly.

---

[22] PCaW Scotland was officially opened by George Foulkes, the then Minister of State at the Scottish office, amidst much local publicity.

[23] The conference was made possible with help from the Chartered Institute of Public Finance and Accountancy (CIPFA), Scotland.

# Funding

PCaW would not have been possible without early and continuing support from a number of charitable trusts,[24] as it receives no state aid. In addition, the charity receives valuable support – through donations and promotion – from a diverse range of organisations, corporations and individuals. However, like many charities in the UK, the more established PCaW has become, the more difficult it is to secure charitable funding. For this reason, and to ensure it maintains its independence, PCaW has always tried to earn part of its income through its consulting and training work.[25] Successful as this has been, PCaW will continue to depend on and seek charitable funding for its community initiative and helpline work. This is clear when one looks at the income sources for 2003. To meet an expenditure of some £300 000 on its London and Scottish offices, it received 50% from earnings and subscriptions, 40% from foundation grants and the balance from individual donations.

# Conclusion

Under the guidance of its trustees and council, the following strategy plan was drawn up in 1993 to cover PCaW's first ten years:

- To promote the positive aspects of whistleblowing and to seek a shift away from the negative meaning of the word;

- To promote individual responsibility by encouraging workers and people generally to speak up about things they think are wrong and thereby to improve the ways in which organisations are – and are seen to be – accountable;

- To give legal and practical advice and help (free of charge) to people concerned about serious malpractice in the workplace;

- To promote legislation to protect public interest whistleblowers;

- To encourage employers to view whistleblowing as welcome and positive;

- To persuade employers to set up safe and effective whistleblowing procedures and to promote them actively to their workforce;

---

[24] These include the Joseph Rowntree Charitable Trust, the Nuffield Foundation, Calouste Gulbenkian Foundation, the Allen Lane Foundation, the Esmeé Fairbairn Charitable Foundation, the Leigh Trust, the Savoy Educational Trust and the Tudor Trust.

[25] In two years – 2001 and 2002 – the charity earned 35% of its income.

- To establish PCaW as the recognised source of independent expertise and authority in this area;

- To encourage insurers to offer premium discounts to organisations which implement effective whistleblowing procedures.

Ten years on (with the sole exception of the last item) PCaW has met or exceeded its targets and, in some areas, made more progress than anyone involved in the first discussions could have anticipated.

Despite the huge strides PCaW has made so far it continues to face the challenge of securing real and lasting cultural change. PCaW's objective remains to offer and make people aware that there is a safe alternative to silence and to ensure that every UK workplace is open and accountable. The charity will also continue to monitor the law and campaign for improvements where necessary and promote this issue overseas.

The UK approach to whistleblowing is fundamentally about individual responsibility and organisational accountability and PCaW will campaign hard to ensure that this approach is in the mind's eye of policy- and law-makers alike as they address these issues in all their manifestations.

# JAPAN: PUBLIC INTEREST SPEAK-UP ADVISERS (PISA)

*By Koji Morioka[1]*

In Japan, in the last two years, information provided by workers and others has increasingly led to the exposure of crimes and malpractice in companies. As a result, a greater emphasis has been placed on the role of public interest disclosures in the workplace. At the same time hotlines acting as "highways" for information within companies have sprung up, and the move to introduce law protection in Japan for people who make public interest disclosures has gained momentum.

The importance of public interest disclosures to consumers was highlighted in July 2000, when Mitsubishi was forced to recall nearly two million cars following information about safety risks received from employees.

In 2002, the conduct of certain companies was deemed far from acceptable as the following frauds and illegalities came to light:

- Snow Brand Foods – meat fraud concealment;

- Sasebo Heavy Industries – illegal acceptance of subsidies;

- Zennoh Chicken Foods – chicken meat fraud concealment;

- Kyouwa Koryo Kagaku – use of non-permitted chemical spices;

- Dasukin – use of unauthorised anti-oxidant;

- USJ – use of expired meats;

- Nippon Ham – meat fraud concealment;

- Tokyo Electric Power – the concealment of nuclear reactor faults.

Under such conditions, and with calls from the *Kabunushi* or shareholders' ombudsman, Public Interest Speak-Up Advisers (PISA), involving lawyers, accountants and academics, was established on 29 October 2002.

PISA discusses with concerned employees the details of alleged wrongdoing in companies or government organisations and offers free advice if necessary. An assessment is made of whether the public interest is at risk and, in such cases, steps are taken to ensure that the incident does not occur again,

[1] I am most grateful to Mr Gerald Dooley and Ms Evelyn Oakley for assisting in the translation of this paper. It goes without saying, however, that the responsibility for any errors and inadequacies there may be rest solely with me.

while respecting the confidentiality of the disclosing individual. The possibility of alerting the relevant regulator or even the media is considered in some circumstances. In its first six months, 130 separate incidents were brought to PISA's attention.

Meanwhile, in December 2002, the Social Policy Council in the Cabinet Office released an intermediate report entitled *Consumer Policy for the 21st Century*. The basis of this report was the establishment of a commission to examine a system of protection for people who make public interest disclosures, as a means of ensuring the protection of consumer interests. In May 2003 a paper entitled "Public Interest Disclosure System" was released, outlining the scope of a possible Act.

This chapter outlines the goals and activities of PISA, and gives examples of disclosures made. Finally, it discusses very briefly concerns about the Public Interest Disclosure Bill in the light of Japan's particular culture.

## PISA's establishment and first six months

The number of public interest disclosures concerning workplace illegalities and malpractice has been increasing, but that does not mean that making a disclosure is becoming any easier. It is clear from statements made at a symposium at the launch of PISA, and earlier discussions, that disclosures of malpractice by senior management lead to many employees suffering severe disadvantages including, in many cases, loss of employment. The perception that a disclosure was a sacrifice has not changed. While incidents where employees disclose information still occur, most disclosures seemed to come from business associates, subsidiary company employees, former part-time workers, temporary workers and independent contractors.

The reality is that in the Japanese business community disclosing information about corporate malpractice is perceived as a betrayal of the company. To break down this perception, public interest disclosure had to be recognised as legally justified and structures to provide protection for those who make public interest disclosures had to be created. At the same time, the need had been demonstrated for a helpline offering advice to concerned employees. The beginning of this process was the creation of the legal advice group, PISA.

In its first six months, PISA offered advice to many employees concerned about grave dangers to people's lives and safety caused by malpractice within companies, government organisations or other groups. Examples are listed below.

## Companies:

- Environmental degradation and pollution;
- Mis-labelling and false advertisement;
- Concealment of chemical contamination;
- Concealment of cases of *karoshi* (death from overwork), sexual harassment or sexual discrimination;
- Corruption among company executives involving violent groups, *sokaiya* (corporate racketeers) and illegal pay-offs;
- Accounting fraud and insider trading;
- Bid-rigging and illegal cartels;
- Concealment or untruthful disclosure of important government facts.

## Government agencies or politicians:

- Acts of illegal collusion among officials, politicians and companies;
- Corruption or acceptance of bribes by public officials and politicians;
- Criminal acts in relation to budgets and management of public funding;
- Negligence by officials;
- Concealment of human rights infringements by immigration and prison officials.

## Other groups (restricted to groups meeting national standards):

- Concealment of health malpractice in medical organisations;
- Illegal acceptance of subsidies;
- Concealment of sexual harassment;
- Incorrect entrance of students into schools;
- Illegal activities in relation to contribution money by industry groups.

PISA does not offer legal advice to individuals who have personal difficulties at work, so individual cases where a person has been dismissed from their job, sexually harassed or been the victim of financial fraud will not be dealt with. However, PISA will take information and offer advice where attempts have been made by organisations to conceal such incidents.

As all work by PISA's lawyers is carried out on a voluntary basis, its capacity is necessarily restricted. There is therefore a focus on listed companies and national bodies, though of course in cases where there is a real threat to consumers or public interests outside these sectors PISA will take details and offer assistance. All information must be received in writing – via email, fax or letter – and, in the first instance, PISA's lawyers and accountants will make an initial decision regarding the importance and level of clarity of the disclosure. If a case is to be taken on by PISA, a lawyer with relevant experience will discuss the details of the disclosure with the individual concerned and give legal advice if necessary.

Some consultations will end there. In certain circumstances PISA will investigate and confirm the information received and attempt to establish the intentions of the individual. It is desirable that, if it is judged necessary and possible, the facts are then reported to the company, while protecting the individual's identity. The company will be urged to take the necessary action to correct the matter. In this case, the company will also be encouraged to make the matter public. Judging from the first six months' experiences, however, it is difficult for PISA to report public interest disclosures by employees to the company, mainly because they strongly distrust the company.

To ensure that the malpractice does not occur again, the company needs to take a positive approach and display a willingness to confront the issue without prejudice towards the claimant. This is not always the case. When the information is disclosed to the company, it is often easy for them to identify the claimant and, without a system of protection for public interest disclosures, many employees fear being victimised or dismissed. In many cases that have been brought to PISA's attention, people make the disclosure despite the realisation that they are likely to be disadvantaged by the employer but, for this reason, many disclosures are made anonymously or under false names. There are also cases where, for fear of reprisals, a person will withdraw the information. In such cases PISA will respect their decision and, even where the incident is considered serious, will not take up the case.

Encouragingly, though, there have been cases where a claimant has voiced his or her concerns within the workplace and the issue has been addressed and rectified. There have also been cases where the claimant has consented to PISA disclosing the information to the media, who in turn bring it to the notice of the public. This has led to the company acknowledging the problem and taking the necessary action to correct it.

# Public interest disclosures in PISA's first six months

There were 113 disclosures to PISA in the six months to the end of April 2003, excluding those not related to the public interest. Below are details of the major problems that have been disclosed.

## Infringements on the interests of consumers

Eighteen separate incidents accounted for 16% of disclosures. The industries affected included insurance, pharmaceuticals, used cars, food production, meat inspection, food product sales, motor vehicles, medicine, electric power, gene alteration medical treatment, money lending, coffee, cosmetics, contact lenses and CATV.

In the case of used car sales, consumers were forced to pay an automobile acquisition tax of between 30 000 and 100 000 yen, despite the fact that the transactions were tax-free. In food production, an order was given by a manager to use expired ingredients. There was sales fraud and incorrect labelling of organic food products that were not, in fact, free of chemicals. Food products containing bacteria were reused. Other food products, banned for domestic use, were used in production. In a medical case, a patient's chart was altered dishonestly and in a power plant inspection documents were falsified. A furniture maker was found to be exporting Chinese products labelled "Made in Japan" when they could not sell them in the Japanese market.

## Illegal acceptance of public funding

Information relating to the illegal receipt of public funding, such as subsidies, through falsified applications and inflated amounts accounted for 17 incidents, or 15% of the total number of disclosures. Organisations involved included government-appointed offices, regional government groups, small and large companies, co-operatives, social welfare corporations, medical corporations, research institutes and universities. There have even been cases of illegal kickbacks from subsidies paid to Diet members.

## Acts of self-profit by managers and senior officials

Incidents of this nature made up 12% of the total number of disclosures. Examples include an accounting division chief who transferred money into his own bank account from a company he had connections with and the son of a company director who illegally took money from the company and used it for his own benefit.

## Other disclosures

Other disclosures include unpaid overtime cases, bid-rigging on public works projects, raising off-the-book-funds, window-dressing and illegal software use. There were also cases of illegalities involving criminal gangs, police and public officials, as well as tax evasion, embezzling money, inaccurate financing, travel expense fraud and interfering with bidding.

On PISA's homepage it is explained that no assistance will be given in cases where the person has been disadvantaged through making a public disclosure without PISA's advice. However, in the six months since PISA's launch, 11 incidents (about 10% of the total disclosures) have been of this nature, where individuals have suffered a reprisal or are in fear of a reprisal in the near future.

The disadvantages they are experiencing are not restricted to loss of employment. A worker for a regional public group disclosed information on a superior who had committed an injustice and the issue was subsequently rectified. However, the superior blocked her application for a transfer and, despite speaking with the person in charge of company compliance, the situation did not change. She now very much regrets making the public disclosure.

An employee of a large listed company disclosed information about the supply of parts and was told that nothing could be done. He discussed the issue with his superiors in the parent company, and was then dismissed for disciplinary reasons. He and his lawyers made a claim of unfair dismissal to the courts who ruled that he remain in the company. However, he was told that no division in the company would accept a person who had made a public disclosure, and he finds job opportunities for him within that company are blocked.

The reality is that if an individual is disadvantaged by an employer after making a public disclosure there is no way that at present this unfortunate situation can be reversed. It is therefore of paramount importance to establish a system which provides protection for a person who makes a public disclosure.

# Conclusion

According to the *Mainichi Newspaper* (13 November 2003), the Public Interest Disclosure Bill, soon to be submitted, clings to the idea that information should be disclosed to the company in question or to government agencies, and sets strict requirements when making disclosures to outside agencies like the media and consumer groups. Such a law will make it more difficult for workers to make public interest disclosures. PISA and other groups want to relax the requirements on disclosures to outside agencies to ensure a strong and effective law.

For those workers who want to make a public disclosure, there is already a deep clash of morals and psychology. Within Japanese corporate culture there has long been a belief that illegality or malpractice should be overlooked or ignored for the sake of the company. Even if a company encourages its employees to use an internal helpline, many people doubt whether anything will change within the company. As mentioned above, almost all informers to PISA do not like to report their information regarding public interest disclosures to their companies.

As a result of this mind-set, most company workers, including those who may wish to disclose information, value the company's interests over those of the consumer or the public interest. People who consider making disclosures face a moral conflict in that, even though the disclosure may be justified, there is a distinct possibility that they may be disadvantaged – that upper management or their colleagues may think they have betrayed the company. This is clear from the calls received by PISA from people who were considering making a disclosure, but then withdrew after considering the consequences of their actions.

But whatever the detail of the new law, it is clear that demand for PISA's advice will grow. However strong or weak legal protection may be, in practice workers will always need confidential advice before they consider how best to blow the whistle.

# SOUTH AFRICA:
# OPEN DEMOCRACY ADVICE CENTRE

*By Alison Tilley and Lorraine Stober*

The Open Democracy Advice Centre (ODAC) was conceived of in mid-1999 by Richard Calland of the Institute for Democracy in South Africa (IDASA) and Lala Camerer, then of the Institute for Security Studies. Camerer was interested in the conceptual link between whistleblowing and access to information and Calland was keenly interested in making two new laws, the Protected Disclosures Act (or Whistleblowing Act) and the Promotion of Access to Information Act, work in practice. Both laws were state-of-the-art legislation, but by then, six years into South Africa's new democracy, a clear trend had emerged: strong law and policy-making alongside weak implementation.

Calland had worked hard in lobbying for both pieces of law, with others in the Open Democracy Campaign Group, which was formed in 1995 and comprised nine other civil society organisations. A major concern for all those working on this legislation was that it would fail at the hurdle of implementation. It was the experience of many of those working on legislation that the parliamentary process was, despite appearances, the easy bit – implementation in a civil service lacking capacity and with a long history of secrecy and authoritarian management was not going to be easy.

At the end of 1999, Calland and Camerer approached the Joseph Rowntree Charitable Trust with the idea of setting up a specialist centre. They were offered a "start-up" grant. ODAC began as a new programme of IDASA, but Calland was keen to sustain the collective energy of the campaign group and so approached the Black Sash Trust and the Public Law Department of the University of Cape Town. Both were keen to be involved.

Once a further grant from the Open Society Foundation was secured in August 2000, ODAC was able to appoint its first manager, Alison Tilley, who started work at the beginning of 2001. Tilley had been the head of advocacy of the Black Sash, a South African human rights and advice NGO, and was also an active member of the Open Democracy Campaign Group. Tilley's first initiative was to explore the intention of providing legal advice. She discovered that it would be necessary for ODAC to qualify as a "law centre," which would require it to be a separate legal entity. The founding organisations agreed and the long process of designing and registering ODAC as a non-profit company began.

The non-profit company is designed so that the founding organisations dominate the shareholding with 30 shares each. There are another seven individual members, drawn from trade unions, further education and human rights organisations, as well as the two founding members, Calland and Camerer.

The executive committee decided at an early stage that it was important to extend the range of opinion and expertise beyond the membership and directors of ODAC by inviting organisations and individuals to be associates. ODAC's current associates include Colm Allan of the Public Service Accountability Monitor, Verne Harris of the South African History Archive, Andrew Puddephatt of Article 19 in the UK, Guy Dehn of the London charity, Public Concern at Work, Chuck Lewis of the Center for Public Integrity, Laura Neuman of the Carter Center and the NGO, MKSS, from Rajasthan, India. The easiest way of describing associates is "friends"; associates have no legal obligation or authority, but are able to provide wise counsel from time to time, and are invited to annual meetings of associates to accompany the annual general meeting.

ODAC's mission is to promote transparent democracy, foster a culture of corporate and government accountability and assist people in South Africa to realise their human rights. ODAC seeks to achieve its mission through supporting the effective implementation of rights and laws that enable access to information and whistleblowing.

## Implementation of a whistleblowing support programme in South Africa

One of our associates, Public Concern at Work, is a highly successful charity based in London. This charity provides training for companies and the public sector to help them install and implement whistleblowing policies. It also runs a helpline for people who are considering blowing the whistle. Public Concern at Work is a model for ODAC, with experience of particular relevance given that the South African Act was largely modelled on the British one. We assumed that the private and public sector would see putting whistleblowing policies into place as useful, and adopted the language of Public Concern at Work in talking about a "common interest" between employer and employee. We recognised that there was little awareness of the concept of whistleblowing and that whistleblowing had a bad reputation in the country. We were also concerned that it would be difficult to sell the concept of a common interest in the workplace to such a heavily unionised and militant society as South Africa – it would also have to meet the challenge of establishing how very different classes with different class interests could find common ground.

We felt that any project of this kind in South Africa would need to place a lot of emphasis on awareness-raising around whistleblowing and what it means. We also saw our relationships with other parts of civil society, particularly the unions, as key to ODAC's success. As a result we made a number of efforts to draw unions into promoting whistleblowing and its protections amongst their members.

The planning for the project envisaged a number of phases in the project cycle.

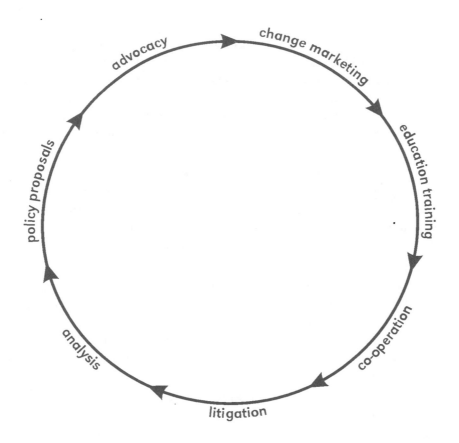

**Project cycle**

The first phase would be awareness-raising and education on the concept of whistleblowing. This would be followed by ODAC trainers assisting companies in the private sector in putting whistleblowing policies in place. We anticipated that following that there would be a fair number of people needing advice on how to blow the whistle and for this purposes some form of free confidential legal advice would be offered. We envisaged that following that the whistleblower would go to court to get the necessary protection and that a jurisprudence would develop. The project would monitor this jurisprudence and analyse it. This knowledge, together with the experience of our training, would enable us to make inputs into the policy processes around the implementation of the legislation. Any changes brought about by those processes would then go back to the trainers who would be able to take those changes back to the public and private sectors.

The minimum staff needed for this process was a trainer, who would deal with marketing, education and training, and a helpline adviser, who would be able to advise potential whistleblowers. The policy work would not need any dedicated staff but rather would be dealt with by the centre manager and other members of staff. In the first phase of the project our PDA trainer came on board and was sent to Public Concern at Work in London for training and to observe how they run their system. A former staff member of Public Concern at Work also came to South Africa to assist with the development of materials.

The centre won a tender to provide consultative workshops around the country on how to implement whistleblowing within the public service. This became one of the first areas of the trainer's work. At this point there were no dedicated staff for the helpline and calls which came in from whistleblowers were referred to the centre manager or the trainer.

While South Africa's Public Service Commission is to be commended for its proactive stance on running workshops in all the provinces the response of the provinces varied. In some cases the workshops were well attended by senior officials and participation was enthusiastic, while in a number of other provinces workshop attendance was very poor and mainly by junior officials. We are not sure how to interpret this in terms of commitment by the various provinces to implementing this legislation.

Initially only a few calls came in and in fact one of the first complex cases the project dealt with was one where the whistleblowers were not actually covered by the legislation. The whistleblowers made a number of sensational allegations of corruption and clearly hoped that ODAC would take up the allegations that they were making. The staff of the centre felt that they were not in a position to do so, that they were there for whistleblowers, and the whistleblowing in this instance was not covered by the Act. The centre staff explained that the matter did not concern whistleblowing and they could not take up a general concern around governance in a particular institution. Although this meant not helping the individuals in the way they wished to be helped, the case laid the foundations for the principles on which the whistleblowing helpline would operate. These would be, firstly, that the whistleblower would not be encouraged to blow the whistle but rather advised of the consequences, and protections provided if she or he chose to blow the whistle.

Secondly, the centre would not take up any campaign around issues that a whistleblower is working on but would rather seek to protect the whistleblower. Thirdly, allegations of mismanagement and corruption would not be taken up by the centre, but we would support the whistleblower in doing so.

In a second case involving a whistleblower reporting the possibility of severe health risks to workers in a particular sector the complainant's purpose was not in fact to raise a public concern, but to elicit a settlement from the employer involved. The individual was emphatic that there was a group of people who had been at risk but was reluctant to identify any of them. The whistleblower did not want to use any of the mechanisms provided in the Act, but rather wanted to threaten the employer with blowing the whistle publicly to obtain some form of compensation. Given the reluctance of the whistleblower to use the provisions of the Act, and given his motive, we felt that we couldn't assist him beyond giving him advice on the legal position. The person concerned was angry at the time and implied that this was the result of corruption within the centre.

The next phase of the project began when the helpline adviser was employed and the helpline launched. Again Public Concern at Work sent one of its staff members to assist with training and a launch was held. A total of 100 000 postcards were printed with the helpline number and distributed in four major metropolitan areas. Extensive media coverage of the helpline and the toll free telephone number resulted in the first week or two in far more calls than we could cope with; all the staff had to stop work on other projects to simply answer the phone. Fairly soon, however, the number of calls dropped off to a reasonable level and remain constant at about 100 a month. The data from calls is captured on a data base and certain cases are monitored through to court level.

The helpline has proved invaluable in informing our understanding of how whistleblowing is experienced by ordinary South Africans. The experience has been a bleak one, with many callers too frightened of retribution to speak out, and those who do subject to occupational detriment. Many are not covered by the protection of the Act. We asked for a meeting with the project committee of the South African Law Reform Commission to share our analysis where we were able to cite the experience of our callers, and urged the committee to recommend broader protections.

The South African Law Reform Commission was instructed by the Minister of Justice to take up the recommendations of the Portfolio Committee of the Department of Justice to research certain issues relating to the Protected Disclosures Act. An issue paper was prepared in the form of a questionnaire to elicit responses from interested people. It served as a basis for the Commission's deliberations, eventually resulting in possible amendments to the law.

All our planning assumed that the "common interest" between employer and employee could be recognised and acted on in the South African workplace. We had not counted on the deluge of legislation that the corporate and public sector would have to digest. Changes to the Labour Relations Act, the introduction of the Employment Equity Act, the money laundering legislation, the Surveillance and Monitoring Act, the Promotion of Access to Information Act, the Public Finance Management Act and the Basic Conditions of Employment Act left employers reeling, and disinclined to do anything more than meet the minimum regulatory requirements.

Repeated calls for the private sector to take up the international move to supported whistleblowing, and local marks of approval such as in the King II report, made little or no impact on the private sector. (In 1994 the King Report on Corporate Governance [King I] was published by the King Committee on Corporate Governance, headed by former High Court judge, Mervyn King S.C. King I, incorporating a Code of Corporate Practices and Conduct, was the first of its kind in the country and was aimed at promoting the highest standards of corporate governance in South Africa.) Over and above the financial and regulatory aspects of corporate governance, King I advocated an integrated approach to good governance in the interests of a wide range of stakeholders. Although groundbreaking at the time, the evolving global economic environment together with recent legislative developments, have necessitated that King I be updated. To this end, the King Committee on Corporate Governance developed the King Report on Corporate Governance for South Africa, 2002 (King II).

King II acknowledges that there is a move away from the single bottom line (i.e. profit for shareholders) to a triple bottom line, which embraces the economic, environmental and social aspects of a company's activities. In the words of the King Committee:

> ...*successful governance in the world in the 21st century requires companies to adopt an inclusive and not exclusive approach. The company must be open to*

*institutional activism and there must be greater emphasis on the sustainable or non-financial aspects of its performance. Boards must apply the test of fairness, accountability, responsibility and transparency to all acts or omissions and be accountable to the company but also responsive and responsible towards the company's identified stakeholders. The correct balance between conformance with governance principles and performance in an entrepreneurial market economy must be found, but this will be specific to each company.*

The public sector was more embracing, and are considering implementation, albeit slowly.

We experience the environment for whistleblowing as being very hostile, more so than we could have imagined. The racial transformations in the workplace, limited as they have been, have not necessarily had an impact on the hierarchical nature of the workplace and South African society generally. The resistance to unionisation has been very dogged, as unions have been seen not only as taking forward the rights of workers, but also the rights of the black majority, who continue to be excluded from ordinary political processes. The workplace remains a site of struggle for democracy.

As a result, the legacy of antipathy and polarisation remains. Some workplaces sound like a battleground between employer and employees, with the classic rhetoric of the "exploitation of the worker" still common currency. Whistleblowers are seen as insubordinate, failing to submerge their concerns in the interests of what the managers see as the greater good. The lack of ability on the part of managers to hear the message without shooting the messenger has meant a distinct shift in policy on our part.

We are focusing less on the positive outcomes of successful whistleblowing for business, e.g. being able to solve problems internally, and are focusing more on the negative outcomes when whistleblowers are not heard. We are using case studies of businesses going under, major industrial accidents and ongoing safety hazards to illuminate the dangers of not giving whistleblowers a safe alternative to silence. We have also developed a policy pack that we are distributing free of charge, containing all the elements needed for implementing a whistleblowing strategy. We continue to engage business, for example at a series of breakfast seminars, which will be followed up by meetings with participants who showed an interest in the work we do. We will also meet people who could not attend the seminars. In addition we will be meeting the Institute of Directors and making presentations at business schools and private sector conferences.

# AUSTRALIA: WHISTLEBLOWERS AUSTRALIA

*By Brian Martin*[1]

In 1973, Bill Toomer was simply doing his job. As quarantine officer at Fremantle, Western Australia, he inspected a ship and ordered it fumigated. This was an expensive operation, unwelcome by some ship owners who had cosy relationships with their regulators. Toomer came under fierce and sustained attack. He lost his job, his family broke up and he ended up destitute and in bad health.

When Toomer first came under attack, the idea of whistleblowing was unfamiliar in Australia. Lots of people thought he had been unjustly treated, but there was no organised network to provide support.

This only changed from 1991 with the setting up of Whistleblowers Australia (WBA), a national organisation whose goal is to promote a society in which it is possible to speak out without reprisal about corruption, dangers to the public and environment and other vital issues, and to help those who speak out in this way to help themselves.

From the start, WBA has been based entirely on volunteers. We have not sought funding from governments, corporations or wealthy individuals. Most of our income comes from $25 annual membership fees. With 200 or so members, that gives an annual budget of less than $10 000. One advantage of relying on volunteers is that everyone who contributes does so because they want to. Another is that there is less temptation to pass all the work to overloaded paid workers. Instead, we're all overloaded!

That's because most members are themselves whistleblowers. Members are not required to be whistleblowers, but that's who gravitates to the group.

Probably the most important function of WBA is to put whistleblowers in touch with each other. Many never set out to blow the whistle but just were doing their jobs, for example by reporting a problem about finances to their boss. Having inadvertently touched a symptom of a deeper problem, they suddenly found themselves under attack.

In the state of New South Wales, which has the largest and most active branch, there are weekly "caring and sharing" meetings that give whistleblowers

---

[1]  Jean Lennane, national president of Whistleblowers Australia, offered useful comments to the author.

an opportunity to tell their stories and obtain support and advice from others. Often it is an immense relief to talk to others who have had similar experiences and to find that the problem lies with complacent or corrupt organisations and not with themselves. In other states, meetings are less frequent but there is considerable person-to-person contact.

Whistleblowers typically hear about WBA through a friend, a newspaper article, radio interview or the Internet. Tracking us down through the telephone directory or the Internet, they may phone or email one of our national committee members or regional contacts. Experienced members provide advice over the telephone, send leaflets and articles by post and sometimes give ongoing support through difficult cases.

Members of WBA include police, teachers, public servants, corporate employees, charity workers, doctors, researchers, church employees and concerned citizens. The word "former" should be attached in many cases because so many have left or lost their jobs. These individuals have raised concerns about corporate fraud, inside appointments, unsafe products, drug deals, protection of criminals, hazardous work practices, lying about government policy, environmental risks, plagiarism, sexual crimes and frame-ups, among other issues.

It is an indictment of social institutions that an organisation like WBA is necessary. After all, if grievance procedures, appeal bodies and the courts could deal with such problems, there would be no need for whistleblowers to band together. Unfortunately, the most common experience of Australian whistleblowers is that formal channels don't help. Many have tried a sequence of channels, from their employer's grievance procedures to an ombudsman, auditor-general, parliamentarian or court. Usually, none of these work. For example, in a court case about unfair dismissal, the employer is able to spend lots of time and money appealing unfavourable decisions while restricting the focus to narrow legal issues. Many whistleblowers spend their life savings and years of effort fighting a case. Meanwhile, the original problem remains unaddressed. Australian researcher William De Maria, in a pathbreaking study, found that whistleblowers reported being helped by formal channels in fewer than one out of ten cases.

Almost all members of WBA who have approached the Independent Commission Against Corruption in New South Wales have been disappointed with its performance and would not recommend that any whistleblower take a complaint there. Similarly, many members of the Whistleblowers Action Group in Queensland – which works closely with WBA – have been extremely disappointed with the performance of the Criminal Justice Commission in that state.

Whistleblower legislation is often touted as protection for those who speak out, but its performance falls far short of its promise. There are a number of whistleblower acts in Australian states and territories, but it is hard to find any whistleblowers who have benefited from them. Although reprisals against whistleblowers are commonplace, not a single employer has ever been prosecuted for such reprisals under any of the acts.

At best, whistleblower legislation signals government support for public interest disclosures and protects a minority of those who make them. More commonly, it channels complaints to dead-end official bodies, giving an illusion of protection while actually nothing changes. Worse still, complainants trying to enforce their rights under the law can have ruinous costs awarded against them, as happened to the only whistleblower yet to try for the "protection" offered by the New South Wales Protected Disclosures Act.

Rather than trying to protect whistleblowers after they suffer reprisals, another approach is to promote a culture of dissent. One WBA campaign was to remove legal restraints on free speech by government employees. WBA worked with trade unions and liaised with Freedom to Care, a kindred whistleblower group in Britain, to bring about an amendment to the International Labour Organisation's convention 111 in order to prohibit discrimination on the basis of making a public interest disclosure.

Australia's defamation laws are draconian, and many whistleblowers are threatened with defamation actions. WBA produced a detailed leaflet on defamation, outlining a number of options for avoiding or challenging the use of defamation law to inhibit free speech.

In New South Wales, many teachers and government employees reported being dismissed after being declared mentally unfit by psychiatrists of a referral body called HealthQuest. WBA branch members collected data, organised media coverage and held rallies outside HealthQuest offices, eventually stimulating a revision of procedures.

WBA set up a formal procedure for assessing nominated whistleblowing cases and declaring individuals to be "Whistleblowers of National Significance," with five individuals so far being so honoured, one of them Bill Toomer. Each case is used to illustrate specific shortcomings in official methods for dealing with public interest disclosures.

Holding together an organisation made up largely of whistleblowers is not easy. Few members have much in common with each other except the whistleblowing experience. Many are highly traumatised, have been let down by organisations and individuals. They often have high expectations of obtaining support, expectations that cannot always be met. WBA has gone through some tense internal battles but we have survived. That is quite an achievement in itself.

Because so many members have their own cases, that leaves relatively few with the energy and experience to advise and support others. Across the country, there are perhaps a couple of dozen individuals who do most of the work: handling queries, organising and running meetings, making submissions and producing materials. Given that WBA might be contacted by several new whistleblowers every week, each with a challenging and complex case, there is no possible way that advocacy can be provided to all comers. Therefore, WBA has a policy of not formally supporting individuals in their whistleblowing cases. Instead, we encourage self-help and mutual support. That means that our primary activities are providing information, offering advice, and putting people in touch with each other.

One thing that does not work very well is to try to decide whether someone is really a whistleblower before providing advice, support or membership. This puts members in the role of judges of newcomers, sometimes leading to further hurt. Promising to offer support to genuine whistleblowers also causes problems, because the demand for individual advocacy far outstrips our capacity to provide it. The New South Wales branch has been highly successful in adopting a policy of welcoming anyone who wants to come along to a meeting. Some who have attended over the years were not whistleblowers but instead better described as disruptive employees or even criminals. Such individuals seldom find what they are after and drop out of WBA. The advantages of a non-judgemental atmosphere outweigh occasionally having to deal with awkward non-whistleblowers. After all, some whistleblowers are awkward too.

Changes in the culture of organisations and society are definitely necessary, since it is amazingly difficult for a whistleblower to obtain vindication through formal channels. In Bill Toomer's case, there have been some 11 inquiries into the affair over two decades, at vast expense to the government and of course Toomer himself. WBA stalwart Keith Potter continues to pursue justice for Toomer, requesting that the federal government formally exonerate Toomer of charges against him and make a compensation payment, as has been recommended more than once by government officials in the long-running saga. But the government continues to stall and resist action.

In contrast to official channels, the media are often extremely helpful, reporting on the whistleblower's plight as well as the issues about which they raised concerns. The media and whistleblowers have a common interest in bringing issues into the open for public scrutiny and in resisting attempts to squash free speech. A number of experienced WBA members have concluded that the two things most helpful to whistleblowers are publicity and talking to other whistleblowers. As well as local meetings and a network of contacts, WBA has regular conferences, a phone number for leaving messages and two websites (http://www.whistleblowers.org.au and http://www.uow.edu.au/arts/sts/bmartin/dissent/).

WBA is part of an informal network of groups and individuals promoting a more open and honest society, including a number of journalists, lawyers, researchers, trade unions and free speech organisations. WBA on its own can't solve the problems of individual whistleblowers but it can be part of a process by which more and more people learn the skills to act effectively against social problems.

# CONCLUSION

## WHISTLEBLOWING AROUND THE WORLD: GIVING PEOPLE A VOICE

### ACCOUNTABILITY AND THE PUBLIC INTEREST: CREATING A SAFE ALTERNATIVE TO SILENCE

*By Richard Calland and Guy Dehn*

In the old days, miners would take a canary underground with them. Gas is highly dangerous underground, but very hard to detect. Canaries apparently have more sensitive capacities and could operate as an early warning system. Whistleblowers have long served a similar sort of role. Unfortunately, like the canary who died in the process, whistleblowers used to be martyrs to their cause. The position has now thankfully changed. Seeing whistleblowers as exercising a "right to warn", they are valued as people who can help organisations and societies avoid disaster.

Usually there is a witness to wrongdoing or negligence. Time and again across the world the story behind scandals and disasters, both large and small, is that people who worked in the organisation had seen the danger but had either been too scared to sound the alarm or had raised the alarm in the wrong way or with the wrong person. Some witnesses are known and some are not; some witnesses choose to stay silent and some choose to speak out. The real question is not whether there is a witness – a potential early warning system – but whether he or she will feel confident both that the climate is safe enough to come forward and that speaking up will achieve something.

Whistleblowing continues to make headlines and impact on public policy around the world. In Europe, Neil Kinnock, vice president of the European Commission, publicly apologised to Dorte Schmidt Brown, whose whistleblowing on major financial abuses at Eurostat had initially been ignored. In the USA, a tip-off from an insider alerted the authorities to a new undetectable anabolic steroid designed to help sports stars cheat their way to the top. In India, Satyendra Dubey, a young engineer who had raised genuine concerns about corruption on a massive road project, was found murdered.

In Australia, an employee at National Australia Bank was praised for blowing the whistle internally on four traders who had covered up losses of $180 million. In the UK, the authorities decided to stop the prosecution of Katherine Gun who admitted she had leaked a top secret request from the US that the UK help spy on plans to avert a rushed invasion of Iraq.

These five incidents from around the world bear out the message of this book; attitudes toward whistleblowing are changing. A decade ago was it imaginable that a vice president of the European Commission would have issued a public apology to a whistleblower? Or that international sporting regulators would admit how easy it is for them to be hoodwinked without information from insiders? A decade ago would a young Indian engineer have written so clearly and so simply about corruption to his prime minister? Had he done so and met with the same tragic consequences, would it have generated such a groundswell of support across the subcontinent for a new approach to whistleblowing? Would a national bank have so willingly admitted that it was the actions of an internal whistleblower rather than its state of the art controls that picked up a major problem? A decade ago would the UK authorities have felt so unsure that a jury of twelve members of the public would refuse to convict someone like Katherine Gun?

While we welcome the fact that whistleblowers are no longer portrayed exclusively or primarily as virtuous victims (a la Jeffrey Wigand in *The Insider*), or as disloyal troublemakers, we do sound a note of caution. While some whistleblowers will be praised for what they do, others will suffer slings and arrows for their principles. While some will succeed in securing change or averting disaster, others won't. While the choices some will face may affect war and peace, others will be concerned by what may at first appear to be innocuous. While some who claim the banner of the whistleblower will be mistaken, others who are whistleblowers will choose to stand on their own and reject any such label. As this book shows, whistleblowing is about basic issues which lie at the heart of human activity. It covers loyalty and the questioning of dubious practices. It concerns communication and silence. It is about practising what one preaches and about leadership. It focuses on responsibility toward others and the accountability of those in charge. It is where public and private interests meet.

So why is it such a difficult issue? In Nirvana, a whistleblower would be free to come forward to raise a concern. The person would be listened to by another human being with due respect and the concern raised taken seriously. The message heeded and acted upon, with an appropriate investigation of the facts, the messenger would then slip quietly back into the humdrum rhythm of normal life. In contradistinction to the history of whistleblowing and whistleblowers, in Nirvana this act of, in Tom Devine's words, "committing the truth" would require no extraordinary departure from ordinary existence.

As this book explains, the British legal approach, emulated by the South African law, attempts to turn this conceptual ambition into reality. In a sense, it seeks to take the bravery out of whistleblowing by "normalising" the act of whistleblowing, taking the "heat out of it" by shifting the debate from one that primarily focuses on the motivation of the whistleblower to one that focuses on the nature of the information and the appropriate recipient for it. At its heart lies a core deal: that in return for the whistleblower making the disclosure internally first, the organisation will take the message seriously and not harm the messenger. When, in the absence of any guidance, whistles are blown externally first or concerns are not raised then unjustified harm can be done to the reputation of the organisation and those it serves. Thus, the stakes are raised – for everyone: for the organisation, for the whistleblower and even for the recipient of the information (consider, for example, what happened to journalist Lowell Bergman in the Wigand tobacco case).

There are significant benefits for the organisation in a system in which the whistle is not, therefore, in the first instance blown externally and employees have an alternative to silence. The corresponding benefit for the employee is that the stakes are lower and that a calmer, less intimidating environment is available for him or her to make the disclosure. But this, in turn, is premised on the organisation not only taking whistleblowing seriously, but having sufficient commitment to the idea, with a longer term vision in mind, to re-shape the internal culture so as to reflect the new "common interest" that is expressed in this model. This core deal reflects the idea that the employees and employer have a shared interest in good corporate governance in its widest possible sense.

That the prevention of loss of business, as well as life and limb, should be in the employees' interest as well as that of the employer is common sense. But, to anyone well disposed to class analysis, the notion that a common interest can exist between the owners of capital and the workers, is anything but common sense. Certainly in a place like South Africa, as noted in Part 3, a harsh history of an adversarial, exploitative relationship between employers and employees represents a huge challenge for the successful implementation of such a model. In the public sector across the world and in the modern consumer economies of the West, however, this approach to whistleblowing – the validity of which is clear from what happened at Enron – recognises that power is exercised not only by those who own capital but also by those who control it.

The evidence from the experiment in Britain is so far relatively encouraging. Slowly organisations have begun to see the value as well as the virtue in a new approach to internal whistleblowing; not untypically for Britain, it has been a "quiet revolution" in the words of our contributor, Anna Myers.

But Satyendra Dubey's case shows how an internal disclosure can go tragically wrong if there is no whistleblowing legislation that guides individuals and organisations on what is expected of them and why. Similarly, the fact that intelligence personnel and the armed forces are the only people not protected by the whistleblowing legislation in the UK may have led Katherine Gun to believe that the only options she had were silence or an anonymous leak. Equally, Lord Hutton's report into the death of David Kelly shows that the fact that such legislation applies is no guarantee in itself that it will impact on the culture of an organisation.

There is, then, a growing recognition that whistleblowers provide an early warning system and that they are crucial to preventing corruption and other forms of wrongdoing by individuals or organisations. That Robin Van den Hende could find that the actions of Chinese whistleblower, Jiang Yanyong, not only saved lives but attracted official praise (not the victimisation suffered by previous Chinese whistleblowers) shows that attitudes are changing everywhere. Providing legal protection and promoting a practical framework for accountability is a necessary step and a number of countries have now passed legislation. Different models are being experimented with and a new body of experience is emerging. The US and UK/South Africa offer distinct approaches to internal whistleblowing, anonymity and rewards. As our contributor, Kirsten Trott, notes in her chapter, Australia's approach to whistleblowing is "ready-made for comparative law study" as eight state legislatures have introduced different regimes to address the same issues.

This wave of activity has attracted some serious research and there is a growing, if still limited, academic literature. When Terry Morehead Dworkin and Janet P. Near asked in 1987: "Whistleblowing Statutes: Are They Working?"[1] their conclusion that "whistleblowing is not an activity amenable to statutory influence" was based on the single model presented by the US approach.[2] Indeed, their concomitant conclusion, that "(t)he most positive thing the statutes may be doing is to influence some companies to change their policies," foreshadowed the alternative model pioneered in Britain and now South Africa.

---

[1] Dworkin T. and Near P. "Whistleblowing Statutes: Are They Working?" *American Business Law Journal*. Volume 25; p 241. 1987. A more recent assessment, from the Public Service Commission of Canada, offers a "primer" comparative analysis of laws in Australia, the United States and the UK: www.psc.-cfp.gc.ca/research/merit/whistleblowing_e.htm

[2] Dworkin and Near, ibid. p 263.

By the year 2000, Dworkin was taking a more sanguine approach,[3] concluding a further review of legislative protections in all 50 US states with the words:

*Encouragement for whistleblowing is no longer a novel concept. All states have statutorily addressed the issue, although in very different ways and with very uneven results...Now that whistleblowing has become a well-accepted mechanism to address organisational wrong-doing, policymakers must take the next step, tailoring their approaches to whistleblowing in order to maximise its benefits and minimise its potentially negative consequences...opportunities for more effective exposure, deterrence, and curtailment of organisational misconduct through spurring whistleblowing are available in every jurisdiction.*

In 2002, she went even further, arguing that:

*Policymakers at all levels of government have embraced whistleblowing as a tool to reduce, deter, and stop corporate wrongdoing. Collectively, their initiatives represent a strong incentive for firms to adopt internal reporting procedures. When appropriately structured and supported, these mechanisms provide significant organisational benefits as well as reduced legal risks. Corporations that do not foster communication within the firm, on the other hand, are more likely to be faced with external disclosures and their consequences.[4]*

The **first conclusion** one can draw from the case studies in this book is that like anybody preparing for a potentially precarious journey a good map and a compass are useful commodities if you are going to arrive safely at your destination. Thus, in addition to the protection the law provides and its signposting for a new culture, the guidance that legislation provides is crucial for whistleblowing. At the very least, as we know from the organisations we run, the guidance the law offers encourages potential whistleblowers to identify their destination or what it is they are trying to achieve.

In working out what that guidance might be it must be remembered that the act of whistleblowing itself is not some magical answer, as all four of the whistleblowers' stories chronicled in this volume show. It cannot operate constructively or effectively, if at all, without the basics of the rule of law and a free press. The rule of law is essential not only because it is a means to protect

---

[3] Callahan E. and Dworkin T. "The state of state whistleblower protection." *American Business Law Journal.* Fall 2000. Volume 38, p 99.

[4] Callahan E., Dworkin T., Fort T. and Schipani C. "Integrating trends in whistleblowing and corporate governance: promoting organisational effectiveness, societal responsibility and employee empowerment." 40 *American Business Law Journal.* 177 (2002).

whistleblowers but, more importantly, because it is a means by which those who damage others and abuse their position can be held responsible for their actions. A free media is essential not because it is or should be the first port of call for whistleblowers, but because it is the means by which the conduct of those in positions of power can be scrutinised. Without these in place, there is little reason to blow the whistle as there is little hope that anything will be achieved as a result.

The **second conclusion** is that whistleblowers and whistleblowing must, therefore, be set in its full context. If its core purpose is to enhance public accountability by enabling individuals to come forward and share information that may prevent harm or stop wrongdoing, then it must be seen as one cog in a bigger wheel. Viewed this way, whistleblower protection can be seen in the context of greater openness and accountability and, therefore, in close relationship to the right to access information. Public interest disclosures and access to information are two sides of the same coin. While right to information laws provide people with the right to access records, it is equally necessary to have someone on the inside who is prepared to speak and act in the public interest as you can only ask for information that you know exists.[5]

The Open Democracy Advice Centre (ODAC) in South Africa, one of the organisations profiled in this book, frames its mission statement in terms of both whistleblowing and access to information, together comprising "the right to know". While this book has focused on whistleblowing in the workplace, the need to question and challenge wrongdoing applies across society. For this reason South Africa is proposing to extend its whistleblowing protection to citizens in all their activities and not just workers. Similarly in Rajasthan, India, this dual conceptualisation is operating powerfully where an activist movement, the MKSS, is using a new right to information law to access official records of, for example, healthcare provision in a particular region or food distribution to the poor through licensed ration dealers. MKSS invites individual members of the community to come forward and present a "community truth" to set alongside the official record obtained under the access law. In this way, at a very local level, allowing the poorest members of society to voice their concerns is a means to hold those in power to account.

The **third conclusion** from this and other examples in the book is the importance of civil society support. Styled in some of the literature as the "third sector", civil society organisations, unencumbered by the need to make profits for shareholders or political and electoral considerations, express a

---

[5] A number of campaigns and conventions now recognise the proximity of this relationship – for example, ARTICLE 19's model access to information law includes protection for whistleblowing and the African Union's convention on freedom of expression includes whistleblowing protection as part of its chapter on access to information.

particular public interest and can provide independent support and expertise on whistleblowing Whether by offering free legal advice to potential whistleblowers or training to organisations serious about instilling a new organisational culture for whistleblowing (Public Concern at Work [PCaW] in the UK or ODAC in South Africa), convening support networks for whistleblowers (Whistleblowers Australia) or campaigning for "free speech advocacy and dissent" (the Government Accountability Project [GAP] in the USA), independent non-governmental organisations (NGOs) have a key role to play. In Japan, civil society has led the call for legal protection for whistleblowers (as noted in Part 3). In India, following the murder of Satyendra Dubey – in whose honour this book is published – a memorial foundation was established to support whistleblowers and campaign for legal reform.[6]

**Fourth**, deriving from a very obvious point about the bluntness of the legal weapon, it has to be recognised that laws protecting whistleblowers are not an end in themselves. As Tom Devine demonstrates, delivering the sort of culture change which recognises public accountability requires organisational leadership and vision, tactical and practical support, and a legislative framework that deters reprisals and cover-ups. In our view, a whistleblowing law should be built with this in mind if it is to have any influence on the culture of organisations, groups or communities and so the legitimate interest of employers is critical. When workplaces recognise and promote the virtue of whistleblowing, not only do the employers benefit but the employees will look afresh at their own values and may question any lingering impulse from school, state or society that silence is the only option.

**Fifth**, as we explain in the Introduction the relationship between whistleblowing and the media is also a vital one. Even where the whistleblower has not gone to the media, its presence can help ensure the message is addressed and its coverage can be a source of support for the whistleblower. This relationship is important to developing a comprehensive strategy to understand and promote whistleblowing. Where the press (be it domestic or international) is sufficiently robust, capacitated and free, a skilful journalist can forge a relationship of great mutual benefit with the whistleblower, in the common, public interest. For this reason, we believe that whistleblowing legislation should try to identify the circumstances when media and other wider disclosures should be protected.

**Sixth**, regulators, whose role as industry watchdogs puts them in a very useful position to support whistleblowing, should be built into any statutory disclosure regime. On one level they are able to foster a whistleblowing culture in the organisations they oversee. As importantly, without whistleblowers

---

[6] www.skdubeyfoundation.org

regulators' jobs would be much harder. Fitting them into the legal and policy equation is every bit as important.

Beyond the academy, a new discourse has also emerged, driven by a growing number of activists and practitioners who value whistleblowing in the wider context of democratic accountability and good corporate and public governance. One of the unique aspects of whistleblowing is that it recognises that through the exercise of an individual right the wider social and economic rights of others can be promoted and protected. **Seventh**, therefore, it is important to apply the language of rights, with all the attendant legal, philosophical, political and strategic implications. Whistleblowing is on a journey: from the harsh hinterland of heroism and victimhood, or worse, the social exclusion of being perceived as an "informer" or "rat", to a new paradigm where whistleblowers are more likely to be listened to and respected not for their bravery but for their voicing of a public concern. This is a journey towards what Harry Templeton calls in his contribution a "more educated and informed society" that will "one day change its perception of whistleblowers and will realise that someone who raises a genuine concern about whistleblowing isn't a sneak or a grass". Speaking of whistleblowers in terms of their rights, as well as their – and all of our – responsibilities, is a helpful part of this collective re-orientation.

There is now a significant activity around the globe directed at supporting whistleblowing. Joining the dots around the world to link up local centres of activity is the next stage towards building a movement that embraces whistleblowing that matches the global movement for the right to information. Part of this strategy is to encourage deeper roots for the understanding and practice of speaking out about wrongdoing. In this context it rightly places whistleblowing not just as a workplace issue but at the sharp end of the vital human right of and struggle for freedom of expression. In small villages in Rajasthan whenever the community now publicly challenges the corruption of ration dealers and bureaucrats, the crowd has begun to sing "We have the right to speak out".[7]

Recognising that the most effective way to deter and detect wrongdoing is to give people a voice to question and challenge it, whistleblowing is now beginning to interest the multi-lateral institutions. As this book shows, civil society is informing these developments. GAP is influencing the approach taken to whistleblowing by the multilateral development banks across the Americas; ODAC is informing developments in Africa; and PCaW continues

---

[7]  Richard Calland visited Rajasthan in January 2004 as a part of the International Transparency Task Force delegation, and attended two *jun sunvais* (public hearings) organised by MKSS. For an account of the proceedings by Calland, see "Opening Up Rural India" at www.opendemocracy.org.za/papers&articles (it first appeared as a column in the *Mail & Guardian* newspaper, South Africa, 20 February 2004).

to promote this message internationally, having helped place whistleblowing on the agenda of the OECD.

As this book was being finalised, an international convention (the UN Anti-Corruption Convention) has for the first time acknowledged the role of whistleblowing. We welcome these first steps and urge multilateral bodies to do two things. The first is to adopt and embed whistleblowing cultures in their own organisations and on their own transactions as this can only demonstrate their accountability and deter abuse. The second is that multi-lateral bodies should use their influence to encourage countries around the world to address whistleblowing and to give people a voice and should seek to learn from the different ways that different countries will do this.

Thus, the promotion and adoption of whistleblowing by developing countries, where the socially and economically excluded are most vulnerable to exploitation and danger, is naturally part of the next phase. The poor and vulnerable need the early warning that whistleblowers can provide most of all; to achieve this they and all conscientious people need to be given the opportunity and assurance to voice their views. One way to start this process and signal and nurture such a culture is through whistleblowing legislation. As one of the leading opinion formers in India wrote soon after the death of Satyendra Dubey,

> *Whistleblower legislation, like the right to information laws, are little known or appreciated in developing countries, while most developed countries have had these for some time now...The U.K.'s Public Interest Disclosure Act of 1998 on the other hand provides protection to employees in the public, private and non-profit sectors...Of the developing countries, only South Africa has followed the U.K. example in providing protection to employees of all organisations through its Protected Disclosures Act of 2000; however other developing countries, including India, need to follow suit.[8]*

As this book shows, whistleblowing is here to stay. Despite the difficulties they faced, each of the four whistleblowers in this book when asked whether they would do it again, answered yes. People of principle and character have and will come forward; their cases help signpost the way, prompt a shift in attitudes and inform legislative solutions. Whistleblowers are essential if we are to forge a new approach to accountability which will help ensure that public and private power is exercised with an eye for the common good. In short, we can't live without whistleblowers. We all need people to speak up – even when we do not agree with what they say – and so we need to give them a safe alternative to silence.

---

[8] *The Hindu*, 3 February 2004.